LIBRARY OF HEBREW BIBLE/
OLD TESTAMENT STUDIES

498

Formerly Journal for the Study of the Old Testament Supplement Series

D1457997

A THEOCRATIC YEHUD?

Issues of Government in a Persian Period

Jeremiah W. Cataldo

t&t clark

NEW YORK • LONDON

T & T Clark International, 80 Maiden Lane, New York, NY 10038

T & T Clark International, The Tower Building, 11 York Road, London SE1 7NX

T & T Clark International is a Continuum imprint.

Visit the T & T Clark blog at www.tandtclarkblog.com

Library of Congress Cataloging-in-Publication Data
Cataldo, Jeremiah W.
  A theocratic Yehud? : issues of government in a Persian province / by Jeremiah W. Cataldo.
    p. cm. -- (The library of Hebrew Bible/Old Testament studies ; no. 498)
  Includes bibliographical references and index.
  ISBN-13: 978-0-567-59934-6 (hardcover : alk. paper)
  ISBN-10: 0-567-59934-5 (hardcover : alk. paper) 1. Jews--Politics and government--To 70 A.D. 2. Yehud (Persian province)--History. 3. Judaism and state--Yehud (Persian province) 4. Judaism--History--Post-exilic period, 586 B.C.-210 A.D. I. Title.
  DS112.C38 2009
  933'.03--dc22
                              2008026809

06 07 08 09 10   10 9 8 7 6 5 4 3 2 1

CONTENTS

ACKNOWLEDGMENTS

It is always difficult for an author to state how he or she "arrived" at the idea for a piece of literary work. That path has as many twists and turns as the dark woods that terrified Dante's poetic "I." Get lost once and live to tell the tale; the clearest memories one will have are of the beginning and the end. My clearest memory of "arrival" for this work was my desire to understand in detail how "theocracy" was or was not an adequate description of Yehud. The province had been described as a theocracy by many and still many others seemed to accept that label uncritically. But what are the implications on the political and historical development of a theocratic Yehud? Without any adequate definition as a guide those implications cannot be accurately or even adequately determined. My desire to understand the "process" of the social-political development of Yehud as an imperial province became my motivation.

As a revision of my dissertation, this work benefited from the care and attention of my own "Virgils": Charles E. Carter, Herbert B. Huffmon, and Jon L. Berquist have each given generously of their time and energy. Without their help and expertise, I would have certainly been lost in the dark woods forever. Theirs was an aid that extended beyond teaching knowledge and skills necessary for this project alone. It has become a crucial part of my development as a scholar. Their patience with my persistence in chasing theocratic and other specters is rewarded, I hope, in this work.

Philip Davies warmly took on the task of reading the dissertation and saw its strengths and potential. His enthusiasm and encouragement of this project are without measure. Andrew Mein, Claudia Camp, and Burke Gerstenschlager and his editorial team at T&T Clark International/ Continuum worked tirelessly and encouragingly to sculpt this project. Duncan Burns has proven himself to be invaluable through his attention to detail to grammar and style.

Jacques Berlinerblau, Diana Edelman, and Heather McKay have also given their support generously. The session leaders of the "Social-Scientific Studies of the Second Temple Period" section of the 2007 Annual Society of Biblical Literature Meeting in Washington, DC, invited me to present a portion of this work when it was being prepared for dissertation. The following discussion between speaker, panel, and participants was enlightening and invaluable. Lester L. Grabbe provided me with an unpublished copy of his presentation "Pinholes or Pinheads," given at the Accademia Nazionale dei Lincei, Rome, March 6–7, 2003.

Though it is a small gesture, this work is dedicated to my wife Susan Christina who was always one step away no matter the turn or twist through the dark woods. Without doubt, she is *de le cose belle che porta 'l ciel.*

To all I am eternally grateful.

ABBREVIATIONS

A   Tablets in the collections of the Oriental Institute, University of Chicago

ABL   R. F. Harper, *Assyrian and Babylonian Letters*. 5 vols. Reprint. Chicago, 1977

ADD   C. H. W. Johns, *Assyrian Deeds and Documents Recording the Transfer of Property*. 2nd ed. Cambridge, 1924

Ag. Ap.   Josephus, *Against Apion* (*C. Ap.* = *Contra Apionem*)

Ana.   Xenophon, *Anabasis*

Ant.   Josephus, *Antiquities of the Jews*

AP   Aramaic papyri

Arrian   Arrian, *History of Alexander*

Art.   Plutarch, *Artaxerxes*

BBSt.   L. W. King, *Babylonian Boundary Stones and Memorial-Tablets in the British Museum*. 2 vols. London, 1912

BE   Babylonian Expedition of the University of Pennsylvania, Series A: Cuneiform Texts

BHT   S. Smith, *Babylonian Historical Texts Relating to the Capture and Downfall of Babylon*. London, 1924

BP   Brooklyn papyri

BRM   Babylonian Records in the Library of J. Pierpont Morgan

CAD   *Chicago Assyrian Dictionary*

COS   *The Context of Scripture*. Edited by W. W. Hallo. 3 vols. Leiden, 1997–

CS   Y. Meshorer and S. Qedar, *The Coinage of Samaria in the Fourth Century*. California, 1991

CT   Cuneiform Texts from Babylonian Tablets etc., in the British Museum

Ctes.   Collected fragments from Photius's *Persica*

Cyr.   Xenophon, *Cyropaedia*

Curtius   Quintus Curtius, *History of Alexander*

Dar.   J. N. Strassmaier, *Inschriften von Darius, König von Babylon (521–485 v. Chr.) von den Thontafeln des Britischen Museums*. Leipzig, 1892–97

DB   Darius Behistun inscription

Diod.   Diodorus

DSf   Inscription F of Darius I at Susa

Hel.   Xenophon, *Hellenica*

Hist.   Herodotus, *Histories*

HSS   Harvard Semitic Series

I.Cyr.	J. N. Strassmaier, *Inschriften von Cyrus, König von Babylon (538–529 v. Chr.) von den Thontafeln des Britischen Museums*. Leipzig, 1890
Justin	Marcus Junianus Justinus, *Epitome of the Philippic History of Pompeius Trogus*
MA	V. Donbaz and M. W. Stolper, *Istanbul Murashu Texts* (Leiden, 1997)
MS	M. W. Stolper, *Entrepreneurs and Empire: The Murashu Archive* (Leiden, 1985)
Oec.	Xenophon, *Oeconomica*
P	Photius, *Persica*
PBS	Publications of the Babylonian Section (University Museum Pennsylvania)
Plut.	Plutarch, *Alexander*
SP	D. M. Gropp, *The Samaria Papyri from Wadi ed-Daliyeh: The Slave Sales*. Cambridge, Mass., 1986
TAD	B. Porten and A. Yardeni, *Textbook of Aramaic Documents from Ancient Egypt*. 4 vols. Jerusalem, 1986–99
TCL	Textes cuneiforms du Louvre
TDOT	*Theological Dictionary of the Old Testament*. Edited by G. J. Botterweck and H. Ringgren. Translated by J. T. Willis, G. W. Bromiley, and D. E. Green. 8 vols. Grand Rapids, 1974–
Thuc.	Thucydides, *Peloponnesian War*
WD	M. J. V. Leith, "Greek and Persian Images in Pre-Alexandrine Samaria: The Wadi ed-Daliyeh Seal Impressions." Ph.D. dissertation. Harvard, 1990
YOS	Yale Oriental Series, Babylonian Texts

INTRODUCTION:
THE PROBLEM OF THEOCRACY

The ever-increasing attention of scholars to Persian-period Yehud is truly exciting. Once only the recipient of brief nods in larger works on Israelite history, the province has increasingly been the subject of conferences and publications. Yet, as I began my own initial study of Persian-period Yehud, I became concerned more and more by the ambiguous and often inadequate use of the term "theocracy" to describe the government or political context of Yehud.[1] Often, the basis for this term seemed to be the testimony of the religiously oriented biblical texts. Those who used the term to describe Yehud's social-political context rarely confirmed the

---

1. To name a few works addressing this generally, see Gösta W. Ahlström, *The History of Ancient Palestine* (Minneapolis: Fortress, 1993), 889; Roland de Vaux, *Ancient Israel: Its Life and Institutions* (trans. John McHugh; New York: McGraw–Hill, 1961), 98; Jonathan E. Dyck, *The Theocratic Ideology of the Chronicler* (Biblical Interpretation Series 33; Leiden: Brill, 1998), 1–4; P. D. Hanson, *The Dawn of Apocalyptic: The Historical and Sociological Roots of Jewish Apocalyptic Eschatology* (1975; repr.; Philadelphia: Fortress, 1979), 210–20; Otto Kaiser, "Freiheit und Bindung in der attischen Demokratie und der jüdischen Theokratie: Ein Beitrag zur Bestimmung der Aufgabe der Religion in der modernen Zivilgesellschaft," in *Vergegenwärtigung des Alten Testaments: Beiträge zur biblischen Hermeneutik— Festschrift für Rudolf Smend zum 70. Geburtstag* (ed. Christoph Bultmann et al.; Göttingen: Vandenhoeck & Ruprecht, 2002), 448–64; Mary J. W. Leith, "Israel among the Nations: The Persian Period," in *The Oxford History of the Biblical World* (ed. Michael D. Coogan; Oxford: Oxford University Press, 1998), 367–419 (407); Otto Plöger, *Theocracy and Eschatology* (trans. S. Rudman; Oxford: Blackwell, 1968), 106–17; Jacobus van Dijk, "The Amarna Period and the Later New Kingdom (C.1352–1069 B.C.)," in *The Oxford History of Ancient Egypt* (ed. Ian Shaw; Oxford: Oxford University Press, 2002), 311–12; Joel P. Weinberg, *The Citizen-Temple Community* (trans. Daniel L. Smith-Christopher; JSOTSup 151; Sheffield: Sheffield Academic Press, 1992), 115–26; Julius Wellhausen, *Prolegomena to the History of Israel* (Edinburgh: A. & C. Black, 1885; Scholars Press Reprints and Translations Series; Atlanta: Scholars Press, 1994), 411–25.

basis for it within the social, economic, or political realms.[2] Instead, there seemed to be contentment in the general and unproven assumption that political authority lay with the religious leaders of the *golah* community.[3]

Dictionaries are sadly enough not generally very helpful.[4] The *Blackwell Dictionary of Political Science*, for instance, cites Israel and Geneva under Calvin as examples of a theocracy but provides no specific time reference for Israel. For a definition it offers that "theocracy" literally means a divine rule by God, though over time it has come to refer to a state dominated by priests and religious rulers.[5] Such a definition seems initially to me to be inadequate, especially without a chronological reference for Israel. Neither Israel nor Judah was a theocracy before the arrival of the Assyrian or Babylonian empires, so a theocracy was not native to the Jerusalem community. Moreover, it is generally known that the Assyrian, Babylonian, and Persian empires used administrative and governing structures already in place, at times altering them to fit an imperial ideal or agenda. Even more, the land was not devoid of people requiring a governing or administrative organization after the Babylonian exile of 586 B.C.E. (cf. 2 Kgs 25:22–24).[6] So, suggesting that the *golah*

2. I will address such uses below and throughout the remainder of this investigation.

3. This assumption is based usually on an uncritical reliance on the biblical texts. See, for example, de Vaux, *Ancient Israel*, 98–99, 141; Dyck, *Theocratic Ideology*, 1–4; Hanson, *Dawn*, 211–20; Plöger, *Theocracy*, 108–16; Weinberg, *Citizen-Temple Community*, 112–26; Wellhausen, *Prolegomena*, 411–22.

4. See also D. Webster ("On Theocracies," *AA* 78 [1976]: 813) who notes that dictionary definitions of theocracy generally are often minimal and ambiguous.

5. Frank W. Bealey, *The Blackwell Dictionary of Political Science* (Oxford: Blackwell, 1999), s.v. "theocracy," online: http://www.xreferplus.com/entry/725874 (accessed March 4, 2005).

6. See also the conversations of Hans M. Barstad, "After the 'Myth of the Empty Land': Major Challenges in the Study of Neo-Babylonian Judah," in *Judah and the Judeans in the Neo-Babylonian Period* (ed. Oded Lipschits and Joseph Blenkinsopp; Winona Lake: Eisenbrauns, 2003), 3–20; Robert P. Carroll, "Exile! What Exile? Deportation and the Discourse of Diaspora," in *Leading Captivity Captive: 'The Exile' as History and Ideology* (ed. Lester L. Grabbe; JSOTSup 278; Sheffield: Sheffield Academic Press, 1998), 62–79; Philip R. Davies, *In Search of 'Ancient Israel'* (JSOTSup 148; Sheffield: JSOT, 1992); idem, "Exile! What Exile? Whose Exile?," in Grabbe, ed., *Leading Captivity Captive*, 128–38; Lisbeth S. Fried, "The Land Lay Desolate: Conquest and Restoration in the Ancient Near East," in Lipschits and Blenkinsopp, eds., *Judah and the Judeans in the Neo-Babylonian Period*, 21–54; B. Oded, "Where is the 'Myth of the Empty Land' to Be Found? History Versus Myth," in Lipschits and Blenkinsopp, eds., *Judah and the Judeans in the Neo-Babylonian Period*, 55–74.

community[7] produced a theocracy upon their arrival in Yehud is not, as I will discuss, without its problems.

Since there is currently no known evidence that a theocratic governing structure was in operation before the Persian empire in Syria–Palestine, and because the empire often maintained the administrative structures already set in place, the structure governing the area of what was Judah must have already been, or have had a tendency toward being, theocratic.[8] If a theocracy or theocratic structure existed in Yehud under the Persian empire, the society must have already contained the social and political components of a theocracy. And unless one argues that the area was devoid of society, for a theocracy to have existed, these components would have also pre-existed the arrival of the *golah* community. Without evidence that the *golah* community effectively restructured the social-political structures of the society (as, e.g., Ayatollah Khomeini did in Iran[9]) in order to impose a theocratic administration, this is a necessity.

Since many recent discussions of Persian-period Yehud maintain that the Jerusalem priesthood was authoritative in the province,[10] the problem,

---

7. For a sustained discussion on a social-scientific definition of the *golah* community, see my "The Crippled Ummah: Toward Redefining *Golah* in Ezra–Nehemiah," *Bible and Critical Theory* 4, no. 1 (2008): 6.1–6.17, esp. 6.11.

8. T. C. Young Jr. ("The Consolidation of the Empire and Its Limits of Growth under Darius and Xerxes," in *The Cambridge Ancient History*. Vol. 4, *Persia, Greece and the Western Mediterranean, c. 525 to 479 B.C.* [ed. John Boardman et al.; Cambridge: Cambridge University Press, 1988], 79) believes that the Persians initially inherited the administrative system and structure from the Assyrians and Babylonians. P. Briant (*From Cyrus to Alexander: A History of the Persian Empire* [trans. Peter T. Daniels; Winona Lake; Eisenbrauns, 2002], 510–11) discusses the political administration of a province from the perspective of law codes. See also Albrecht Alt, *Die Rolle Samarias bei der Entstehung des Judentums* (Kleine Schriften zur Geschichte des Volkes Israel 2; Munich: Beck, 1953), 329 n. 2; Muhammad A. Dandamaev and Vladimir G. Lukonin, *The Culture and Social Institutions of Ancient Iran* (trans. Philip L. Kohl; Cambridge: Cambridge University Press, 1989), 96–97. Lisbeth S. Fried (*The Priest and the Great King: Temple–Palace Relations in the Persian Empire* [Biblical and Judaic Studies 10; Winona Lake: Eisenbrauns, 2004], 31) notes that Cyrus used the traditional modes of, for example, Babylonian kingship to legitimate his authority within an already existing administrative system. See also Chapter 2 of this work.

9. The case study in Chapter 4 discusses this process in Iran in more detail. To summarize briefly, Khomeini was successful because his actions were part of a social revolution in Iran that unified the social majority by a common desire to remove the social-economic-political oppression of the shah in power.

10. D. Janzen ("The 'Mission' of Ezra and the Persian-Period Temple Community," *JBL* 119 [2000]: 619–43), for instance, merely assumes a temple community when he discusses the authenticity of Ezra's mission. According to Wellhausen, this

in part, is due to the immediate association of priests assumed to be authoritative with the existence of a theocratic governing structure. This problem is especially significant because the social and political authority of the priests has yet to be firmly established. At least three aspects of Yehud's governing structure(s) require further attention: the social, economic, and political implications of a theocracy within the society; the development(s) of the society that could have led to a theocracy; and a clearly articulated definition of the term "theocracy."

It is a working hypothesis of this work that a theocracy, because it is a system of government, must be rooted or confirmed in the social, economic, and political realms of a society.[11] In addition, it is also a basic hypothesis that the definition of theocracy must be more than a priest having power or the ruling authority linked to the divine realm in some manner. These hypotheses are influenced by an understanding that governments and governing systems are products of their societies; are rooted in the social, economic, and political realms of their societies; and hold authority over the physical and symbolic powers.[12] It may be

problem was present even in past scholarship: "Writers of the present day play with the expressions 'theocracy,' and 'theocratic' without making it clear to themselves what these words mean and how far they are entitled to use them" (*Prolegomena*, 411). Note also, his claim regarding Yehud (425) that while the social-political structure during the time of Moses may be considered a theocracy, the leaders of the cultus of the later Persian period borrowed these theocratic terms and ideas to preserve an identity defined within its own religious tradition. According to him, the Mosaic constitution was an ideal representation, and this period—i.e. Persian—marks the first attempt to realize the structure of a theocracy outwardly (411).

11. I am motivated in this regard by Webster, "On Theocracies," 812–28.

12. My own conclusion follows one that has long been generally accepted. The following are more recent discussions on the relationships between government and societies. A. Norgaard and T. Pallesen ("Governing Structures and Structured Governing: Local Political Control of Public Services in Denmark," *Journal of Public Administration Research and Theory* 13 [2003]: 543–61) analyze the social and political impact of central and local governments upon their societies. V. Paglaia ("Poetic Dialogues: Performance and Politics in the Tuscan Contrasto," *Ethnology* 41 [2002]: 135–54) analyzes how Italian literary production, being a cultural product, reflects the political divisions of the same society. D. Lane ("What Kind of Capitalism for Russia? A Comparative Analysis," *Communist and Post-Communist Studies* 33 [2000]: 485–504) discusses the post-communist transformation of government and society in Russia, and the attempted transition into capitalism. He concludes Russian policy should head toward a state-run "negotiated" type of capitalist system. D. Hamilton ("Organizing Government Structure and Governance Function in Metropolitan Areas in Response to Growth and Change: A Critical Overview," *Journal of Urban Affairs* 22 [2000]: 65–84) notes the effect a metropolitan area has on a governing structure. J. Simon ("Electoral Systems and

understood, then, that from a social-scientific and political standpoint, no social structure can emerge without some foundation in or "genetic" ties to the society that legitimates it.[13] Thus, the purpose for this investigation will be to define adequately the term "theocracy" as a system of government in terms of its social, economic, and political requirements and to determine based on this new definition whether a theocracy is an appropriate description for Persian-period Yehud.

Outline of Chapters and Procedure

From a methodological perspective, the subject of this investigation is the social-political context of Persian-period Yehud, specifically whether or not Yehud was a theocracy. To be true to social-scientific method, it is necessary to explain how that subject is constituted in not only the terms of the external forces and systems acting upon it but also in terms of its internal systems and forces.

Therefore, because it is my hypothesis that at a theocracy is rooted in the various realms (be they social, economic, and political, etc.) of a society it governs, I will begin by discussing how the society of Yehud has been described by various scholars (Chapter 1). In the course of this process, I will analyze the strengths and weaknesses of the various descriptions. Comparatively, this will illustrate the complexity of the task before us. It should also help clarify some of the main areas of focus—drawn in part from those common strengths and weaknesses—in developing a definition of theocracy. In addition, because it is my understanding

Democracy in Central Europe, 1990–1994," *International Political Science Review* 18 [1997]: 361–79) analyzes the transition of post-communist societies into democracy. P. Chhibber and M. Torcal ("Elite Strategy, Social Cleavages, and Party Systems in a New Democracy: Spain," *Comparative Political Studies* 30 [1997]: 27–54) observe how social class has affected politics in Spain. J.-G. Gros ("The Hard Lessons of Cameroon," *Journal of Democracy* 6 [1995]: 112–27) analyzes Cameroon's postcolonial history, social structure, and political dynamics. Gros believes one will find in the results of these analyses the reasons behind the undermining of democracy in Cameroon.

13. One would need, at the very least, to see the works of Pierre Bourdieu, *The Field of Cultural Production* (ed. and trans. Randal Johnson; New York: Columbia University Press, 1993); idem, *Practical Reason: On the Theory of Action* (Stanford: Stanford University Press, 1998); Anthony Giddens, *Central Problems in Social Theory: Action, Structure, and Contradiction in Social Analysis* (Berkeley: University of California Press, 1979); Max Weber, *The Protestant Ethic and the Spirit of Capitalism* (1930; trans. Talcott Parsons; repr.; New York: Routledge, 1999).

that Yehud should be first considered an imperial province, I will address
the character of Persian administration throughout the empire (Chapter
2). My purpose here is to explore the extent to which the Persian administration was active in the administration of the empire's local provinces.
This discussion will also pay attention to the possible parallels (looking intently at the interaction between Yahwistic religious ideology and
the surrounding society) between Yehud and other imperial provinces.
For this section, I will rely on scholars such as P. Briant, J. Cook,
M. Dandamaev, S. Hornblower, and others to offer a view of the Persian
empire that extends beyond the unique focus of ancient Israelite/Judean
scholars.

I will address the variety of leadership models given to Yehud
(Chapter 3). My intent here is to discuss the complexities of the province
and to offer models of the primary contours of leadership. The problems
regarding the dating and interrelationships of such models are complex,
but I can, and will, question these models for an answer to who (governor, priest, or other) governed Yehud. Additionally, I will ask what sort
of influence social factors revealed through attainable evidence may have
had on the governing structure(s) and the society more generally. Here, a
discussion of archaeological and textual information such as, coins, seals
and seal impressions, as well as papyri, will supplement a discussion of
primary biblical texts. I will address the supplemental sources for not
only a perspective on Yehud's governing structure(s) different from that
of the biblical texts, but to offer as well a limited comparative study of
Yehud and other provinces.

In preparing for the task of defining the term "theocracy," I will make
use of social-scientific analysis of contexts previously described by
others as theocracies, building on the work of anthropologist D. Webster
(Chapter 4).[14] There are two primary steps in this process. The first will
focus on a representative sampling of definitions and how they have been
applied to various historical contexts in the ancient Near East. This rather
structuralist approach will not only offer a representative history of the
use of the term in studies of the ancient Near East, it will look for the
strengths and weaknesses of the various definitions and look specifically for those strengths that are common to all the definitions. The second part will take a more macrosocial approach and analyze case studies
of contexts (Classic Maya, Yathrib/Medina, Geneva, and Iran) previously
described as theocracies. Where this is most helpful is through defining
those elements that are common to theocracies, regardless of historical or
social situation. Positive or negative results, revealing the presence or

14. Webster, "On Theocracies," 812–28.

absence of structural elements common to theocracies, are mutually beneficial. It is these elements combined with the common strengths of the first step that will become structural components for a working definition of theocracy. Finally, I will apply the working definition of theocracy to Yehud (Chapter 5).

My primary literary sources for this investigation will be the biblical texts of Ezra–Nehemiah, Haggai, and Zechariah. I will selectively use Herodotus for his portrayal of history from a (Greco-)Persian perspective, and Josephus—selectively as well—for his portrayal of history from a (Roman-)Jewish perspective. From the Wadi-Daliyeh and Elephantine papyri, I will seek a comparison from communities similar to Yehud and the nature of any interaction they may have had and/or what light they might be able to shed on the ways Yahwism as a religion interacted with the society in which it was located. From other archaeological evidence, I will review the bullae, seals, and coins of Yehud in the Persian period,[15] which I will examine for what they might offer to a discussion of the economic and political contexts of Yehud.[16]

15. For instance, see Nahman Avigad, "A New Class of Yehud Stamps," *IEJ* 7 (1957): 146–53; idem, *Bullae and Seals from a Post-Exilic Judean Archive* (Qedem 4; Jerusalem: Hebrew University, 1976); Arnold Spaer, "Some More 'Yehud' Coins," *IEJ* 27 (1977): 200–203.

16. The bullae and seals have proven to be more promising than the coins for determining governors within Yehud. On the practice of minting coins during the Persian period, see Dandamaev and Lukonin, *Culture and Social Institutions*, 197–200.

Chapter 1

EVIDENCE AND INTERPRETATION

Was Yehud a theocracy? Answers to this question have generally been assumed to the detriment of precise analysis. Perhaps that is because, though simply put, it is a complex and demanding question requiring simultaneous analyses. The term "theocracy" has yet to receive adequate definition. Evidence from Persian-period Yehud is scant, leaving us without a complete picture of the social-political context. And so one must somehow reconstruct a model of Yehud that is sound social-scientifically but without being able to observe the system and processes of the society at work. Investigators have made do by engaging cross-cultural comparisons of similar Jewish or Yahwistic groups living during the time of the Persian empire or very near it. And while this work has been unquestionably important, these investigations and their sometimes fragile reconstructions have never formulated the question of theocracy with any articulation.

The time is right to ask thoroughly the question, an objective to which this investigation engages. To start, I have divided this chapter into two primary sections: one section introduces the evidence that will be discussed throughout this investigation; another section introduces interpretations of the social-political context in Yehud—many of which make use of the evidence discussed. For the benefit of this investigation, I locate common elements in various interpretations or theories and place those into a heuristically defined category with others that share a notable degree of similarity. In "Religious Groups in Power Struggles" (p. 12), I examine those theories that have tended to see power struggles between various religious groups as defining the social-political context of Yehud. In "The 'Social Infrastructure' in Yehud" (p. 19), I group those theories that have sought to define attributes of the social and economic structures in Yehud. In turn, these theories have offered proposals of the social-political context based on the defined attributes as fundamental to this context. In "Remote Administration from Babylonia" (p. 25), I place those theories that define the social-political context as being under the authority or guidance of the Jewish diaspora in Babylon. In "Impact of Persian Imperial Policies" (p. 26) I treat those theories that define the social-political context in Yehud as a context directly affected by policies of the Persian imperial government.

Introduction to the Aramaic Papyri and Bullae

Since I will discuss this evidence in more detail throughout this investigation, I provide only a brief introduction here. The Elephantine papyri, a collection of predominantly legal texts, contain, within the collection, certain correspondences to and from Yedanyah and his colleagues the priests.[1] These letters, or memoranda, deal with Yedanyah and colleagues' petitions for aid with which to rebuild the temple of Yahu in Elephantine. They were sent to Bagohi, to Yehohanan the high priest and his colleague the priests in Jerusalem, to Ostanes, brother of Anani, to the Judean nobles, and to Delayah and Shelemyah, sons of Sanballat, governor of Samaria. Even though Yedanyah and colleagues claim to have written to the high priest in Jerusalem for aid, they received no response. Different arguments can be made regarding the lack of response: perhaps the high priest in Jerusalem, being the authority over Yahwism, showed his disregard for a polluted cult by not answering.[2] Perhaps there was a reply but it was lost. Alternatively, perhaps the high priest was not *the* religious authority for Yahwism (though possibly an authority only in Jerusalem) but was petitioned as an aristocrat. The latter argument, portions of which will be addressed in Chapters 2 and 3, is part of a larger one that proposes that the temple in Elephantine was not under the authority of the Jerusalem priesthood, and that the Elephantine temple was without extended religious obligations, allowed by the imperial government for the soldiers there.[3]

---

1. For some collections of the texts, see Emil G. Kraeling, *The Brooklyn Museum Aramaic Papyri: New Documents of the Fifth Century B.C. From the Jewish Colony at Elephantine* (New Haven: Yale University Press, 1953); James M. Lindenberger, *Ancient Aramaic and Hebrew Letters* (ed. Kent H. Richards; SBLWAW 4; Atlanta: Scholars Press, 1994); Bezalel Porten, "The Religion of the Jews of Elephantine in Light of the Hermopolis Papyri," *JNES* 28 (1969): 116–21; B. Porten and Ada Yardeni, "Ostracon Clermont-Ganneau 125 (?): A Case of Ritual Purity," *JAOS* 113 (1993): 451–56.

2. Briant, *From Cyrus to Alexander*, 586.

3. Cf. Fried, *Priest and the Great King*, 92–107.

F. M. Cross published some papyri found at Wadi ed-Daliyeh in 1963 and 1969.[4] The badly worm-eaten papyri are primarily legal texts.[5] Within the papyri, several name-types have been found, though a significant number of the name-types are Hebrew-Yahwistic.[6] The papyri and their seals offer evidence that while many of the provincial officials and aristocrats of Samerina practiced a form of Yahwism, neither the religion nor its priesthood controlled the social-political context of the province.

Cross has reconstructed a list of governors of Samerina from the papyri and seals as based on the practice of papponymy.[7] This construction, however, is not without its detractors.[8] Nevertheless, he uses the reconstructed list to verify the listing of high priests in Jerusalem during

4. F. M. Cross, "Discovery of the Samaria Papyri," *BA* 26 (1963): 110–21; idem, "Papyri of the Fourth Century B.C. From Dâliyeh: A Preliminary Report on Their Discovery and Significance," in *New Directions in Biblical Archaeology* (ed. David N. Freedman and Jonas C. Greenfield; Garden City: Doubleday, 1969), 41–62.

5. Douglas M. Gropp, *The Samaria Papyri from Wadi Daliyeh*. Vol. 28, *Introduction* (Wadi Daliyeh II and Qumran Cave 4: The Samaria Papyri from Wadi Daliyeh/Miscellanea, Part 2; ed. Emanuel Tov et al.; Oxford: Clarendon, 2001); Paul W. Lapp and Nancy L. Lapp, *Discoveries in the Wâdi Ed-Dâliyeh* (AASOR 41; Cambridge, Mass.: Annual of the American Schools of Oriental Research, 1974).

6. As discussed in Deniz Kaptan, *The Daskyleion Bullae: Seal Images from the Western Achaemenid Empire*. Vol. 1, *Text* (ed. Pierre Briant et al.; Achaemenid History 12; Leiden: Nederlands Instituut voor het Nabije Oosten, 2002); Leith, "Israel among the Nations," 367–419.

7. F. M. Cross, "A Reconstruction of the Judean Restoration," *JBL* 94 (1975): 5, republished in *From Epic to Canon: History and Literature in Ancient Israel* (ed. F. M. Cross; Baltimore: The Johns Hopkins University Press, 1998), 152. A number of scholars have accepted Cross's proposal to varying degrees: Nahman Avigad and Benjamin Sass, *Corpus of West Semitic Stamp Seals* (Jerusalem: Israel Academy of Sciences and Humanities, Israel Exploration Society, and Institute of Archaeology, Hebrew University, 1997); Briant, *From Cyrus to Alexander*; Graham Davies, *Ancient Hebrew Inscriptions: Corpus and Concordance* (Cambridge: Cambridge University Press, 1991); M. Leith, *Wadi Daliyeh: The Wadi Daliyeh Seal Impressions* (DJD 24; Oxford: Clarendon, 1997). On the other hand, G. Widengren ("The Persian Period," in *Israelite and Judean History* [ed. John Hayes and J. Maxwell Miller; Philadelphia: Westminster, 1977], 489–538) discusses a number of reasons why one cannot accept Cross's theory.

8. Lester L. Grabbe ("Pinholes or Pinheads in the *Camera Obscura*? The Task of Writing a History of Persian Period Yehud" [paper presented at the Accademia Nazionale dei Lincei, Rome, March 6–7, 2003]) argues that Cross's reconstruction fails because it is based on a hypothetical practice of papponymy and on an assumption that the governorship of Samerina was always held by the Sanballat family. Diana Edelman (*The Origins of the 'Second' Temple: Persian Imperial Policy and the Rebuilding of Jerusalem* [London: Equinox, 2005], 64) offers a similar argument.

the Persian and early Hellenistic periods.[9] He makes a political connection between Jerusalem and Samaria when he accepts Josephus's description of the relationship between the officials in Samaria and the high priests in Jerusalem and his comment that they intermarried (cf. *Ant.* 11.5–8). He posits that these marriages were political marriages.[10] Thus, he interprets the evidence as confirmation that the high priests were the authorities in Yehud—an interpretation that is based in part on a hypothetical Sanballat III (to whom he sees the Wadi ed-Daliyeh 22 bulla linked).[11]

The Wadi ed-Daliyeh papyri and seals offer at best incomplete glimpses into the society of Samerina. From what little we have, however, we can conjecture that Yahwism was present in the society but that it was not the dominant and controlling ideology. The presence of Yahwism is shown by the papyri and the seals that contain Yahwistic names.[12] But since the legal proceedings detailed in the papyri do not appear to be exclusively Yahwistic in nature, one can theorize that Yahwists engaged in legal proceedings within a legal context that was not defined by Yahwistic religious law.[13]

In 1976, N. Avigad published a collection of bullae and seals from a Judean archive that he dated to the Persian period.[14] His findings have since been cited in almost every work addressing Palestine in the Persian and Hellenistic periods. A number of scholars accept Avigad's dating of the bullae and seals to the Persian period.[15] Others, however, argue that

9. Cross, "Reconstruction," 5.

10. Ibid., 6.

11. Some argue that there is no conclusive evidence for this third Sanballat. For instance, see Edelman, *The Origins of the 'Second' Temple*, 51–53; Lester L. Grabbe, "Josephus and the Reconstruction of the Judean Restoration," *JBL* 106 (1987): 231–46.

12. Kaptan, *The Daskyleion Bullae*; Leith, *Wadi Daliyeh Seal Impressions*; idem, "Israel among the Nations," 367–419.

13. Gropp (*Samaria Papyri*, 5) argues that the papyri provide a counterbalance to a predominant reliance on the Elephantine papyri to reconstruct the early development of Jewish law. Based on the topics discussed in the papyri, that conclusion seems dubious. The papyri from Wadi ed-Daliyeh and Elephantine have almost nothing to say about Jewish law. In addition, the "Jews" of both locations probably had perceptions of "Jewish law"—if anything can even be defined as such—that differed notably.

14. Avigad, *Bullae and Seals*.

15. For example, Joseph Blenkinsopp, *Isaiah 56–66: A New Translation with Introduction and Commentary* (New York: Doubleday, 2003); Charles E. Carter, *The Emergence of Yehud in the Persian Period: A Social and Demographic Study* (JSOTSup 294; Sheffield: Sheffield Academic Press, 1999); Stephen L. Cook,

the significance of the findings reflects more of a Hellenistic context: E. Stern and G. Garbini, for example, have both argued that the use of Hebrew script on the bullae and seals does not fit the context of the Persian period.[16] However, if A. Lemaire is correct, that it is believable that Judean provincial officials used Hebrew script during the Neo-Babylonian period and later,[17] then neither Stern's argument nor Garbini's argument is enough to reject a Persian-period dating.[18] If Avigad's bullae and seals can be dated to the Persian period, then it is possible to establish a sequence of governors to that time.

Interpretations of the Social-Political Context in Yehud

Table 1. *Thematic Division of the Interpretations of the Social-Political Context in Yehud*

Religious Groups in Power Struggles	*The "Social Infrastructure" in Yehud*	*Remote Administration from Babylonia*	*The Impact of Persian Imperial Policies*
O. Plöger	J. Weinberg	P. Bedford	K. Hoglund
P. D. Hanson	D. Smith	J. Kessler	J. Berquist
M. Smith			J. Schaper

Religious Groups in Power Struggles
Based on the biblical texts, O. Plöger found sociological and religious evidence of a developing apocalypticism in Yehud. He argued that the province was rife with theocratic aspirations.[19] For Plöger, a theocratic

Prophecy and Apocalypticism: The Postexilic Social Setting (Minneapolis: Fortress, 1995); Fried, *Priest and the Great King*; Carol L. Meyers and Eric M. Meyers, *Haggai, Zechariah 1–8* (AB 25B; Garden City: Doubleday, 1987).

16. For example, see Giovanni Garbini, "Nuovi Documenti Epigrafici Dalla Palestina," *Henoch* 1 (1979): 396–400; Ephraim Stern, *Archaeology of the Land of the Bible*. Vol. 2, *The Assyrian, Babylonian, and Persian Periods (732–332 B.C.E.)* (New York: Doubleday, 2001).

17. His argument deals directly with a jar handle from the Palestine area upon which *Mōsah* is inscribed. Nevertheless, if he is correct that Judean provincial officials from the (Neo-) Babylonian period used Hebrew script, then by extension the conclusions can be applied more generally to the Persian period. See André Lemaire, "Nabonidus in Arabia and Judah in the Neo-Babylonian Period," in Lipschits and Blenkinsopp, eds., *Judah and the Judeans in the Neo-Babylonian Period*, 293. The jar handle was published by Avigad in "Two Hebrew Inscriptions on Wine-Jars," *IEJ* 22 (1972): 5–9.

18. Lemaire, "Nabonidus," 285–98.

19. This section provides a brief discussion of Plöger's argument. See also the section, "O. Plöger: Theocracy and Eschatology," in Chapter 4 (p. 130).

context provided the necessary conditions for the social-religious development of apocalypticism. The rise of apocalypticism resulted in part from a conflict between the priestly (theocratic) group and the anti-establishment (prophetic) group, both of whom sought to control the theocracy in Yehud.[20] According to Plöger's deprivation theory, the priestly group isolated the prophetic group from the center of power, which he argued resulted in a developing eschatological hope for a future restoration of prophetic power.[21]

> The only way to neutralize such influences [i.e. of restoration eschatology] was not by combating or discrediting living eschatological hopes, which might perhaps only have provoked fresh tensions, but by burying them in the foundations of the community which was to be rebuilt, the unique and incomparable significance of which could be understood *inter alia* as the fulfillment of prophetic promises.[22]

According to Plöger, an initial eschatological faith developed into apocalypticism.[23] He writes of the groups who held this faith, "[H]owever much these groups felt that they were members of the theocracy, they must have regarded it as their task to foster the hope of a more comprehensive restoration of Israel. This must have involved differences with the leaders of the theocracy."[24] For Plöger, the religious belief of the community provided the undercurrent to Yehud's governing mechanism, and the politics of the province and the society itself were ideologically bound to the existence of an eschatological belief—in either an attempt to manifest the faith or react against it.[25] The catalyst for this

20. Cook argues, however, that this theory is not completely appropriate (*Prophecy and Apocalypticism*, 153). He concludes that apocalypticism (and eschatology) was not always the result of deprivation. It was, in part, the result of groups allied with or identical to the priests at the center of the "restoration society" (2).
21. Plöger, *Theocracy*, 109–10.
22. Ibid., 109.
23. In this sense, Plöger's apocalypticism is primarily religious and only secondarily social. Yet the reverse would seem more accurate: apocalypticism originates first from the social and only secondarily from the religious situation. Religion provides the vocabulary to a society attempting to provide some relief to the dissonance of a social crisis—most often oppressive in nature. One should also note Cook's discussion of apocalyptic groups (*Prophecy and Apocalypticism*, 19–54). In addition, Cook criticizes Plöger's "coventicle approach" to the rise of apocalypticism: "A 'coventicle approach' sees proto-apocalyptic texts as written within small religious communities that meet secretly for fear of those in authority" (ibid., 1 n. 1). Plöger's approach was followed and elaborated by Hanson (*Dawn*).
24. Plöger, *Theocracy*, 111.
25. Ibid., 116.

development was the Babylonian exile, a watershed moment according
to Plöger that created a theocracy:

> One has the impression that in every dimension of Israel's revelation
> right back to the very beginning of mankind the witnesses worked as
> witnesses of the apocalyptic world-view. This reveals a completely differ-
> ent type of mentality from that discernible in the anonymous eschatologi-
> cal additions within the prophetic literature, a new type of mentality
> which can only be explained as a result of a new understanding of what
> Israel represents in the world. How did this change come about and how
> can the initial factors which led to this change be traced? They took shape
> during the period when the structure of Israelite society underwent other
> momentous changes also, namely the time, almost unparalleled in history,
> when Israel ceased to be a political state and became a religious com-
> munity, a theocracy instead of a nation.[26]

P. D. Hanson continues Plöger's argument. Discussing the origins of
what he believes to be a "post-exilic hierocracy," Hanson writes, "The
events of 597 and 587 B.C. represent a type of crisis which is of decisive
importance in the history of social institutions. Through the trauma of
national disaster, the traditional community structures which supported
the social life of the people suddenly collapse."[27] In the wake of this
collapse, two primary groups (the visionaries and the hierocrats [compare
Plöger's prophets and theocrats]) competed for a position of dominance
through which to legitimate their respective models for social reconstruction.[28] The prophetic tradition assumed the mode of apocalyptic eschatology in the radically altered situation of the "post-exilic" community
in Yehud.[29] This was due in part to the dissonance created by unfilled
prophecies and an attempt by the tradition to maintain a continued
relationship between Yahweh and the people.[30]

   According to Hanson, the plan of the visionaries (those who were
outside the power structure dominated by the hierocrats) for restoration
focused on the centralization of the community and of Yahweh's presence within that community.[31] The restoration of the religious community
could not occur within the social structures in existence—which had
already shown themselves to be drawn to division and failure—but

26. Ibid., 29.
27. Hanson, *Dawn*, 211.
28. Ibid., 212.
29. Ibid., 10, 17–26.
30. Ibid., 30, 219–20. R. Carroll (*When Prophecy Failed: Cognitive Dissonance
in the Prophetic Traditions of the Old Testament* [New York: Seabury, 1979], 204–
13) discusses this in detail, with a focus on the role of dissonance.
31. Hanson, *Dawn*, 79–100.

restoration required the "cosmic" actions of Yahweh.[32] The hierocrats' plan for restoration focused on the centralization of society on the temple and on regulating the cultic life of the province. According to Hanson, this plan would ultimately give the hierocrats social–political–religious authority.[33] He states that as the hierocrats, who were from the Zadokite tradition, rose in power, they alienated many Levites.[34]

Hanson proposes that these groups were the result of a logical distinction brought on by divisions of social class and religious ideologies.[35] In other words, religious ideology between the classes differed according to economic status: "The ruling classes, because of their vested interest in the institutional structures of the immediate past, construct a program for restoration on the basis of those recently disrupted structures so as to preserve their positions of supremacy."[36] As for the lower end of the social-economic scale, "The alienated and oppressed classes look to the more distant past for models which call into question the position of power claimed by the ruling classes, and readily adhere to prophetic figures calling for revolutionary change on the basis of such archaic models."[37]

He argues that the lower classes looked to religion to usher in a social transformation and to put an end to oppression—"Having no worldly power, the sect understandably denounces the idea of world domination"[38]—while the upper classes saw in it a legitimization of their present place and role in society.[39] Thus, for Hanson, religion appears to be the dominant source of legitimation for the society.

32. Ibid., 373–89.
33. Ibid., 79–100.
34. Ibid., 220–28.
35. Hanson (ibid.) relies on Plöger (*Theocracy*) who argued the post-exilic theocratic group was primarily interested in cult and law. Blenkinsopp criticizes both proposals when he writes, "One of the most problematic aspects of both of these essays in religious history is the attempt to create a trajectory covering some four centuries with generally inadequate data. Both authors also write as if millenarian, messianic, and apocalyptic movements are peculiar to Judaism, which of course is not the case" (*A History of Prophecy in Israel* [2d ed.; Louisville: Westminster John Knox, 1996], 213–14). See also Blenkinsopp, *Isaiah 56–66*, 63–66, 146–47. See also Carroll's informed analysis of Hanson's argument ("Twilight of Prophecy or Dawn of Apocalyptic?," *JSOT* 14 [1979]: 3–35), which includes a discussion of the argument's strengths and weaknesses.
36. Hanson, *Dawn*, 212.
37. Ibid.
38. Ibid., 216.
39. Ibid., 214.

According to Hanson, the hierocratic (one could even say theocratic)[40] structure in Yehud was backed by the Persian imperial government, giving the priests an unquestionable advantage over the visionaries in their competition for power. He conjectures that the priests, or hierocrats, inhabited the center of power and exercised power over the community.[41] Apocalypticism was the result of a social outcry by the visionaries against hierocratic oppression.[42]

Hanson's social transformation and classes center almost entirely on religion—more specifically, the Yahwism of the Jerusalem cult. His discussion of the models desired by each group does not show an awareness of the variety of social components and variables extant within Palestine to which M. Smith, for example, has pointed.[43]

Based on an analysis of the sociology of the Zechariah group, S. Cook argues that Plöger's and also Hanson's deprivation theories are flawed:

> Study of Zechariah does not confirm the idea of Plöger and Hanson that apocalyptic eschatology arose out of increasingly deprived prophetic circles. Rather, Zechariah 1–8 evidences a millennial and messianic worldview among priests in power in the early days of the restoration… It must be concluded that an apocalyptic worldview need not be a fringe phenomenon. In the case of Zechariah 1–8, apocalyptic literature was produced from the center, both theologically and sociologically. Plöger's thesis that the priestly elite had a noneschatological theology which opposed the views of opposition circles cannot be maintained.[44]

---

40. Ibid., 212, 226. A hierocracy, as defined by M. Weber (*Economy and Society: An Outline of Interpretive Sociology* [ed. Guenther Roth and Claus Wittich; trans. Ephraim Fischoff et al.; New York: Bedminster, 1968], 1163–64), creates an autonomous administrative apparatus, tax system, and legal forms for the protection of ecclesiastical landholdings. In addition, a hierocracy seeks to turn the political leader into a vassal, as much as political control is compatible with its own interests. Thus, Hanson's argument that a hierocracy governed Yehud is virtually an argument that Yehud was a theocracy. Note for example: "When we speak of the hierocratic party, we refer to the leading priestly group of the post-exilic period *whose center of power* was the Second Temple in Jerusalem…" (*Dawn*, 220 [emphasis mine]).

41. Ibid.

42. Cook's work (*Prophecy and Apocalypticism*) questions Hanson's fundamental assumption when he (i.e. Cook) argues it is possible that apocalypticism can originate from a socially central group. He does not deny the position of the priests at the center but adds that the proto-apocalyptic Hebrew texts were not all the products of an oppressed minority but rather of the central priests.

43. Morton Smith, *Palestinian Parties and Politics that Shaped the Old Testament* (2d ed.; London: SCM, 1987).

44. Cook, *Prophecy and Apocalypticism*, 153.

M. Smith suggested that the political leadership of Yehud after Nehemiah's governing activities alternated between the Separatists and the Assimilationists—both of which were controlled by religious groups (Levites and priests).[45] He traces this struggle to the Assyrian conquest of Israel and to the subsequent ripples that the event had on the society of Judah (i.e. pre-586 B.C.E.). Smith states that the process of assimilation in Samerina included religion (cf. 2 Kgs 17:24–28).

Smith observes that after conquering the Northern Kingdom and settling deported peoples in the area, the Assyrian king reportedly sent a Yahwistic priest back to Bethel to teach the new settlers the משפט אלהי הארץ. He proposes that while the empire restored the temple and cult in Bethel, the empire probably also restored the cults of other shrines in the area. Based on the conclusions of K. Kenyon, he argues that some temples in Beth-Shan continued in use down to the Persian period,[46] and worshipers of Yahweh still made pilgrimages to Jerusalem.[47] This shows not only that Yahwism continued to exist in Samerina but also that the cultures of Samerina and of Judah were not entirely separate from one another. This interaction continued into the Persian period. Ezra–Nehemiah even testifies to this in its discussion of Sanballat, Tobiah, and others (cf. Ezra 4:1–2; Neh 13:28). Moreover, the various ethnic and religious groups, native to the area or supplanted into the area by the Assyrian and Babylonian conquests,[48] intermarried. This practice led to the concern shared by Ezra and Nehemiah.[49]

Note the following statement:

> In sum, the ethnic history of the country seems to have been…a history of conquests and reconquests, of deportations of native stock and importa-tions of aliens, of campaigns and encampments of armies, billeting of garrisons, penetration of the country by foreign traders and government agents, and the establishment of estates, agricultural colonies and entire cities dominated by aliens. To suppose that throughout such a history the native population retained its ethnic purity (which it probably never had) would be fantastic, even if there were no specific evidence to the contrary.[50]

---

45. Ibid., 117–19.
46. Ibid., 63. See also Kathleen M. Kenyon, *Archaeology in the Holy Land* (3d ed.; New York: Praeger, 1971), 251–52, 273.
47. Smith, *Palestinian Parties*, 63–64.
48. Ibid., 63. See also Ahlström, *The History of Ancient Palestine*, 822–23.
49. Smith, *Palestinian Parties*, 64–66.
50. Ibid., 66.

According to Smith, the social context of Palestine was diverse, as was the religion in the area. Discussions should consider this diversity and not rely primarily upon the *golah* community to define the society of Yehud.[51] He does argue, however, that the Separatists were given their own administrative district within the empire—a district, he posits, whose identity was defined by religious ideology. As Smith puts it, "Most of the people of that district were now marked off from those of neighbouring districts by exclusive devotion to Yahweh, limitation of their sacrifices to Jerusalem, peculiar customs (the observance of Sabbath), an attitude of hostility and a tradition of self-segregation."[52]

Smith states that once the Separatist party was established as the head of their administrative district, it no longer depended on administrative officials from the Persian administration developing an administration from among its own members. "Its leadership was no longer drawn from officials in the Persian administration, but from those few members of the Jerusalem priesthood and gentry who had gone over to Nehemiah's side and, mostly, from the levites whom Nehemiah had established as temple police and who had a vested interest in maintaining this tradition."[53] For Smith, Nehemiah's break with the high priest Eliashib, however, united the bulk of the priesthood and the gentry against the Separatists. "The union was made lasting by the priesthood's resentment of the levites' supervision in the temple, and by the gentry's intermarriage with the leading families of neighboring territories, as well as by their hostility to the poor."[54] The Assimilationists and the Separatists continued to struggle for control of the district, and this struggle marked the context of Yehud through the Hellenistic period.[55]

Smith argues that following Egypt's successful rebellion against Persia in 401 B.C.E., the parties aligned themselves with either Egypt or Persia, and control of power in Yehud depended upon which realm,

51. Ibid., 81.
52. Ibid., 110.
53. Ibid., 118.
54. Ibid.
55. One might note as a related issue that even into the Hellenistic period not all Yahwists accepted the absolute authority of the Jerusalem temple. In fact, as Josephus claims (*Ant.* 13.3), the Samaritan Yahwists under the directorship of Onias believed their temple at Gerizim to be more in line with the Mosaic tabernacle than was the Jerusalem temple—a claim directed toward claims of religious purity. See also Edward F. Campbell, "Jewish Shrines of the Hellenistic and Persian Periods," in *Symposia Celebrating the Seventy-Fifth Anniversary of the Founding of the American Schools of Oriental Research* (ed. Frank Moore Cross; Cambridge, Mass.: American Schools of Oriental Research, 1979), 161.

Egypt or Persia, held control over the area.[56] For example, after Tachos invaded Palestine in 360, the pro-Egyptian Separatist party held power. After Artaxerxes III Ochus reconquered the area, the pro-Persian Assimilationist party held control.[57]

Smith states that the two parties developed their own circles of literature, which they sought to establish as authoritative for the religious and "national" tradition. These literatures promoted the ideologies of each group and sought to lay claim to the religion's intellectual traditions.[58] Even more,

> Besides religious and political divisions, a rift developed between persons who held to the old, Palestinian cultural forms (of language, decoration, costume, diet, exercise and so on) and those who adopted the newly fashionable Greek ones. The resultant differences…were conspicuous among the causes of the Maccabaean revolt.[59]

Smith sees here a competition and struggle between the two groups for dominance in religion and political authority. The texts portray a context characterized by a struggle for religious, social, and political independence. The temple, symbolizing both religion and authority, was the vehicle for power in Yehud and for its independence.[60]

The "Social Infrastructure" in Yehud

In a series of published articles—articles that were later collected into a single volume by Smith-Christopher—J. Weinberg argues that the Jerusalem cult, through its leaders, subsumed the economies of the communal-private and state sectors when the sectors merged, resulting in a theocratic state, the *Bürger-Tempel-Gemeinde* (translated Citizen-Temple Community).[61] He posits that the priesthood of the Jerusalem

---

56. The Assimilationists, connected to the so-called *am ha'aretz*, advocated acceptance of Persian authority and assimilation with the peoples of the land. The Separatists, on the other hand, rejected Persian authority and assimilation (Smith, *Palestinian Parties*, 118). Each party sought to control the area by controlling the temple and the administrative district it was in (110–12).

57. Ibid., 119.

58. Ibid., 120–24. According to Smith (76–77), the Separatists wrote or at least shaped Ezekiel, Second Isaiah, the Deuteronomic and Priestly traditions, and the Holiness Code. The Assimilationists produced or preserved Proverbs, Job, Ecclesiastes, Ruth, Jonah, Judith, Tobit, Esther, and the Song of Songs.

59. Ibid., 119.

60. I will discuss Smith's argument in further detail in Chapter 3.

61. Weinberg, *Citizen-Temple Community*, 92–93.

temple was the central authority of the *Bürger-Tempel-Gemeinde*.[62] That was so, he argues, because the priests controlled the bulk of private property in Yehud, and, as a result, they controlled the economic, social, and political structures—an argument based on archaeological evidence that has since been superseded.[63] His uncritical use of the biblical texts to reconstruct the social, economic, and political contexts of Yehud produced unconvincing results.[64]

Weinberg argues that the *bet abot* was a post-exilic social structure based loosely on the pre-exilic *bet ab*.[65] After the Babylonian deportations, he concludes, the *bet abot* became the defining trademark of the post-exilic social identity.[66]

The *bet abot* represented a social unit or a communal unity,[67] which Weinberg confirms in part through the use of the term *abot* in the Qumran writings.[68] He finds a further parallel in the "general agnatic group" that dominated Iran in about the sixth century B.C.E.[69] Social units within this group were structured under specific heads or leaders. The identity of each member within a unit became linked to the name of the head, which was also the name of the group.[70]

62. Ibid., 111–13. See also the German article, "Das Bēit ʾAḇōt im 6.–4. Jahrhundert v.u.Z.," *VT* 23 (1973): 400–414. For critiques on the suitability of Weinberg's model, see Carter, *Emergence of Yehud*, 294–307; Jeremiah Cataldo, "Persian Policy and the Yehud Community During Nehemiah," *JSOT* 28 (2003): 240–52. While I offer a preliminary discussion of Weinberg's theory here, I will discuss the theory further in Chapter 3.

63. Cf. Carter, *Emergence of Yehud*, 294–307.

64. Weinberg (*Citizen-Temple Community*, 117) seems to suggest that the Persian authorities held what might be termed a "theological function." "It was acknowledged that thanks only to the help and support of the Achaemenids the community was organized, the temple rebuilt and a *geder* (refuge) given. The word *geder* is frequently used in the Old Testament to refer to God's protection over his people, which brought about the isolation of God's people (e.g. Mic 7:11; Ezek 13:5; Ps 80:13). Ezra 9:9 is also to be read in this sense and indicates that for the community, the most important result of the edict of Artaxerxes was the separation and formation of the citizen-temple community." See also Carter, *Emergence of Yehud*, 297–300.

65. Weinberg, "Das Bēit ʾAḇōt."

66. Ibid., 400. According to Weinberg, the *bet abot* groups made up about 75 per cent of the returning collective (406).

67. Weinberg suggests that the terms are not strictly indicators of a blood-relations group but can refer to social groups which have split off from a parent group (ibid., 405–6).

68. Ibid., 401.

69. Ibid., 401, 405.

70. Ibid., 408.

Weinberg argues that the *bet abot* structure initially designated work-groups in Babylonia—social units that were defined by vocational designations.[71] The structure of the *golah*—a group to which the theocratic leaders belonged—and the *Bürger-Tempel-Gemeinde* by extension, was based in part on this blueprint.[72] Weinberg argues that Ezra 4:2—where the representatives of Samaria seek out Zerubbabel and the heads of the *bet abot* for permission to aid in the construction of the Jerusalem temple—confirms this thesis.[73]

His insistence upon a *Bürger-Tempel-Gemeinde* structure within Yehud is based on his belief the Persian government gave the community a measure of self-government.[74] Self-governing groups based on land ownership led to a merging of the sectors controlled by the priesthood with those controlled by other non-cultic *bet abot* heads into one *Bürger-Tempel-Gemeinde* structure.[75]

Weinberg's thesis oversimplifies the social and political complexities of Yehud. He acknowledges that an amount of complexity existed more generally in the relationship between the central bureaucratic administration, i.e. the Persian government, and its local organs: satrapies, provinces, and the self-governing institutions contained within them.[76] In contrast, he reconstructs the social-political context of Yehud based on an uncritical reliance on the biblical texts. While Weinberg claims, without substantiating evidence, that citizen-temple communities existed throughout Babylonia, Syria, Asia Minor, Armenia, Phoenicia and

71. Ibid., 409. Priests, for instance, belonged to the *bet abot* designated for priests (414). He also argues (402) that the heads of families indicated in Ezra 8:1–14 were the heads of the *bet abot*. The *bet abot* was a segment of the *batei abot*, the greater body politic which derived from the house of Hezekiah (406).

72. Ibid., 403.

73. Yet scholars still hold in question whether Ezra contains actual historically valid information. For instance, in opposition see Ahlström, *The History of Ancient Palestine*, 877, 886–87; Bob Becking, "'We All Returned as One!': Critical Notes on the Myth of the Mass Return," in *Judah and the Judeans in the Persian Period* (ed. Oded Lipschits and Manfred Oeming; Winona Lake: Eisenbrauns, 2006), 6; Carroll, "Exile! What Exile?," 75; G. Garbini, *History and Ideology in Ancient Israel* (trans. John Bowden; New York: Crossroad, 1988), 151–69; Grabbe, "Pinholes or Pinheads"; J. Alberto Soggin, *A History of Israel: From the Beginnings to the Bar Kochba Revolt, AD 135* (London: SCM, 1984), 277.

74. See also P. Dion, "The Civic-and-Temple Community of Persian Period Judaea: Neglected Insights from Eastern Europe," *JNES* 50 (1991): 283.

75. Dion (ibid., 286) writes that for Weinberg, the *bet abot* controlled land-ownership within Yehud, dividing it among the *bet abot* members.

76. Weinberg, *Citizen-Temple Community*, 105–6.

Palestine,[77] Palestine, according to Weinberg, "is an outstanding example of the citizen-temple community, and thus can be referred to for conclusions about this type of 'local administration', with, however, certain reservations."[78] Unfortunately, he does not specify what these reservations are. Yehud is "an outstanding example" because it is the only analyzable example of his theoretical model. Beyond the biblical texts, Weinberg's theory fails to find corroborating evidence. Furthermore, he hides within the complexities of an empire-province relationship the unavoidable tension of justifying how an autonomous, self-governing province might exist within and under the political jurisdiction of an empire—a relationship that does not appear to lend itself easily to provincial self-autonomy.[79]

D. Smith expands upon Weinberg's *bet abot* model.[80] Through social-scientific analysis, Smith examines the structural identity as a survival mechanism of the Judean diaspora in Babylon. He concludes:

> The preservation of an identity under threat calls for 'defensive structure.' If, as we have suggested, 'ethnic identity' is preserved by conscious choice in circumstances of intercultural contact…then an analysis of the social mechanisms of the Judean exiles in Babylon ought to reveal creatively structured identities in order to be 'the people of God' in a foreign land.[81]

The community's survival depended upon its ability to create a solid community with social boundaries.[82]

---

77. D. Janzen ("Politics, Settlement, and Temple Community in Persian-Period Yehud," *CBQ* 64 [2002]: 490–510) also argues, based on the work of G. McEwan (*Priest and Temple in Hellenistic Babylonia* [Freiburger Altorientalische Studien 4; Wiesbaden: F. Steiner, 1981]), that temple communities existed in Babylonia. He believes, however, that the Babylonian temple communities served as archetypes for the assembly, or temple community, in Jerusalem.

78. Weinberg, *Citizen-Temple Community*, 106.

79. I will deal more extensively with Weinberg's theory in Chapter 3.

80. Daniel L. Smith, *The Religion of the Landless: A Sociology of the Babylonian Exile* (Bloomington: Meyer-Stone Books, 1989), 93–126.

81. Ibid., 63.

82. In *A Biblical Theology of Exile*, which continues his work from *The Religion of the Landless*, Smith-Christopher focuses more specifically on the communal formation and social solidarity of the "diaspora groups" in Babylonia and Yehud (*A Biblical Theology of Exile* [Overtures to Biblical Theology; Minneapolis: Fortress, 2002]). He suggests that an understanding of these groups and how they interacted with each other and others around them presents a better picture of the reformulated traditions of the biblical texts (6). Because his focus is primarily upon the social development of the "exilic" community under the Babylonians, he does

The role of the elders—who previously headed the pre-exilic *bet ab* groups[83]—maintained a similar function in the *bet abot* construction, though with some changes reflecting structural adaptation.[84] For instance, while the *bet abot* was loosely based on the *bet ab*, in size and function they were more similar to the משפחות.[84] New leaderships, which became known as the ראשים,[85] were established from the elders, who were motivated by ideologies such as the one that advocated Jeremiah's call to nonviolent social resistance.[86] In addition, the role of ritual within the community functioned as a method of group preservation and for symbolic resistance of the community to the society around it.[87] Another response, folklore, particularly hero stories addressing endurance through a life-threatening test, especially in a foreign society (e.g. Daniel, the Joseph story), preserved hope and identity as it offered the community a new sense of continuity and strength in situations seen as threatening to the community.[88] Smith posits:

not address the significant influence of the Persian empire. He infers, instead, that the Persian empire did not interact much with Yehud, leaving the society to fend for itself (137–38).

83. C. Meyers describes *bet ab* as a term for the household unit in ancient Israel, including both biologically related individuals as well as those connected through other social ties. As an extended family, the *bet ab* in its "economic aspect" included structures, property, animals, and people. She concludes that the "family household" is a suitable translation for *bet ab* because it includes basic kinship orientation while simultaneously allowing for and fulfilling the various functions of a household ("'To Her Mother's House': Considering a Counterpart to the Israelite *Bet Ab*," in *The Bible and the Politics of Exegesis* [ed. David Jobling, Peggy L. Day, and Gerald T. Sheppard; Cleveland: Pilgrim, 1991], 40–41). See also L. Stager ("The Archaeology of the Family in Ancient Israel," *BASOR* 260 [1985]: 22–23) who also describes the *bet ab* as the constitutive social unit of the משפחות.

84. Smith, *Religion of the Landless*, 99. N. Gottwald (*The Tribes of Yahweh: A Sociology of the Religion of Liberated Israel 1250–1050 B.C.E* [Maryknoll: Orbis, 1979], 285, 292) describes the *bet ab* as a living extended family that includes some members with affinal ties and excludes some with consanguineous ties. The basic composition of the *bet ab* was the head and his wife, or wives, sons and their daughters, including children, and unmarried daughters. Furthermore, he believes the *bet ab* to be the basic economic unity of pre-exilic society characterized by self-subsistence, producing its own basic means for all members and consuming nearly all it produced.

85. Smith, *Religion of the Landless*, 99. Smith suggests that the ראשים terminology was part of the development of the *bet abot* as a structurally adaptation response.

86. Ibid., 127–37.

87. Ibid., 139–49.

88. Ibid., 153–74.

> [W]hile I do not believe that the post-exilic *Bēt ʾĀbôt* was continuous with the pre-exilic *Bēt ʾĀb*, which was a smaller, real biological family unit, the use of the *Bēt ʾĀbôt* terminology to refer to a structure that was, in fact, more similar in size to the pre-exilic *Mišpᵉḥôt* (clan) is itself highly significant. The familial terms and 'close-knit' nature of the pre-exilic *Bēt ʾĀb* were used to impose a familial fiction on a sociologically necessary unit of survival—the bands of the 'remnants' in Exile who settled together. Post-exilic sources show such changes occurring for social and political reasons (1 Chr 23:11).[89]

While this social structure was affected by the Babylonian deportations, it maintained its continuity through what Smith claims were traceable associations with the society of the pre-deportation Judah. He argues that Ezra 2:59–63 testifies to the social upheaval brought on by the exile and that previous groups were separated in their settled locations. Groups previously unified by genealogy were divided. Maintaining solidarity within a foreign setting demanded that the people redefine the structural nature of the group.[90] Thus, the term *bet abot* became the designation for work-groups and groups defined by vocation.[91]

Smith suggests further that the structure developed in Babylon continued to be useful in Yehud, which was to some extent another unfamiliar social-political context for the immigrating *golah* community.[92] Based on this, his proposal provides one possible manner for understanding the ideological background for the exclusivist tendencies of the *golah* community in Yehud.[93] The exclusivism of the Haggai and Ezra–Nehemiah texts, he claims, reflects this survival mechanism rather than portraying "whimsical religious fanaticism."[94]

---

89. Ibid., 115.
90. Ibid., 106.
91. Weinberg argued this originally in "Das Bēit ʾAḇōt," 409–14.
92. Smith, *Religion of the Landless*, 119–20.
93. "Cultural oppression" in this sense is being used to describe the power of a dominant culture or society to deny any cultural expressions of a minority group. This (un)conscious "fear" of oppression begins, Smith believes, even before the community returns to Palestine. He writes, "[T]he role of discrimination and domination has a clear impact on social formations. Among the relevant aspects of the Babylonian Exile community was the fact that it was not only a minority, but it was a *conquered* minority, *under domination*" (ibid., 60). The self-identity of the community developed under domination, a situation that began to develop the very social structures and responses that would later manifest the "exclusivism" of the biblical texts.
94. Ibid., 197.

Remote Administration from Babylonia

Based on the text of Ezra–Nehemiah, P. Bedford argues that the *golah* community in Yehud continued to depend upon the Babylonian diaspora for leadership—which appointed Sheshbazzar, Zerubbabel, Ezra, and Nehemiah as community leaders.[95] He writes, "With the homeland devoid of Judeans, the first generation of repatriates is sent as a colony of Judeans from the Babylonian diaspora to re-inhabit the homeland (Ezr. ii)."[96] Yet, as previously noted, arguments based on an assumption of "empty land" are problematic because they are based on unconvincing assumptions.[97]

The repatriation of the *golah* community and their rebuilding the Jerusalem temple do not signify, for Bedford, the end of exile; these events were merely a beginning of a larger process of restoration. This restoration was possible, he argues, because the Persian government supported the Babylonian diaspora *golah* ideology and legitimated the community's claim to authority over those who "repatriated." While the Babylonian diaspora community held to the authoritative traditions and "knew how to live correctly," the repatriates, or "community in the homeland," were at risk of "undermining its identity through intermarriage with non-Judeans, whose only claim to legitimacy lies in residence in the homeland."[98] Because the Babylonian diaspora and the repatriate communities formed a single people, social-political authority resided in the diaspora community, who governed the repatriates.[99] It did not act on issues of major social and political natures without the parent community's expressed direction.

Bedford's conclusion that the Babylonian diaspora maintained social, religious, and political authority over the community in Yehud avoids any real discussion of governing structures in the province. According to his argument, the *golah* community did not belong to a society unique to Yehud but was a sort of satellite society of the Babylonian diaspora— the diaspora being, for Bedford, a Judean community living within a

---

95. Peter R. Bedford, "Diaspora: Homeland Relations in Ezra–Nehemiah," *VT* 52 (2001): 151, 158.

96. Ibid., 153.

97. For a few works on the subject, see Barstad, "After the 'Myth'," 3–20; Carroll, "Exile! What Exile?," 62–79; Davies, "Exile! What Exile? Whose Exile?," 128–38; Garbini, *History and Ideology*; Oded, "Where Is the 'Myth'," 55–74; Charles C. Torrey, "The Exile and Restoration," in *Ezra Studies* (New York: Ktav, 1970), 285–335.

98. Bedford, "Diaspora," 156.

99. Ibid., 158.

Babylonian-Persian (Elamite) society. Bedford reduces the *am haʾaretz* to Samarians and other non-Judeans, while defining "Judean" as the Babylonian-Elamite diaspora.

J. Kessler concludes that the Judeans in Babylonia maintained control over Yehud by maintaining authority and control over the "Golah Returnees."[100] He defines the *golah* as a charter group and enfranchised elite who were placed in this position by the Babylonian Diaspora and indirectly, by the Persian government.[101] In turn, the "returnees" dominated the major institutions of Yehud, creating a province of their own design.[102] Yehud, it seems, enjoyed autonomy because of imperial oversight, and it was the *golah* who occupied a central place of control and whose authority consequently defined this autonomy.[103] Kessler points out that rather than being a strictly religious phenomenon, the exclusionary practices found in the texts of this period were the result of threats to the *golah* authority.[104] Thus, the religious overtones of *golah* actions legitimated the "rightness" of the *golah* group before Yahweh and the Persian empire. This assumes a certain universality to *golah* Yahwism, however, and also that both the empire and the people of Yehud accepted the authority of this religious legitimation.

The Impact of Persian Imperial Policies
Based in part on the architectural remains of what he designates as fortresses, and in part on the pottery remains (that he describes as Iron Age II) found on the floors of these remains, K. Hoglund concludes that Yehud received imperial attention as part of a larger Persian imperial refortification policy.[105] He concludes that the missions of Ezra and Nehemiah were part of this larger imperial refortification policy, and that Nehemiah's activities during 445 B.C.E. occurred during the employment of imperial garrisons throughout the Levant.[106] Hoglund argues that

100.   John Kessler, "Persia's Loyal Yahwists: Power, Identity, and Ethnicity in Achaemenid Yehud," in Lipschits and Oeming, eds., *Judah and the Judeans in the Persian Period*, 103.
101.   Ibid., 99–100.
102.   Ibid., 104.
103.   Ibid., 105–7.
104.   Ibid., 110–12.
105.   Kenneth G. Hoglund, *Achaemenid Imperial Administration in Syria-Palestine and the Missions of Ezra and Nehemiah* (SBLDS 125; Atlanta: Scholars Press, 1992), 191–98.
106.   Ibid., 210. Ahlström (*The History of Ancient Palestine*, 835) states that the garrisons of the inland areas of the Levant were intended more to "keep people in line" than to serve an aggressive military purpose. But compare the argument of

the Egyptian revolt of 465 B.C.E. posed a serious threat to the security of the Levant. Succeeding events connected with the revolt—namely, the establishment and actions of the Delian League, along with the continued presence of Greek naval operations in the Eastern Mediterranean—required the empire to change its attitude toward the importance of territories in Syria-Palestine and other areas. This change prompted the Persian government to send Nehemiah to Jerusalem so that he might refortify the city and create an imperial garrison.[107]

Hoglund posits that the Persian empire also established Jerusalem as a location to collect and store imperial revenues.[108] He conjectures that this was most likely due to Darius' administrative restructuring; the city-wall system, portrayed in the narrative of Ezra–Nehemiah, represented Jerusalem's establishment as an urban center within the imperial system.[109] The appointment of a commander over the garrison by Nehemiah (Neh 7:2), he suggests, implies that Nehemiah's mission was to strengthen imperial control over Jerusalem and Yehud by extension.[110] In addition, he considers the prohibition against foreign marriages found in Ezra–Nehemiah to be a social mechanism[111] used by the Persian empire to control the stability of the area.[112] For Hoglund,

I. Eph'al ("Syria-Palestine under Achaemenid Rule," in Boardman, et al., eds., *Cambridge Ancient History*, 4:139), who argues that Syria-Palestine became a vital bridge for maintaining power in Egypt and for the empire's continual struggle against Greece.

107.   Hoglund, *Achaemenid Imperial Administration*, 212.
108.   Ibid., 224.
109.   Ibid.
110.   Ibid., 225–26.
111.   This purpose, of course, differs from Smith's proposal, discussed above, which contended ethnic purity was a *golah* survival mechanism.
112.   According to Hoglund (*Achaemenid Imperial Administration*, 226), the empire, rather than having a context rife with internecine conflict, sought to minimize quarrels by establishing social boundaries. Moreover, marriages, which he argues were the results of alliances between the authorities in Samerina and Yehud, were sources of confusion for Yehudean social identity, a result that increasingly threatened to become counterproductive (233). The employment of terms such as תועבתיהם and ראשונה, Hoglund argues (232), were aimed at creating a web in which intermarriage was inextricably linked in the minds of the people to religious infidelity. By supporting a social structure in tune with religious ideology, the Persian empire created a context in which obedience to Yahweh was beneficial for the empire: fidelity to Yahweh, in theory, maintained a trouble-free social context. He believes, in other words, that the concern over intermarriage was not strictly a religious concern, but that religion became a means through which to legitimate a broader social concern, viz., social stability (239–40).

> There is clear evidence from Mesopotamia that the Achaemenid court
> practiced a form of imperial domain, treating land gained by conquest as
> imperial territory and disposing of it to courtiers and various officials...
> [A]ny group of returning exiles, such as the Neirabians of Syria or the
> various groups of Judean exiles who returned to Yehud, were not reclaim-
> ing a right to land tenure based on past land allotment systems but were
> being allowed to reside in a homeland by the graciousness of the empire.
> Such systems of allocating territories to dependent populations will work
> as long as the imperial system is capable of maintaining some clarity as to
> who is allowed access to a particular region and who is not. Intermarriage
> among various groups would tend to smudge the demarcation between
> groups.[113]

While some suggest that Hoglund has misread the evidence,[114] others find
his reading of the evidence acceptable.[115] At the very least, however,
Hoglund has appropriately demonstrated the need for scholars to address
the role of the imperial policies in the province of Yehud. Moreover, if
his analysis of an imperial land tenure system is correct, then we have

---

113. Ibid., 238–39.
114. Edelman, *The Origins of the 'Second' Temple*, 319, 326–30; Alexander
Fantalkin and Oren Tal, "Re-Dating Lachish Level I: Identifying Achaemenid
Imperial Policy at the Southern Frontier of the Fifth Satrapy," in Lipschits and
Oeming, eds., *Judah and the Judeans in the Persian Period*, 187; Oded Lipschits,
"Achaemenid Imperial Policy, Settlement Processes in Palestine, and the Status of
Jerusalem in the Middle of the Fifth Century B.C.E," in Lipschits and Oeming, eds.,
Judah and the Judeans in the Persian Period, 35–40. Fantalkin and Tal argue that
not a single site in Hoglund's list of fortresses can be dated to 450 B.C.E. Lipschits
argues that the imperial government had no interest in establishing urban centers and
their accompanying fortresses in the hill country of Yehud. Jerusalem, he continues,
could not have been an urban center because the return was gradual, the area was
poor, and "[t]here are no architectural or other finds that attest to Jerusalem as an
urban center during the Persian period" (Lipschits, "Achaemenid Imperial Policy,"
30–32). Alternatively, Edelman conjectures that the location of the Persian-era free-
standing forts suggests the buildings better represent fire signal stations. She accepts
(*The Origins of the 'Second' Temple*, 319) Briant's proposal (*From Cyrus to Alexander*, 371) that the string of forts from Beersheva to Jerusalem, for example, were
tightly spaced to facilitate passing messages through fire signals. Both Lipschits and
Edelman argue that it was unnecessary to defend the borders of Yehud because there
was no regular threat of invasion. Edelman, *The Origins of the 'Second' Temple*,
329; Lipschits, "Achaemenid Imperial Policy," 38–39.
115. Jon L. Berquist, *Judaism in Persia's Shadow: A Social and Historical
Approach* (Minneapolis: Fortress, 1995), 144 n. 1; Carter, *Emergence of Yehud*,
passim; Edwin M. Yamauchi, "The Reconstruction of Jewish Communities During
the Persian Empire," *The Journal of the Historical Society* 4 (2004): 1–25.

evidence that the imperial government maintained social, economic, and political control over its territories, which included Yehud.[116]

Similar to Hoglund, J. Berquist[117] sees a general imperial push to strengthen the Persian empire's loyal territories that bordered rebellious ones. He argues that Artaxerxes I increased Persian outposts to strengthen its territories that bordered Egypt and Greece in response to the rebellions of Egypt and the Delian League.[118] To help meet this end, the Persian government established the Jerusalem temple as a revenue storage center for Yehud.[119] He argues that the temple became the physical center of the "new state" (i.e. Yehud) and functioned as the civic and political locus. The imperial government supervised the collection of taxes through the temple.[120]

For Berquist, the Jerusalem temple was a sign of Yehud's "state" status. It served not only as a symbolic legitimation of the relationship between the Persian empire and Yehud, but also as the physical center for the new state of Yehud, as a functioning civic and political locus.[121]

116.   Hoglund's land tenure theory offers a different interpretative framework for reading Ezra–Nehemiah than the one proposed by Smith above—that exclusionary tactics were part of a coping mechanism.

117.   It is important to point out at the beginning of this section that Berquist has himself seen certain deficiencies in his 1995 argument. He writes, "Thus, the search for patterns is warranted—but we must not confuse these patterns with categories into which we could place different types of societies or social situations. Patterns are themselves patterns of force, and the forces are vital to understanding the patterns. This moves our search for social patterns beyond the older categories of political anthropology and its theories of state formation. *My concentration on secondary state formation recognized the relevant forces of imperialism and autonomy but still searched for a category into which to place Persian Yehud. This was my error: obsessed with locating the right category, I failed to attend adequately to the forces themselves.*" J. Berquist, "Constructions of Identity in Postcolonial Yehud," in Lipschits and Oeming, eds., *Judah and the Judeans in the Persian Period*, 61 (emphasis mine).

118.   Berquist, *Judaism in Persia's Shadow*, 108. For instance, he writes, "Yehud suffered from the economic weakness of Artaxerxes' time and also experienced the increasing influence of the Greek city-states and other Mediterranean powers. Yehud's orientation began to shift from east to west... During the early years of Artaxerxes I, the Persian Empire attempted to place additional resources on its western border to support its campaigns against Egypt and Greece. Later, the general weakening of the Persian imperial economy removed Persia from concerns in the southeastern Mediterranean and drove Yehud closer to Greece's economic sphere of influence" (108).

119.   Ibid., 131–46.

120.   Ibid., 135.

121.   Ibid.

"[C]olonial Yehud," he writes, "took advantage of the Persian system of administration to create its own distinctive temple system as a dominant social institution, to establish the training of sages with distinctive traditions as a significant social influence, and to canonize large portions of still-extant scripture."[122]

The Jerusalem temple represented the symbolic legitimation of this Persian Empire–Yehud relationship—a relationship that further outlined Yehud as a unified state.[123] He conjectures that Darius' "energetic funding" of the temple project in Jerusalem produced an upper class of priests and governmental officials that became dependent upon the Persian empire for its power and wealth.[124] Note also:

> The Persian Empire used a legal, bureaucratic style of imperial management in order to create Yehud as a Persian colony… Whereas the inhabitants of the Jerusalem area had been a relatively nonorganized group before the beginning of the Persian Empire, the advent of imperial organization allowed Persia as a state to encroach upon that populace and to transform this group of people into a state of its own, albeit highly dependent upon the more extensive structure of the Persian Empire.[125]

The Persian empire, Berquist argues, gave to Yehud its own centralized governmental agencies. "From the perspective of its inhabitants, Yehud functioned as its own state."[126] Substantial variety marked these inhabitants, of whom Berquist writes, "There was no general, natural harmony among the inhabitants of Yehud but instead a politically managed unity enforced through the powers of the state, whether the state of Yehud or that of the Persian empire."[127] Despite his questionable conclusion that Yehud was a "state,"[128] Berquist's assertion that Yehud was a politically

---

122.   Ibid., 233.
123.   Ibid., 135. According to Berquist, Yehud was a state by extension because the Persian empire was a state. He defines "state" as a "community of communities that could exist outside of a state structure, however related with the larger structure they happen to be" (132).
124.   Ibid., 113.
125.   Ibid., 131.
126.   Ibid., 132–33. This conclusion is somewhat difficult. The only voice of the inhabitants we currently have is the biblical texts. Therefore, utilizing the texts as sources for all of Yehud's inhabitants of Yehud dramatically confines one's definition of Yehud to the perspective of these texts.
127.   Ibid., 133.
128.   See, for instance, Carter's discussion (*Emergence of Yehud*, 214–48) of Yehud as being a small province primarily containing un-walled villages. See also Hoglund's 1991 study ("The Achaemenid Context," in *Second Temple Studies 1: Persian Period* [ed. Philip R. Davies; Sheffield: Sheffield Academic Press, 1991],

managed unity is important. He is careful to demonstrate that Yehud cannot be separated from the imperial policies imposed upon Syria-Palestine or from the broader social forces set in motion by those policies. Not only were these policies possibly military,[129] as Berquist argues, they were financial as well.[130] These are vital issues concerning the social, economic, and political realms of Yehud. While most modern commentators would agree generally with Berquist's points noted here, it is interesting that most discussions of theocracies do not fully consider them.[131]

J. Schaper argues that the Jerusalem temple served as a financial center for the province, operating as a type of bank.[132] Drawing a parallel to Babylonian temples, Schaper points out that Nabonidus maintained a "king's chest" in the temple, the supervision of which was the task of an official appointed by the king, the *rēš šarri bēl piqitti*.[133] Through this

---

54–72), of which Carter provides an informed analysis. It should also be noted again that Berquist has himself ("Constructions of Identity," 61) pointed out certain shortcomings of his 1995 study. He defines state in the following manner: "[S]tates contain groups that identify themselves as groups separate from others inside the same state. For individuals, membership in a "state" is in addition to membership in a smaller social circle; a state is therefore a community of communities that could exist outside a state structure, however related with the larger structure they happen to be" (*Judaism in Persia's Shadow*, 132). But compare Weber (*Economy and Society*, 56), who writes that a state possesses a legal and administrative order—subject to change by legislation—that establishes a system of order. This system claims binding authority over the citizens and largely all actions taking place within its jurisdiction. Weber observes that a state is a compulsory organization with a territorial basis. A state controls, permits, and prescribes the use of force for its citizens and for all who present themselves within its territory; the state holds a monopoly over force (Weber, *Economy and Society*, 56, 65). Bourdieu (*Cultural Production*, 125) adds more: "The state…has the power to orient intellectual production by means of subsidies, commissions, promotion, honorific posts, even decorations, all of which are for speaking or keeping silent, for compromise or abstention." The state guarantees the values of currency and product (242).

129. Berquist, *Judaism in Persia's Shadow*, 61–62, 91–94.

130. Ibid., 141.

131. This deficiency will be addressed more extensively throughout this investigation.

132. Joachim Schaper, "The Jerusalem Temple as an Instrument of the Achaemenid Fiscal Administration," *VT* 45 (1995): 528–39; idem, "The Temple Treasury Committee in the Times of Nehemiah and Ezra," *VT* 47 (1997): 200–206.

133. Schaper, "Jerusalem Temple," 529. He builds his argument in part from the conclusions given by Dandamaev and Lukonin, *Culture and Social Institutions*, 361–62; A. Leo Oppenheim, "A Fiscal Practice of the Ancient Near East," *JNES* 6 (1947): 117; Mariano San Nicolò, "Parerga Babylonica XVII. Ein Mühlenbannrecht des Tempels Eanna in neubabylonischer Zeit," *ArOr* 7 (1935): 367 n. 2.

individual, the king exercised control over the temple finances and supervised the correct distribution of income.[134] This practice, Schaper observes, was not lost with the Persian empire. When Cyrus conquered Babylon, he continued the practice set up by Nabonidus; temples included foundries and their personnel served as collectors and administrators of temple and state taxes.[135] Collected gold and silver were melted down in these foundries and cast into more convenient and consistent forms, whose value was determined by purity and weight. Schaper argues that the imperial use of temples in Babylonia parallels the purpose of the Jerusalem temple. The Jerusalem temple, he states, also operated as an outlet for the royal mint and as a collection agency.[136]

Thus, according to Schaper, temples in general served a dual purpose: to maintain loyalty by allowing local territories their cults and to simplify the administration and collection of taxes.[137] Because the temples were also imperial institutions, the temple personnel—Schaper speaks specifically of the priests and Levites in Yehud—received royal stipends.[138] Yet, he cautions, one should not conclude from this that the imperial government gave cult officials autonomous or semi-autonomous political authority and control. He writes further, "Concerning those taxes which the temples collected for and passed on to the Persian king and his administration, it must be stressed that the sanctuaries—amongst them the Jerusalem temple—merely acted as outlets of the imperial 'Inland Revenue.'"[139] The imperial government appointed an additional administrator—a guardian of the "king's chest" (a parallel to the Babylonian *rēš šarri bēl piqitti* originally introduced by Nabonidus)—who was not normally a priest, to manage and facilitate the imperial/state taxes of the province.[140]

134.   Schaper, "Jerusalem Temple," 529.
135.   Ibid., 532–36. He discusses three types of state tax: *middā* (cf. Ezra 4:20; 6:8; Neh 5:4; or *mindā* [Ezra 4:13; 7:24]), *belō* (cf. Ezra 4:13, 20; 7:24), and *halāk* (cf. Ezra 4:13, 20; 7:24). *Middā* was a tribute tax paid to the king, *belō* was a poll tax, and *halāk* was a land tax. The taxes correspond to the Akkadian *mandattu, biltu*, and *ilku* (535).
136.   He draws in part from Herodotus (*Hist.* 3.96) and the Murashu texts and compares the use of the terms for various taxes paralleled in the biblical texts (see the previous footnote, n. 135). Ibid., 530–39.
137.   Ibid., 535.
138.   Ibid., 537. He bases this conclusion on an analysis of the various taxes mentioned in Babylonian texts and in the Persian-period biblical texts (e.g. Neh 13). See also Schaper, "Temple Treasury Committee," 200–206.
139.   Schaper, "Jerusalem Temple," 539.
140.   Ibid., 529; see also 531–36.

Chapter 2

THE FACE OF THE PERSIAN EMPIRE
AND ITS ADMINISTRATION

The Persian empire was a large and complex entity. All of its provinces were not content to exist under Persian authority, and the empire's history shows a number of territories actively pursued self-governance.[1] This active pursuit, marked by revolt and rebellion, demonstrates one reason why the Persian imperial government was not in the practice of granting autonomy to its provinces. In 1948, A. Olmstead wrote,

> Cyrus was now monarch of the greatest empire yet known to history. For the government of this wide-extending territory, he adopted in principle the organization first devised by the Assyrians, who replaced the states they had conquered by formal provinces. Each was ruled by a governor with a full staff of subordinates, and all kept in close touch with the central power through frequent exchange or orders and reports. The chief difference between these Assyrian provinces and the twenty satrapies established by Cyrus lay in the fact that the satrapies took the place of far larger independent monarchies.[2]

When the Achaemenids expanded their empire, they did not restructure every local administration.[3] The Aramaic, Egyptian, and Greek texts, as well as other archaeological documents, testify to the manners by which the imperial government established its authority.[4] As evidenced in the western territories of the empire—Asia Minor, Egypt, Babylonia,

---

1. See Briant, Cook, and Olmstead for more general discussions/overviews of the Persian empire: Briant, *From Cyrus to Alexander*; John M. Cook, *The Persian Empire* (New York: Schocken, 1983); A. Olmstead, *History of the Persian Empire* (Chicago: University of Chicago Press, 1948).

2. Olmstead, *History of the Persian Empire*, 59.

3. Stern, *Archaeology*, 2:369; Matthew W. Stolper, *Entrepreneurs and Empire: The Murašû Archive, the Murašû Firm, and Persian Rule in Babylonia* (Publications de L'institut historique et Archéologique Néerlandais de Stamboul; Leiden: Nederlands Historisch-Archaeologisch Instituut te Istanbul, 1985), 2–5.

4. Briant, *From Cyrus to Alexander*, 422–73 (472).

Samerina, among others—the Persian government used, where available, the administrative structures already set in place—often by either the Assyrian or Babylonian empires.[5]

Rebellions Within the Empire:
Stopping Pursuits of Self-Governance

After Darius's ascension, Elam and Babylon rebelled in 522 B.C.E. Açina, son of Upadarma, proclaimed himself king in Elam (DB 1 §16), and Nidintu-Bel claimed to be the legitimate son of Nabonidus, Nebuchadnezzar III (DB 1 §§18–20). Within two to three months, Darius successively quelled the rebellions.[6] The delay may have been due to the amount of time that it took him to organize a response. Another attempt at the Babylonian throne was made a year later by Arkha, who claimed to be Nebuchadrezzar, the son of Nabonidus (DB 3 §49). Darius carried out administrative and financial reforms in 519 that among other things was intended to better organize the empire.[7]

Darius died in 486 B.C.E.[8] while making military preparations to reconquer Egypt, who had risen in rebellion (*Hist.* 7.5). Xerxes, who succeeded him, regained the territory only two years later in 484 with an army headed by Megabysos (Bagabukhsha).[9] Herodotus wrote that

5. For example, see Hoglund, *Achaemenid Imperial Administration*, 234–35; Adam Zertal, "The Province of Samaria (Assyrian *Samerina*) in the Late Iron Age (Iron Age III)," in Lipschits and Blenkinsopp, eds., *Judah and the Judeans in the Neo-Babylonian Period*, 377–412.

6. See also Briant, *From Cyrus to Alexander*, 114–15.

7. Dandmaev and Lukonin (*Culture and Social Institutions*, 222) write that the empire was additionally divided into military toparchies. Administrative restructuring, however, was not primarily for military purposes. Dandamaev (*Persien unter den ersten Achämeniden [6. Jahrhundert V. Chr.]* [trans. Heinz D. Pohl; Wiesbaden: Reichert, 1976], 144–65) states further that Darius restructured the empire to give the Persian nobles (who were instrumental in his rise to the throne) more of a role within the imperial government. Eventually, this division of the empire into administrative units headed by Persian nobles may have led to the empire's eventual downfall; nobles increasingly sought independence, as argued by Jack Martin Balcer, *Sparda by the Bitter Sea: Imperial Interaction in Western Anatolia* (Brown Judaic Studies 52; Chico, Calif.: Scholars Press, 1984), 123.

8. Based on Herodotus's proposal of a 36-year reign (*Hist.* 7.4–5).

9. Cook, *Persian Empire*, 168. According to Dandamaev and Lukonin (*Culture and Social Institutions*, 95), Egypt may have received aid for their rebellion from Athens, a city maintaining a long resistance to Persian control. For a more specific discussion of the relationship between Athens and the Persian empire, see E. D. Francis, "Oedipus Achaemenides," *The American Journal of Philology* 113 (1992): 333–57.

Xerxes put Egypt under a heavier yoke than it endured under previous kings (*Hist.* 7.7). In addition, Xerxes confiscated temple lands, showing imperial authority over the cult and its properties. To control the area, he placed his brother, Archaemenes, in charge as satrap.

The Babylonians also rebelled. Tablets from the city and its environs speak of two uprisings, the first by Bel-shimanni and the second by Shamash-eriba (see also Ctes. §§52–53 [= P 18.52–53]).[10] Megabysos crushed the revolt and the symbols of Babylonian autonomy were systematically removed and/or destroyed. Military fortifications were razed, the temple at Esagila was partially destroyed, local priests were killed, and the statue of Marduk was melted down.[11] Herodotus writes that Xerxes carried off the statue and melted it down into 800 talents of gold (*Hist.* 1.183).[12] Cook states that the statue was carried off but not melted.[13] M. Stolper writes that the Babylonian manuscripts confirm Persian soldiers damaged temple buildings,[14] but it remains questionable whether the soldiers sacked and burned the main temple and carried off its god.[15] Briant, representing an additional possibility, concludes that one cannot be certain it was the statue of Marduk and not a different

10. For instance, tablets from Dilbat and Borsippa and dated to August 10–29, 482 B.C.E., were written under Bel-shimanni's name. See Olmstead, *History of the Persian Empire*, 236. Dandamaev and Lukonin (*Culture and Social Institutions*, 95) date the two Babylonian rebellions to 486 and 484 B.C.E. Cook (*Persian Empire*, 100), however, dates them after the end of the Egyptian revolt, and finds them in the years 484 and 482 B.C.E. Young ("Consolidation," 74) is unsure, dating either one or both of the rebellions to 482/1 B.C.E., but claims in the very least the rebellions occurred before Xerxes invaded Greece in 480/79 B.C.E. Overall, Cook's dating seems more plausible when one recognizes the title, "King of Babylon," is no longer used of Xerxes. Stolper (*Entrepreneurs and Empire*, 8–9) concludes that this was by choice of Xerxes and the following kings. Following the revolts, Xerxes systematically destroyed any remaining symbols of Babylonian autonomy, including the political recognition of Babylonia as an imperial state, shown in the title itself. After this point, Babylonian documents referred to the Persian king as, "King of the Land."

11. These were the extents of the damages, as Young ("Consolidation," 74) understands them.

12. Olmstead (*History of the Persian Empire*, 237) accepts Herodotus's account, which included Xerxes killing the priest who told him not to touch the statue of Marduk (see again, *Hist.* 1.183).

13. Cook, *Persian Empire*, 100.

14. M. Stolper, "The Governor of Babylon and Across-the-River in 486 B.C.," *JNES* 48 (1989): 296. Also, note a correction to the previous article in "Babylonian Evidence for the End of the Reign of Darius I: A Correction," *JNES* 51 (1992): 61–62.

15. Stolper, *Entrepreneurs and Empire*, 8–9.

statue that was melted down.[16] In the end, the symbolic power of the Babylonians was cut at its source because Xerxes effectively destroyed or controlled the symbols of Babylonian identity and autonomy.[17] One can gather from the punishments exacted upon the temples that the Persian government did not tolerate the participation of temples in rebellions, and that temples symbolically represented the freedom of the people. While temples appear to have been permitted as symbols of religious and social identity, the Persian authorities monitored them. The destruction of temples in response to rebellions suggests that the imperial government only permitted local cults as long as the province remained loyal.

Artaxerxes I took the throne in 465 B.C.E., and in 460, a Libyan by the name of Inaros induced a large portion of Egypt to rebel against him (cf. Thuc. 1.104). In turn, Megabysos, after leading successful campaigns against Egypt and the Athenians, sought autonomy and rebelled against Artaxerxes when he returned to Syria, territory the imperial king had given him (cf. Ctes. §§34–42 [= P 72.34–42]).[18]

Xerxes II took the throne in 424 (cf. Ctes. §§23–24 [= P 72.23–24]), but Sogdianus (Secydianus) murdered him 45 days later as he lay drunk in bed (Ctes. §48 [= P 72.48]).[19] Ochos, son of Cosmartidene and the satrap of Hyrkania (appointed by Artaxerxes), raised an army, and Arbarius, commander of the cavalry, and Arxanes, the satrap of Egypt, joined him (Ctes. §50 [= P 72.50]). After reigning for six and a half months (424–23[20]), Sogdianus was forced to surrender and was subsequently put to death. Ochos took the throne under the name of Darius II Nothus and reigned from 424–405/4 B.C.E. (Ctes. §§48–56 [= P 72.48–56]). Still desiring autonomy, Egypt rebelled again and the empire did not recapture it until approximately 58 years later in 342 B.C.E., under Artaxerxes III Ochus. Diodorus writes that Artaxerxes responded by demolishing the walls of the important cities, plundering the shrines for

---

16. Briant, *From Cyrus to Alexander*, 544.

17. If Diodorus is correct, we see a similar reaction given by Artaxerxes III to an Egyptian rebellion (Diod. 16.51.2).

18. Cook (*Persian Empire*, 169) dates this to sometime during the early 440s— an acceptable date if one concedes that it was Megabysos who led the armies in Cilia in 450 B.C.E., and that the revolt was over before the mission of Nehemiah in 445 B.C.E.

19. See also the discussions of Cook and Olmstead regarding Xerxes II's short reign: ibid., 129; Olmstead, *History of the Persian Empire*, 355.

20. Cook (*Persian Empire*, 129) writes that Ctesias refers to 424–23 as the "Year of the Four Emperors" (Artaxerxes I, Xerxes II, Sogdianos, and Darius II).

silver and gold, and carrying off inscribed records from the temples—records that Bagoas later ransomed back to the temples for large sums (Diod. 16.51.3).

Within a few years Darius' brother, Arsites, encouraged by Megabysos' son, Artyphios, led a revolt (Ctes. §52 [= P 72.52]).[21] In consequence, both Arsites and Artyphios were put to death. Pissuthnes, a Persian satrap of Lydia, also revolted against Darius. Tissaphernes incited a rebellion in Pissuthnes's own ranks, resulting in the latter's surrender. As a consequence of his actions, Pissuthnes was "thrown into the ashes" (Ctes. §53 [= P 72.53]). The last five years of Darius' reign were marked by rebellions.[22]

In 338/7 B.C.E., Bagoas had Artaxerxes III Ochus poisoned and placed Arses, Artaxerxes' son, on the throne (Diod. 17.5.3–4). Yet, because Arses made known his ill-feelings toward Bagoas's actions, Bagoas killed Arses and his family in 336 (his third regnal year) and the satrap of Armenia took the throne under the name of Darius III Codomon. Two years later Alexander and the Macedonians marched against the empire. On October 31, 331 B.C.E., the Persians suffered a near total defeat at the hand of Alexander near Gaugamela in Syria (Diod. 17.57.1–17.64.3 [compare also, Curtius 4.12–16; Arrian 3:11–15; Justin 11.13–14.3; *Alex.* 32–33]).[23]

Rebellion was not uncommon in the Persian empire. The imperial government's response provides a counterargument to proposals of provincial self-governance. That temples were affected by punishments meted out shows they were not outside imperial jurisdiction or control; they were permitted in societies as long as the society demonstrated its loyalty to the empire.

Imperial Administration and Governing Officials

Darius's desire for a more efficient administration of tax income led to a more obvious imperial administrative structure throughout its territories, including specified amounts of tribute. According to Herodotus, no such fixed-amount tribute existed during the reigns of Cyrus and Cambyses; the various peoples brought donations. Darius set up twenty provinces/satrapies with a fixed tribute each was supposed to pay (*Hist.* 3.89).

21. According to Cook (ibid.), all this happened after 417 B.C.E.
22. Ibid., 130.
23. See also the following discussions on the impact of the battle: ibid., 227–28; Dandamaev and Lukonin, *Culture and Social Institutions*, 96.

The Dandamaev–Lukonin Reconstruction (of a Self-Governing System)
As a comparison to the more unified political system this investigation is proposing, Dandamaev and Lukonin suggest that the remarkable levels of social-economic diversity that existed within the Achaemenid empire created difficulties in establishing a central administrative system. They believe the Persian government achieved success by using the traditional forms of administration and business organization from local areas. Each territory remained its own social-economic unit, whose systems seemed for the most part uninterrupted by the Persian empire. In turn, the empire existed as a parasite living off each system's products.[24]

According to them, after the conquests of Media, Babylonia, and Egypt, "the Achaemenid kings attributed to their conquests the nature of a personal union with the peoples of these countries, crowned themselves according to local customs, and used the traditional systems of dating and methods of administration that had developed historically."[25] This union was symbolized in the affirmation by the cults that the imperial king was appointed by the national deity.[26]

Dandamaev and Lukonin proposed that the empire would not have survived had it not used the already existing administrative and economic structures.[27] That the empire made use of the already existing structures is not being debated. The extent to which these structures maintained their own power revenue, however, *is* being held up for discussion. For instance, no occurrence of self-governance can be found when Egypt was under the control of the Persian imperial government.[28] Egypt was, however, more difficult for the Persian empire to control effectively.

The imperial structure under which central power was established and upheld was hierarchical. As Fried notes, "all power was in the hands of the king and his representatives."[29] Imperial representatives held power only under the authority of the imperial king. In Babylonia, Cyrus acted with the same authority as previous Babylonian kings, replacing top temple and city officials with his own appointees.[30] Gubarvaya, a later Persian satrap, appointed judges, and civil and temple officials.[31] Further,

24. Dandamaev and Lukonin, *Culture and Social Institutions*, 96–97.
25. Ibid., 97.
26. Ibid.
27. Ibid., 116.
28. Fried, *Priest and the Great King*, 106.
29. She qualifies (ibid., 6) power as the ability to control both human and material resources.
30. As noted by ibid., 24, 29–30.
31. Thierry Petit, *Satrapes et Satrapies dans l'empire achéménide de Cyrus le Grand à Xerxés 1er* (Bibliothèque de la Faculté de Philosophie et Lettres de

"The judges appointed by Cyrus and his officials were the vehicle through which royal edicts were enforced. The ubiquitous Mesopotamian law codes did not restrict these decisions."[32]

Xenophon claims that it was the responsibility of each satrap to imitate the king in everything they saw him do (*Cyr.* 8.6.10–13). When the satrap was at home, the hyparch functioned in part as a garrison commander. When the satrap was away, the hyparch ran the satrapy.[33] Garrison commanders reported to the king, not the satrap, in order to prevent open insolence or disobedience by the satraps (8.6.1).

The function of judicial systems throughout the empire also prohibited self-government. The local law collections of territories within the empire were not oblivious to imperial law. In other words, a local law code had to fit the criteria for being also the law of the king.[34] As noted above, the arbiters of laws, judges, were appointed by the Persian government and became the means through which royal edicts were enforced.[35] Thus the Persian government, while allowing local laws to remain for the most part in place, ultimately controlled the judiciary system.[36]

Even the book of Ezra attempted to draw authority from a proposed decree of Artaxerxes—an act that sought to establish the autonomy and authority of the *golah* community. Ezra 7:25–26 reads:

> And you, Ezra, according to the God-given wisdom you possess, appoint magistrates and judges who may judge all the people in the province Beyond the River who know the laws of your God; and you shall teach those who do not know them. All who will not obey the law of your God and the law of the king, let judgment be strictly executed on them, whether for death or for banishment or for confiscation of their goods or for imprisonment.

l'Université de Liège; Paris: Les Belles Lettres, 1990), 55–56 nn. 183–88. As cited by Fried (*Priest and the Great King*, 32), this conclusion is based on more than 20 texts.

32. Fried, *Priest and the Great King*, 33.

33. Ibid., 126.

34. On this see Briant, *From Cyrus to Alexander*, 511.

35. Note also Fried, who points out that the judges, who were appointed by the king, were not bound to the written laws. These laws were instead arbitrary laws—assurance to the people that laws existed—and judges made decisions of right or wrong based on socially constructed values (*Priest and the Great King*, 33–35).

36. Fried (ibid., 91) states that the judicial system in Egypt was completely Persian.

Since Persian imperial law, or "the law of the king," set the standard for jurisprudence in the empire, local laws were permitted as long as they fit within the "law of the king" and did not counteract imperial law. The law referred to in Ezra would have been no different.

Arbitration of law also fell under imperial control. Like the system/structure of government, the judicial system was structured hierarchically. Judicial decisions made at Elephantine, for instance, could be appealed to a higher court located in Thebes. If the decision at Thebes was unsatisfactory, one could appeal further to the satrap in Memphis.[37] Order was maintained through a system that was either set up by or incorporated into the Persian government. In either case, the system was always subject to Persian control.

An example from Egypt may well demonstrate how judicial systems were not specific to a particular nationality. As Fried points out, "there were no Egyptian judges for the Egyptians or Jewish judges for the Jews."[38] The judges were either royal appointees, or appointed by the province (cf. *TAD* A.5.2:4, 7; B.5.1:3).[39] "The use of Persian loanwords suggests a completely Persian judicial system in the Egyptian satrapy, with provincial judges, police, and intelligence officers appointed by Persian officials. Indeed, in both the Elephantine archives and the Arsames letters, nearly every named judge is Iranian."[40] While her argument seems to me to be correct, it is not clear that these judges were "Iranian" rather than simply having "Iranian" names.

Therefore, even though local laws were used, the imperial government appears to have maintained control over the judicial system. When the imperial government codified local laws in the empire, the laws were made uniform within the limits of their social and political contexts, and at some points changed to fit the policy of the king.[41] In 445 B.C.E.—according to the biblical accounts (cf. Neh 8:1–13)—Nehemiah declared that the laws collected and codified by Ezra were the laws of Yehud. The Demotic Chronicle states that the laws of Egypt were codified in 518. Neither one of these territories reached this point without the direction of the imperial government or the imperially appointed functionaries.

Finally, the position of the satrap within the Persian administrative system was not available to locals. From the time of Darius on, the

37. Ibid., 94.
38. Ibid., 91.
39. Ibid., 91–92.
40. Ibid., 91.
41. Ibid., 34–35; Hoglund, *Achaemenid Imperial Administration*, 234–35; Simon Hornblower, *Mausolus* (Oxford: Clarendon, 1982), 117.

satraps were Persians,[42] and the satraps controlled their satrapy's military.[43] (It is most likely this level of power that aided many a satrap in their decision to rebel against the central authority.) "It would seem then," Cook writes, "that in the normal way the jurisdiction of the satraps embraced the spheres of both civil and military activity."[44] They were responsible for tribute, military levies, justice, and security. The satrapal courts were modeled after the Persian king's and were frequented by Persian grandees in the provinces. They employed Aramaic-speaking scribes through whom they maintained correspondence with the central court and with local and regional authorities.[45]

Satraps may have also appointed provincial judges and top officials to the temples in Egypt. Fried argues that the local garrison commanders appointed second-level priests. "This is not consistent with a model of self-governance or even a model of imperial authorization of local norms... The temples—and the entire satrapy—were run by the Persian rulers as a fiefdom for the king."[46]

Provincial Governors/Administration

Part of the confusion over the responsibilities of satraps and governors derives from the closely related terminology for the two offices.[47] In the MT, פֶּחָה refers both to the heads of satrapies and to the heads of provinces (cf. Ezra 5:3, 6, 14–17; 6:6, 7, 13; 8:36; Neh 2:9; 3:7; 12:26; Hag 1:1, 14; 2:2, 21).[48] "Province," in this sense, refers to a territory within a larger satrapy. Ezra 5:14 states Sheshbazzar was appointed פֶּחָה.

42. Cook, *Persian Empire*, 173.

43. Ibid., 85; Dandamaev and Lukonin, *Culture and Social Institutions*, 101, 111; S. Hornblower, *The Greek World 479–323 BC* (New York: Routledge, 1991), 69.

44. Cook, *Persian Empire*, 85.

45. Cook (ibid.), locates these at Persepolis, Memphis, and Daskyleion, and also at, what he terms, sub-centers in Samaria and in Lagash (southern Babylonia).

46. Fried, *Priest and the Great King*, 106.

47. "Satrap" comes from the Greek designation (σατράπης) for the Old Persian *xšaçapāvan*. The Persian word may itself be a Median loanword.

48. Briant (*From Cyrus to Alexander*, 487) concludes that while *pḥh* is a general title, *piḥātu* (an Akkadian loan word [see also from CAD, BRM 1 101:5; *Dar.* 27:3; 338:4, 14]) and its derivatives refer to a governor over a satrapy while *peḥā* refers to a governor over a province. This conclusion is dubious, however, because the MT (Aramaic and Hebrew) uses פֶּחָה for both (cf. Ezra 5:3, 6, 14; 6:6, 7, 13; 8:36; Neh 2:2–9; 3:7; 5:14–17; 12:26; Hag 1:1, 14; 2:2, 21). In addition, various forms of *pḥt* in Akkadian denote responsibility, the bearing of responsibility, and province (cf. BE 9 83:18; 9 84:11; PBS 2/1 1:14, 34:13 [as cited in CAD]). In the construct, *bēl pḥt*, a provincial governor is meant (cf. BRM 1 101:5; *Dar.* 27:3; 338:4; KAJ 103:6; 106:5; 191:3 [as cited in CAD]).

Ezra 5:3, 6; 6:6, 13 describe Tattenai as פחה over ʿabar-nahara(h) (*Ebir
Nāri*).[49] ʿAbar-nahara(h), while it corresponds to Herodotus's fifth
nome/province (*Hist.* 3.91),[50] does not appear to be a unique or autonomous satrapy but is somehow connected to the satrapy of Babylonia.[51]
The exact nature of the relationship between the governors of Babylonia
and ʿabar-nahara(h), however, remains unclear. As Briant points out, no
available document speaks clearly to this relationship.[52] Yet despite the
uncertainty, one can note that the ʿabar-nahara(h) satrapy was divided
into provinces (*medinah*), one of which was Yehud. Ezra 7:25–26 seems
to give Ezra authority within the whole of ʿabar- nahara(h).[53] Haggai
refers to Zerubbabel as פחה (Hag 1:1, 14; 2:2, 21). And the term is used,
of course, of Nehemiah (Neh 12:26). The books of Jeremiah and Ezekiel
link the term, פחה, to סגנים (Ezek 23:6; Jer 51:23).

In the Murashu archive, *pehā* designates both major and minor
officials.[54] Stolper writes that the Babylonian texts normally identified
the Persian governors with Babylonian titles, such as *bēl pīḫāti, pīḫatu*,
and *pāḫātu*.[55]

Regarding governors in Samerina, Briant suggests that the Sanballat
family held a "true" local dynasty in Samaria, based on references to
multiple Sanballats (cf. SP 7, 9; CS 29–30; *Ant.* 11.302).[56] However,
there is currently no available evidence that conclusively demonstrates
that the Sanballats referred to were related; they may have simply been
officials taking on an "official" name, thereby claiming legitimate affiliation. This practice was not uncommon and was demonstrated in the
imperial court by the number of kings who took on names such as Darius
and Artaxerxes.

---

49. There is also an interesting ancestral character named פחת־מואב that shows
up throughout Ezra–Nehemiah (cf. Ezra 2:6; 8:4; 10:30; Neh 3:11; 7:11; 10:15).

50. Herodotus writes that the territory stretched from the town of Posideium
(Ras-el Bassit) to Egypt, excluded the Arabian territory, and encompassed Phoenicia, Palestinian Syria, and Cyprus.

51. As a point of reference, Herodotus defined Babylon and "the rest of Assyria"
as the ninth province (*Hist.* 3.92).

52. Briant, *From Cyrus to Alexander*, 487.

53. Note further: "Reading through the 'reports' about Ezra and his mission, one
is struck by the contrast between Ezra's appointment, as a special Persian emissary
with authority that was on a par with that of a satrap, and his cultic and social actions
in Jerusalem. The presentation of Ezra is less 'historical' than that of Nehemiah."
Ahlström, *The History of Ancient Palestine*, 877, 886–87.

54. Stolper, *Entrepreneurs and Empire*, 39, 58.

55. Ibid., 58.

56. Briant, *From Cyrus to Alexander*, 713–15, 1016.

If we find ourselves concluding the Sanballats, like the Hekatomnids in Karia, were a dynasty, they were an exception to the rule.[57] As a general policy, the Persian government did not allow dynasties to exist in satrapal or provincial governments, in order to control any build-up of power.[58] Briant writes, based on a passage from Herodotus (*Hist.* 6.43), "Cependant il apparaît que, fondamentalement, la nomination ou destitution des satrapes et généraux reste du ressort exclusive du roi."[59] It is possible some sons succeeded their fathers, yet these occasions seem to be very few because the central (imperial) government tried to prevent satraps and governors from acquiring too much power.[60] As Leith shows, seal impressions from Samaria show the imperial government was actively involved in administrative concerns.[61] This example of active involvement demonstrates the empire's desire to control the administrative systems in its territories.

In general, officials appointed by the imperial king were allowed to remain in place as long as they remained loyal.[62] Loyalty was expressed in part through payments of tributes and expressed allegiances to the imperial government.[63] The power structure was centralized in the imperial government, and Briant asserts that the Greek sources insist on direct imperial control over the empire's territories.[64] If the Sanballats of Samaria maintained a dynasty then one can conclude that they showed no signs of disloyalty. Should a governor show disloyalty, the governor was replaced. If, as Briant suggests, the Sanballats maintained their dynasty up to Darius II (perhaps even Darius III), then their loyalty to the imperial government must have been without question.[65] In addition, they would also be one of a small number of dynasties in the Persian empire.[66]

57. See Briant's discussion of the Sanballats and the Hekatomnids. He states (ibid., 713–15) that the manner of succession was parallel between the two "dynasties."

58. Ibid., 338–44.

59. Pierre Briant, *Histoire de l'empire perse de Cyrus à Alexandre* (Paris: Librairie Arthème Fayard, 1998), 351 (see also 339–40 of the ET [cited p. 3 n. 8]).

60. See also, Edelman, *The Origins of the 'Second' Temple*, 62.

61. Leith, *Wadi Daliyeh Seal Impressions*, 7–8.

62. Briant, *From Cyrus to Alexander*, 586–87.

63. Ibid., 423.

64. Briant, "Pouvoir central et polycentrisme culturel dans l'empire achemenide," in *Achaemenid History.* Vol. 1, *Sources, Structures and Synthesis* (ed. Heleen Sancisi-Weerdenburg; Leiden: Nederlands Instituute voor het Nabije Oosten, 1987), 1–2.

65. Briant, *From Cyrus to Alexander*, 713–15.

66. Persian policy toward governors, as argued by Edelman ("Dangerous Liaisons: How Hypothetical Sinuballits are Skewing the Dating of Sidonian and

Another possible dynastic succession, as previously mentioned, existed in Karia under the Hekatomnids—to which Briant parallels the Sanballats; although, this dynasty (i.e. in Karia) might be explained by the tenuous relationship of the Persian imperial government with the territories of Asia Minor.[67]

References to Sanballat/*snblṭ*[68] are found on coins and bullae from Samaria. Three series of coins can be connected to Sanballat/*snblṭ* as the property of the governor's office.[69] A fourth series has been proposed by Y. Meshorer and S. Qedar.[70] Cross argues that the *snblṭ* of Wadi-ed-Daliyeh papyrus 11[71] was a descendant of Samerina's governor.[72] He believes that this *snblṭ* was the third in a dynastic line of governors who held office over Samerina for about 100 years.[73] Cross's 100-year (dynastic) continuity is based partially on an acceptance of Josephus's reference to a second Sanballat, Sanaballetês (Σαναβαλλέτης).[74] He accepts

Samarian Coinage" [paper presented at the University of Sheffield, 2005]), tended to be non-dynastic in order to prevent families from accruing too much power. But compare Briant's statement of imperial and dynastic power in Asia Minor. He observes, "À l'intérieur de l'Asie Mineure, la conquête et l'occupation perses n'avaient pas signifié l'annexion et la fusion de tous les territoires dynastiques au sein de la nouvelle organisation impériale" (*Histoire de l'Empire perse*, 514–16 [514] [see also 497–500, esp. 498 of the ET]). Briant posits additionally that Paphlogonie was another example of a dynasty.

67. For an informed discussion of the Hekatomnids in the fourth century B.C.E., see Hornblower, *Mausolus*, 137–38.

68. For the purpose of clarity, I use Sanballat to refer to the unquestioned governor of Samerina and *snblṭ* to refer to the second and third figures that remain in question.

69. Ya'akov Meshorer and Shraga Qedar, *Samarian Coinage* (Numismatic Studies and Researches 9; Jerusalem: Israel Numismatic Society, 1999), 93 nos. 51–54. For a general discussion of the different series of coins, see Edelman, *The Origins of the 'Second' Temple*, 38–50.

70. Meshorer and Qedar, *Samarian Coinage*, 92 nos. 49, 50.

71. For a reproduction of the papyrus, see Gropp, *Samaria Papyri*, pl. XI. Another reference to *snblṭ* is found on Wadi-ed-Daliyeh bulla 22, which was attached to papyrus 16 (see Gropp's pl. XVII). This was one of two seals bearing a personal name in the collection (see Leith, *Wadi Daliyeh Seal Impressions*, 21).

72. F. M. Cross, "The Papyri and Their Historical Implications," in Lapp and Lapp, eds., *Discoveries in the Wâdi Ed-Dâliyeh*, 18.

73. See also Briant, *From Cyrus to Alexander*, 713–14.

74. Meshorer and Qedar (*Samarian Coinage*, 14–15) have adopted Cross's hypothesis. J. Elayi (*Sidon, cité autonome de l'Empire perse* [Paris: Idéaphane, 1990]) has published a work on Sidonian coins that uses Meshorer and Qedar's Samarian dating.

Josephus's accounting of Nikaso's, Sanballat's daughter, marriage to Manasseh, brother of Yaddua, the high priest of Jerusalem ca. 375 B.C.E. (*Ant.* 11.302–12, 321–25).[75] He assigns Wadi-ed-Daliyeh bulla 22 to this *snblṭ* rather than to the first. The coins and bullae from Samerina show that various individuals named Sanballat/*snblṭ* were governors, though they do not provide much more information beyond that.

Administration in Yehud. Briant believes that the *golah* community in Jerusalem enjoyed an internal autonomy. Fried, however, concludes that Yehud as a whole was not self-governing. Local officials held little real power, which remained in the hands of the imperial government and its appointees. She writes, "Persian-period Judah was not self-governing: There were no assemblies, no Jewish lay bodies to advise the governor, no sanhedrins. There was no vehicle for local control. Neither was Judah a theocracy. Local officials, whether priest or lay, held little real power."[76]

No local body of people held power over the politics of Yehud outside the control of the imperial government. While the imperial government probably did not concern itself over the local minutia of a province, those who managed the administration of a province did not act outside imperial control. Briant's "internal autonomy" is problematic because it allows such to occur in Yehud, whereas no known evidence supports this. The only sources one could draw support from are the biblical texts, but at many points those seem to have been written to legitimate *golah* control. These biblical sources do not even feign to discuss an imperial context, but a context centered on Jerusalem and the city's temple.[77]

Governors governed territories composed of smaller districts and answered to a satrap. These governors were often related locally to the area (cf. Ezra 5:14; 6:7; Neh 5:14–17; 12:26; Hag 1:1, 14; 2:2, 21). For example, the governors of Yehud all appear to be Jews. Were provinces self-governing? What seems initially to be the issue is a definition. If by "self-governing" one means local bodies that wholly controlled their provinces, then the answer seems to be negative. If one intends instead to show that the imperial government allowed local individuals to sit in the position of provincial government, as well as district and sub/half-district governments, then one might answer in the affirmative.

---

75. Cross, "Papyri," 17–24. Edelman ("Dangerous Liaisons") argues that the conclusion is tenuous, based on a different conclusion that Josephus's story is a variant of Neh 13:28–29.

76. Fried, *Priest and the Great King*, 233.

77. These conclusions will be discussed further throughout Chapters 3 and 5.

District Governors and Other Officials

A. Zertal writes of the administrative-structural development in the Levant preceding Persian control, "Administratively, the Assyrian provinces replaced the former independent sates of the Levant. A governor (Assyrian *bēl piḫati* or *šaknu*) was appointed head of each province/ *piḫati*, and the conquered populaces became Assyrian citizens."[78] This structure parallels that existing under the Persian administration.[79] The Assyrian title *bēl piḫati* [80] suggests *piḫati* refers to the area or officials over which a *bēl piḫati* holds administrative jurisdiction.

Stolper states that in the Murashu archives the term *pāḫātu* (LÚ.NAM) refers in part to an official appointed over a canal (cf. PBS 2/1 43, 59, 72).[81] Apla, son of Bel-Kašir, was appointed *pāḫātu* (LÚ.NAM) *ša ÍD LÚ Simmagir*: "officer in charge of the *simmagir* (official's) Canal." Napsanu, son of Iddin-Nabu, was appointed *pāḫātu ša Nār* ᵈ*Sîn*: "officer in charge of the left side of the Sin Canal."[82]

Thus the imperial government, through those in its employ, appears to have had a significant amount of control over its territories. Even "canal managers," Stolper writes, "were agents of the crown; they controlled the use of waterways and crown properties, agricultural equipment, and even field workers; they leased their holdings to others."[83] These canal managers were subordinates to the *mašennu* officials (cf. MA 9, 40).[84] The Murashu texts from Babylonia (esp. nos. 9, 40) indicate that *mašennu* officials were placed in charge over the area's canal districts.[85]

Two additional positions appear in the administrative structure. In Samerina, references to *rāb alāni* ("district governor") and *ḫazannu* ("city governor") are found (cf. ABL 91:12; ADD 166:2; 169:2; BBSt. No. 5 iii 2; No. 7 i 32; HSS 5 67:57).[86] The Aramean papyri, seals, seal impressions, and monies found to date from Samaria demonstrate a

78. Zertal, "Province of Samaria," 381, who cites KAJ 191:2.
79. Hornblower (*Mausolus*, 140) concludes the Persian government did not actively appoint Persians to political or administrative offices below the level of satrap or hyparch. Where non-Persian satraps were already in office, the imperial government replaced the satraps with Persians of its own choosing.
80. See BRM 101:5; Dar. 27:3; 338:4, 14; BHT pl. 13 iii 20; see also KAJ 103:6; 106:5; 191:3; 182:10; 184:8 (as cited by CAD).
81. Stolper, *Entrepreneurs and Empire*, 38–39.
82. PBS 2/1 43 and PBS 2/1 59, 72, respectively (as cited by ibid.).
83. Stolper, *Entrepreneurs and Empire*, 45.
84. Ibid., 47.
85. Veysel Donbaz and Matthew Stolper, *Istanbul Murašû Texts* (Leiden: Nederlands Instituut voor het Nabije Oosten, 1997), 4.
86. Zertal, "Province of Samaria," 381.

well-established and authoritative Persian presence.[87] Thus, the evidence from Samaria suggests the imperial government did not overlook territories in Syria-Palestine.

Even though the imperial government incorporated pre-existing administrative structures, a general framework of hierarchy existed. We must first situate the administration of any context within this framework, especially those "created" under the Persian empire. Officials employed by the imperial government exist at even the local levels, therefore denying the potential for a power vacuum.

Temples in the Empire

Both local temples and local elites lost power during the Persian period,[88] indicating a growing control by the empire. Dandamaev and Lukonin, however, argue that autonomous temple communities existed in Asia Minor in Mylasa under the Hekatomnids from the fifth century B.C.E. on.[89] Likewise, Dion, drawing on Weinberg's work, argues that this particular type of society was well represented in Asia Minor, Syria, and Mesopotamia.[90] But in his extensive work on Mausolus, Hornblower does not note a temple community under the Hekatomnids or any other area.[91] Hekatomnid-run Mylasa was a part of Karia. In the late nineties of the fourth century, Karia was formed into a separate province—before that time it had been part of Sardis.[92] Only in 360 B.C.E., when Karia took part in the 'Revolt of the Satraps,' did it pursue political aims at odds with those of the Persian empire.[93] That a dynasty was allowed to remain in place suggests the officials, as well as the area itself, remained loyal.[94]

---

87. See, for instance, Briant's informative discussion (*From Cyrus to Alexander*, 713–15). Cross has published a study ("Reconstruction," 4–18) drawing upon the legal papyri found in Wadi ed-Daliyeh, but he focuses on the genealogy of Jerusalem high priests and on the "Judean Restoration."

88. Fried, *Priest and the Great King*, 155.

89. Dandamaev and Lukonin, *Culture and Social Institutions*, 106.

90. Dion, "Civic-and-Temple," 283–84; Weinberg, "Das Bēit ʾAbōt"; idem, "Die Agrarverhältnisse in der Bürger-Tempel-Gemeinde der Achämenidenzeit," *Acta Antiqua* 22 (1974): 473–86; idem, "Bemerkungen zum Problem 'Der Vorhellenismus im Vorderen Orient'," *Klio* 58 (1976): 5–20; idem, "Zentral- und Partikulargewalt im achämenidischen Reich," *Klio* 59 (1977): 25–43.

91. Hornblower, *Mausolus*, 34–51. See also his *Greek World*.

92. Hornblower, *Mausolus*, 138.

93. Ibid.

94. Briant, *From Cyrus to Alexander*, 667–68. Also note the statements of Diodorus and Josephus that posit the imperial king (in this case, Artaxerxes III) confirmed satraps and officers (Diod. 11.71.1; *Ant.* 11.185). Therefore, if a dynasty

The temples erected in Lycia, after Lycia became part of Karia, a Persian satrapy, do not establish Persian support for local gods. Fried posits that the temples dedicated to King Kaunios at Xanthus and to Zeus Labraunda at Lymra were built for the new landowners of the Karian bureaucracy and the members of the Karian garrison and their families.[95] It is quite possible that the bureaucracy petitioned the Persian government for the cult in much the same manner as Udjahorresnet did for temples in Egypt. Even if that were so, however, it does not prove the autonomy of the cult; rather, it may show the influence of an aristocratic elite. Fried argues that the temples and their relative cults were used by the satrap Pixodarus to draw the Lycians more tightly into the Karian sphere of influence; religion was used as an instrument of political control.[96]

Likewise, in Babylonia, Cyrus allowed the various priesthoods to revive the ancient cults Nabonidus had neglected.[97] The cults responded by proclaiming Cyrus the chosen of Marduk and appointing him to the Babylonian throne, thus establishing Cyrus's legitimacy. This was, in fact, the normal Babylonian process for legitimating a ruler. Once he became a Babylonian king through the local process, he was no longer considered a foreign leader. To maintain good relations, Cyrus sought to patronize the cults in as many ways as possible.[98]

"With Babylon, then," writes Cook, "the whole of Abarnahara...fell to Cyrus by right of conquest, so he ruled from the Syrian Gates on the Cilician border to Gaza."[99] After his conquest of Babylon and its provinces, Cyrus turned the area over to Cambyses in 538 B.C.E. However, during the New Year's festival Cambyses refused to change his costume or lay down his arms. In a ceremony that some kings may have found degrading, the kings acted out symbolic submission to the Babylonian deities.[100] The ceremonial formula generally followed a "standard" pattern:

existed in Karia, one may conclude the officials were loyal until they took part in the "Revolt of the Satraps."

95. Fried, *Priest and the Great King*, 154–55.

96. Ibid., 129–37, 54–55.

97. E. Yamauchi (*Persia and the Bible* [Grand Rapids: Baker, 1996], 91) suggests Cyrus repaired the Eanna temple at Uruk, the Enunmah temple at Ur, and temples in Babylon.

98. Dandamaev and Lukonin, *Culture and Social Institutions*, 90.

99. Cook, *Persian Empire*, 32.

100.   See the text of the New Year's festival translated by A. Sachs (*ANET*, 331–34). See also the *akitu*-festival discussions of Cook and Olmstead. Cook, *Persian Empire*, 32; Olmstead, *History of the Persian Empire*, 86–87.

When he (that is, the king) reaches [the presence of the god Bel], the *urigallu*-priest shall leave (the sanctuary) and take away the scepter, the circle, and the sword [from the king]. He shall bring them [before the god Bel] and place them [on] a chair. He shall leave (the sanctuary) and strike the king's cheek. He shall place the...behind him. He shall accompany him (that is, the king) into the presence of the god Bel.... [H]e shall drag (him by) the ears and make him bow down to the ground. The king shall speak the following (only) once: "I did [not] sin, lord of the countries. I was not neglectful (of the requirements) of your godship. [I did not] destroy Babylon; I did not command its overthrow. [I did not]...the temple Esagil, I did not forget its rites. [I did not] rain blows on the cheek of a subordinate... I did [not] humiliate them. [I watched out] for Babylon; I did not smash its walls." ... [The *urigallu*-priest speaks:] "...Have no fear...which the god Bel... The god Bel [will listen to] your prayer...he will magnify your lordship...he will exalt your kingship... On the day of the *eššešu*-festival, do...in the festival of the Opening of the Gate, purify [your] hands...day and night... [The god Bel], whose city is Babylon..., whose temple is Esagil...whose dependents are the people of Babylon... The god Bel will bless you...forever. He will destroy your enemy, fell your adversary." After (the *urigallu*-priest) says (this), the king shall regain his *composure*. The scepter, circle, and sword [shall be restored] to the king. He [i.e. the *urigallu*-priest] shall strike the king's cheek. If, when [he strikes] the king's cheek, the tears flow, (it means that) the god Bel is friendly; if no tears appear, the god Bel is angry: the enemy will rise up and bring about his downfall.[101]

From the portion above, one may speculate along with Cook that while Cambyses may have found the ceremony degrading, his greater aversion was to being confirmed on the throne by the priests. Whatever the reason, by the next year, Cambyses no longer used the title, "King of Babylon."[102] While Cyrus had chosen religion as a tool to influence social and political control in Babylonia, Cambyses seems to have relied on his own imperial authority.[103] This is a choice that may have prompted the following response:

The fourth day, as Cambyses, son of C[yrus], went to the Egidri-kalama-sumu, [on his] arrival, the one in charge of the Egidri of Nabû who [...] the scepter, [did not let him take (?)] the hand of Nabû because of his Elamite dress.[104]

101. *ANET*, 334, trans. Sachs.
102. Cook, *Persian Empire*, 32.
103. Dandamaev and Lukonin, *Culture and Social Institutions*, 90.
104. Jean-Jacques Glassner, *Mesopotamian Chronicles* (ed. Benjamin R. Foster; SBLWAW 19; Atlanta: Society of Biblical Literature, 2004), 238–39.

Although the great sanctuaries of Babylonia were important social and economic centers, owning land and slaves, imperial superintendents still exercised financial control.[105] The temples were given substantial freedoms but the Persian government did not give temples complete autonomy, using them as instruments of imperial control.[106] In Egypt the reliance of the temples upon the policies of both Cambyses and Darius suggests that temples within the Persian empire were still bound to the "Law of the King."

It also appears that temples, as they have been since our earliest written records, were imperial organs of taxation and redistribution.[107] Schaper believes, based on the tax-collection process in Babylonia, *quppu ša šarri* (king's chest),[108] that the temple was responsible for collecting royal taxes and delivering them to the king.[109] He argues that this model was used even more aggressively by the Persian administration, which set up temples as fiscal administrative centers in its provinces: "The temple or temples of a given Achaemenid province or *mᵉdīnā* were responsible for collecting the taxes according to the targets set by the central government."[110] The individual(s) in charge of the royal taxes remained royal employees though the individuals were most likely stationed in local temples. The tax was always an imperial tax paid through a sanctuary, never a temple tax.[111] Because the imperial government desired a fiscal system that operated efficiently, the priests (and Levites in Jerusalem) "seem to have been given a regular stipend."[112] Nevertheless, one should not interpret the presence of a royal payroll in the temples as proof that the temples, or cults, governed their respective provinces. "[I]t must be stressed that the sanctuaries—amongst them the Jerusalem temple—merely acted as outlets of the imperial 'Inland Revenue.'"[113] In other words, the temples functioned as ancient banks.[114]

---

105. Cook, *Persian Empire*, 174.
106. Fried, *Priest and the Great King*, 129–37.
107. Ibid., 55.
108. For further reference on the *quppu ša šarrî*, see also, as cited by CAD, Dar. 216:3; *I.Cyr.* 271:14; CT 22.131.10–11; TCL 9 147:6–7; 12 117:8; YOS 7 19:19, 59:17, 140:25, 190:17, 198:2.
109. Schaper, "Jerusalem Temple," 529.
110. Ibid., 535.
111. Ibid., 534, 539.
112. Ibid., 537.
113. Ibid., 539.
114. This proposal seems to work well with an understanding of the financial and military obligations of satrapies and provinces. Imperial revenues required

Schaper's argument is related to those previously made by Briant, R. Descat, and A. Kuhrt.[115] Kaptan also argues, based in part on the Persepolis texts, that not all taxes went directly to the royal treasury; some most likely passed through provincial treasuries functioning as storehouses.[116]

Other Imperial Policies: The Military and Miscellaneous Taxes
Though the Persian empire relied heavily upon hired mercenaries, it still maintained its own armies. Aside from conscript soldiers, the 10,000-man army known as the "Immortals" stood as a central symbol within the collective Persian army. Herodotus states that the Immortals were so called because their numbers never changed. As soon as one died or was no longer able to serve, another replaced him. Comprised entirely of Persians, the Immortals were given the "most brilliant equipment" and were considered the best in the army.[117] Their equipment was laden with gold, and provisions were carried for them separate from the rest of the soldiers (*Hist.* 7.83). Cook claims that of the 10,000 soldiers, 1,000 were designated as the battalion closest to the king. They were identified by the golden apples on their spear butts.[118]

To build its more extended army, the Persian government set in place a land tenure system through which individuals/families granted land were required to serve as conscripts for a specified period.[119] According to Dandamaev and Lukonin, the stability of the Achaemenid empire depended to a large extent on the conscripted army "which was distributed in garrisons and, in case of an uprising or war in any country, was transferred along roads that had already existed for a long time or had

storehouses in locations near areas of collection. On the financial and military obligations of satrapies and provinces, see Briant, *From Cyrus to Alexander*, 63–64.

115.   Briant, *Rois, tributs et paysans*, vol. 43 (Centre de recherches d'histoire ancienne: Paris, 1982), 292–96; idem, "L'histoire achéménide: Sources méthodes, raisonnement et modèles," *Topoi* 4 (1994): 109–30; idem, *From Cyrus to Alexander*, 410–35; Raymond Descat, "Mnesimachos, Hérodote et le Système Tributaire Achémèmide," *Revue des etudes anciennes* 87 (1985): 97–112; Amélie Kuhrt, *The Ancient Near East c. 3000–330 B.C.* (Routledge History of the Ancient World 2; London/New York: Routledge, 1995), 690.

116.   Kaptan, *The Daskyleion Bullae*, 22–23.

117.   Cook (*Persian Empire*, 105) points out that while the Immortals were indeed pampered, the select Persian cavalry was not "unappreciated."

118.   Ibid., 101.

119.   The Persian king was perceived to own all land and reserved the right to distribute it. For an extended discussion, see Briant, *From Cyrus to Alexander*, 415–21.

been built especially for this purpose."[120] Hornblower, however, is not convinced and notes: "A fundamental question may be asked, without hope of a final answer: did these obligations encumber the land (that is, its possessor for the time being) or were individuals personally liable down the generations?"[121] According to Briant, the Persian king owned all land once the area was conquered.[122] "Possession" of the land entailed meeting stated military obligations.[123]

Dandamaev and Lukonin state that by the fifth century B.C.E., the Persian infantry, paid with land, was replaced by Greek mercenaries who were paid in silver and gold coins.[124] The transition to hired soldiers, along with Darius' administrative and tax restructuring, led to an increased social stratification that brought the empire into what Dandamaev and Lukonin describe as the beginnings of a feudal system.[125]

Dandamaev and Lukonin also claim that the Achaemenids set up military forces in provinces with people not local to the area. The Elephantine military colony, for example, was populated by Persians, Medes, Choresmians, Babylonians, Phoenicians, Aramaeans, Jews, and others.[126] Military settlers in Elephantine lived with their families and were divided into subdivisions of 100 men each.[127]

The dinners of the king, for which satraps were responsible, were yet more examples of the power of the Persian king's political authority.

---

120.   Dandamaev and Lukonin, *Culture and Social Institutions*, 222.

121.   Hornblower, *Mausolus*, 160.

122.   Young ("Consolidation," 96) argues that to claim the king owned all land within the empire, and that taxes were nominally rent, is an extrapolation backwards from Sasanian legal forms. However, the idea that the king owned the land in his kingdom or empire does not necessarily require that taxes be considered "rent." The taxes of the Persian empire do not appear to be over land, but more generally requirements imposed upon the empire's subjects. Thus, it is possible to say that the king owned the land without concluding that taxes were "rent" for use of the land.

123.   Briant, *From Cyrus to Alexander*, 405.

124.   Dandamaev and Lukonin, *Culture and Social Institutions*, 199, 202, 229.

125.   "It is the opinion of these scholars that the Achaemenid kings, by creating military colonies in the conquered countries and by distributing land allotments to their civilian and military servants, had promoted the development of feudalism. Thus, feudalism is regarded in Western scholarship not as a distinct socio-economic formation: any society is considered feudal where political decentralization or a hierarchical dependence of subjects is observed" (ibid., 177). Balcer (*Sparda*, 123) argues that the empire set up a vassal system, as demonstrated in the legal strictures of taxation and military service.

126.   Dandamaev and Lukonin, *Culture and Social Institutions*, 230–31.

127.   Ibid., 231.

Dinners were large affairs that could economically break a satrapy.[128] When the military passed through a province, the subject peoples were required to provide victuals for the king's table.[129] One can note from Herodotus that the requirements necessary here were quite extreme and most locales were fortunate the king did not require provisions for more than one meal. As the military departed, the king took the required silver and gold vessels (*Hist.* 7.118–20).

Dandamaev and Lukonin suggest that the cohesiveness of the Persian army was related to the apparent lack of a strong class division. This was the result, they propose, of an empire defined primarily as an agrarian-based society.[130] Strict class division, as they argue, would have resulted in the avoidance of the menial tasks, such as military service, by the upper class and the obligatory fulfillment of these tasks by the lower class, and a more pronounced reliance by the Persian empire on Greek mercenaries. Yet Briant notes that the development of class division can be seen in the existence of corvée laborers.[131] In the case of Babylon, the temples were furnished through labor requisitioned by the satrap. Construction and maintenance of canals also required the use of laborers, designated as the service of the *urāšu* in Neo-Babylonian texts (cf. MA 9, 40; MS 59).[132] The existence of corvée labor in itself implies a division of society between upper and lower classes and illustrates a stratified society.[133] Lords or landowners used forced labor in lieu of monetary payment, a situation most commonly found in feudal societies. Monarchies also used corvée labor as a responsibility/requirement for citizenship or, in the case of the Persian empire, as an obligation.

Not only were subjects required to meet imperial taxes, they were also required to pay the various taxes of the satraps. Briant observes that satraps mirrored the image of a king in their provinces not only in figure but also in lifestyle.[134] Plutarch even suggests that a belief existed that

---

128. Briant, *From Cyrus to Alexander*, 286–97.
129. Cook, *Persian Empire*, 105.
130. Dandamaev and Lukonin, *Culture and Social Institutions*, 229.
131. Even Dandamaev and Lukonin (ibid., 224) admit that the military was divided between nobility and farmers. While the cavalry was comprised of nobility, the infantry were the farmers.
132. See also Briant, *From Cyrus to Alexander*, 401–2.
133. For instance, Briant writes, "Il est également probable que le creusement du canal de Suez fut réalisé grâce à la conscription de paysans." And, "[L]es paysans étaient en règle générale soumis et au tribut et aux corvées (dont étaient exempts les jardiniers d'Apollon en raison d'un privilège royal)" (ibid., 413).
134. Ibid., 414.

Cyrus the Younger, a satrap, rebelled against his brother because he was not receiving enough for his meals each day (*Art.* 4.1). While Plutarch claimed that this was absurd, it does demonstrate the weighty requirements of a satrap's table. Xenophon described one territory as being so impoverished it no longer had enough provisions for even one more meal (*Hel.* 4.1.33). Nehemiah 5:15–17 suggests that even the governors of Yehud required provisions for their own tables, as it is this context that could make sense of his claim to not have taken the "food of the governor."[135] In sum, provinces were required to pay imperial taxes and to provide for the satraps and governors.[136]

Xenophon's *Oeconomica* offers a further glance into the level and type of authority the Persian empire held over its provinces. According to him, because Darius was fond of art and gardens (*Oec.* 4.4), the imperial king required satraps to create and maintain gardens within their provinces (*Oec.* 4.8). Briant (referring to *Oec.* 7.6, 12) echoes that each satrap was effectively ordered to create and maintain a "paradise" for the king.[137] While royal gardens may not seem to have much to tell about politics and governing structures, the mandatory royal gardens point to the authority of the Persian king over his territories.[138] Control by the means of taxes and military power is normally considered part and parcel of empires. When that control extends to more seemingly insignificant areas, such as gardens—in terms of politics and stability—it is harder to argue that the Persian empire operated with a *laissez-faire* policy. That the king actively controlled land and material is also evident in Nehemiah, where the text speaks of the king's forest (Neh 2:8).

Briant maintains that there is no doubt that Yehud, like the other provinces, was subject to imperial tribute among the variety of other imperial, satrapal, and provincial taxes.[139] He appears, however, to give the Persian-period biblical texts significant credibility when he writes that the community of Jerusalem enjoyed an internal autonomy it had known since Cyrus; the Persian authorities merely required the community to manifest its loyalty, especially in tribute, to maintain its permitted autonomy.[140] He speaks to the relative "freedom" that the Persian king gave to its provinces and explains that the internal autonomy of a

---

135. Dandamaev and Lukonin, *Culture and Social Institutions*, 184.
136. Ibid., 192.
137. Briant, *From Cyrus to Alexander*, 232–34.
138. See also ibid., 584.
139. Ibid., 487–88.
140. Ibid., 488.

2. The Face of the Persian Empire

community subject to royal domination implies that the Persian king took on the role of protector and guarantor of local customs if the localities, or provinces, did not conflict with Persian interests.[141]

During the fourth century B.C.E., according to Dandamaev and Lukonin, collection of taxes turned into direct robbery and coercion and resulted in numerous uprisings throughout the empire.[142] They characterize the Persian empire as a "parasite" living off the labor of the people in the land,[143] distributing large chunks of the land to Persian nobility and royal soldiers. The monetary taxes and grain requirements for the upkeep of the garrison troops all had a negative effect on the development of productive forces within the provinces.[144] "In addition to paying taxes, the subjects had to hand over their children to perform domestic work for the Persian kings, as bakers, cooks, wine-waiters, eunuchs, etc. According to the Book of Esther, the subjects had to send hundreds of concubines to the Persian kings."[145]

Briant shows that the variety of taxes was considerable. A decree found at Aegae reveals a rather extensive listing of taxes and their percentages on fruits, sheep, goats, deer, wild boar, and so on. Briant, however, is not convinced that this type of list existed during the time of Darius, noting that the necessary documentary proof is missing.[146] It is possible that the introduction of this type of structured taxation was due in part to Darius's reorganization.

According to Herodotus (*Hist.* 3.89), Darius divided the empire into twenty provinces,[147] established satrapies, and appointed the tribute that each should pay. Herodotus states further that under the reigns of Cyrus and Cambyses there had been no regular fixed tax, only a collection of so-called gifts.[148] With the construction of the administrative tax system,

141.   Ibid., 584.

142.   Dandamaev and Lukonin, *Culture and Social Institutions*, 193.

143.   This reflects a Marxist view of empires in general.

144.   Dandamaev and Lukonin, *Culture and Social Institutions*, 194.

145.   Ibid. As is generally accepted in biblical studies, however, the book of Esther is not always a reliable source (cf. Susan Niditch, "Legends of Wise Heroes and Heroines," in *The Hebrew Bible and Its Modern Interpreters* [ed. Douglas A. Knight and Gene M. Tucker; Chico, Calif.: Scholars Press, 1985], 445–46).

146.   Briant, *From Cyrus to Alexander*, 399–400.

147.   It should be noted that Herodotus's list and the Behistun Inscription differ. See Dandamaev and Lukonin, *Culture and Social Institutions*, 98–99.

148.   Herodotus notes that because of the tax system, the Persians had a saying that Darius was the shopkeeper, Cambyses a master of slaves, and Cyrus a father. In other words, Darius kept petty accounts for everything, Cambyses was a tyrant, and Cyrus sought out everything for the good of the provinces (*Hist.* 3.89). Though

those paying in silver were required to use the Babylonian talent and those paying in gold were required to use the Euboic standard.

In conclusion, this section shows that the Persian empire held and sought to hold a strong grip on its territories. This is an important realization for the broader picture of the nature of the relationship between the imperial government and its provinces, because in light of the preceding evidence, the conclusion that Yehud maintained political and economic autonomy is difficult to sustain.[149] It was, after all, a province of the Persian empire.

Imperial Administration and Presence in Territories Near Yehud

Asia Minor and the Persian Empire

The relationship between the Persian empire and Asia Minor was tenuous; Asia Minor seemed often to be just out of the imperial reach. To what extent, then, do the administrative officials and imperial territories in Asia Minor parallel the other areas of the empire?

Of all the areas within the empire, this area may be the most unique. It was from Asia Minor, after all, that the sword that would strike the Achilles heel of the Persians came, inaugurating a change from a Persian

---

perhaps a bit tongue-in-cheek, Herodotus's statement does give an indication of the type of individuals the three kings were. Cyrus, for example, allowed himself to be crowned King of Babylon by Marduk. Cambyses refused to partake in the New Year's Festival (though he did end up conceding to portions of the ceremony), and Darius, following his troublesome ascension, sought to create a more stable and consistent empire through a structured administrative system. Herodotus also notes that the tax for Babylonia was 1,000 talents, in addition to the annual provision of 500 boys as eunuchs to serve in the imperial court (*Hist.* 3.92). The only province proper not taxed within the Persian empire was that of Persia (*Hist.* 3.97). The Ethiopians, Colchians, and Arabians were also not taxed because they regularly offered "gifts" to the king. None were included under a satrapy or among the taxpayers of a province (*Hist.* 3.97). The nature of the "gifts" as described by Herodotus, however, presents striking similarities to a tax.

149.   Hoglund (*Achaemenid Imperial Administration*, 207–40) and Berquist (*Judaism in Persia's Shadow*, 131–46) propose that, while not a doorway, Yehud held some military, economic, and political strategic purpose for the Persian empire. Fortresses established in Yehud offered ready access to surrounding areas, such as Egypt. In addition, note T. Eskenazi and E. Judd ("Marriage to a Stranger in Ezra 9–10," in *Second Temple Studies. Vol. 2, Temple and Community in the Persian Period* [ed. Tamara C. Eskenazi and Kent H. Richards; Sheffield: Sheffield Academic Press, 1994], 277), who identify Yehud as a strategic doorway for the empire's dealings with Egypt and Greece.

empire to a Greek empire under Alexander. It is also from investigations of this area that scholars have developed theoretical models that can be used for analyses of Yehud: *synoecism*[150] and tyranny.[151]

Cook holds that what Xenophon calls hyparchs (cf. *Hel.* 6.1.2, 3)[152] can probably be regarded as large fief-holders.[153] In comparison, Fried describes the relationship of Egyptian satrapies to the Persian empire as fiefs.[154] In Egypt, hyparchs functioned as acting-satraps when the satrap was away, but they generally appear to be officials administering the provinces.[155]

D. Stockton proposes that oligarchic structures preceded democratic ones in portions of Asia Minor.[156] For example, in 413 B.C.E. a group of revolutionaries proposed to capitalize on the anti-democratic sentiment growing in Athens by setting up an oligarchy. He states that the Persian government supported the revolutionaries, preferring an oligarchic form of government to a democratic one.[157]

The seeming variety of possible governing structures in Asia Minor led Hornblower to conclude that the Persian empire did not suppress local autonomy in Asia Minor,[158] though what benefited one area often dispossessed another.[159] In light of Persia's dominating concern with the Greeks, any action or decision taken in Asia Minor on the part of the empire should be read primarily as political. Though one might conclude that the empire permitted significant levels of autonomy in Asia Minor, the current analysis of imperial actions suggests that this was not the case.[160] What is more, throughout its existence the empire sought to

150. A. Alt, *Judas Nachbarn zur Zeit Nehemia* (Kleine Schriften zur Geschichte des Volkes Israel 2; Munich: Beck, 1953); David J. A. Clines, *Ezra, Nehemiah and Esther* (NCB; Grand Rapids: Eerdmans, 1984), 211; Wilhelm Rudolph, *Esra und Nehemia samt 3. Esra* (HAT 20; Tübingen: J. C. B. Mohr, 1949), 181.

151. Smith, *Palestinian Parties*, 138–39.

152. For example, Xenophon defines Alcetas from Epirus as a hyparch, thereby disagreeing with Diodorus, who refers to Alcetas as "King of the Molossians" (Diod. 15.13, 36).

153. Cook, *Persian Empire*, 178.

154. Fried, *Priest and the Great King*, 106.

155. Cf. *Ana.* 4.4.4; *Hel.* 6.1.2, 3; *Hist.* 3.70, 126; 4.166; 6.1. For further discussion, see ibid., 136.

156. David Stockton, *The Classical Athenian Democracy* (Oxford: Oxford University Press, 1990), 142.

157. Ibid., 145–56.

158. Hornblower, *Greek World*, 70.

159. Hornblower, *Mausolus*, 142–43.

160. E. Dusinberre, for example, believes local culture was altered by the political transformations resulting from Persian presence, as specifically illustrated

control Asia Minor, as can be shown in its constant battles with the Greeks (from which the Greeks would ultimately emerge victorious).

It is possible that democracies existed in portions of Asia Minor, but that they existed outside the Persian sphere of control—for example, in the city of Athens. Apparently, the Persian empire opposed democratic polities as a means of gaining political control and in 413 B.C.E. lent its support and resources to Sparta in its struggle against Athens.[161] After a level of calm had been reached, the conflict was renewed in 408 when Athens provoked Sparta and affronted the Persian king by assisting the rebel satrap Amorges.[162]

The imperial government changed loyalties and lent its support at this point to Athens in 392,[163] but in this tentative time the attempted alliance between democratic Athens and the Persian empire did not survive, taking but a few staggering steps before it collapsed. Hornblower notes that a subsequent anti-Persian revolution at Rhodes followed the example of Athens by establishing a democracy.[164] What can be said with certainty is that the Persian empire did not favor a democratic system of government in its provinces, as too much control would be taken out of the hands of the Persian government.

M. Austin believes that tyrannies proliferated in Greek cities and that the Persian government under Darius supported individual tyrants.[165] But compare Hornblower, who believes that the Persian empire did not suppress local, autonomous authorities in the area.[166] He does, however, suggest the empire restricted the freedoms of imperial subjects by imposing subjection to satraps and exacting of tribute, which included personal military service.[167] How then should one understand "tyrant"? Was it an autonomous ruler, or a strong-armed "satrap" who remained loyal to the imperial government? Given the general distaste of the Greeks for the Persians, the latter is a viable definition.[168]

by the example of Sardis, capital of Lydia ("Satrapal Sardis: Achaemenid Bowls in an Achaemenid Capital," *AJA* 103 [1999]: 73–102).

161. Stockton, *The Classical Athenian Democracy*, 157.
162. Ibid., 145.
163. Hornblower, *Mausolus*, 126.
164. Ibid.
165. M. M. Austin, "Greek Tyrants and the Persians, 546–479 B.C," *CQ* 40 (1990): 300; see also 304. Young ("Consolidation," 68) posits that Darius placed some tyrants in power, including Coes, who was a tyrant in Mytilene, and Histiaeus, who was a tyrant in Miletus.
166. Hornblower, *Greek World*, 70.
167. Ibid., 69.
168. Cf. Hornblower, *Mausolus*, 90, 117.

The reliance upon Greek tyrants by the Persian empire led to the series of revolts in Asia Minor.[169] Young writes that when Darius put down the revolts in 494, he deposed most of the tyrants. Herodotus's statement that all tyrants[170] were deposed (*Hist.* 6.43) cannot be entirely true and Herodotus's claim most likely refers only to Ionia proper.[171]

A. Momigliano argues that the Greeks generally perceived Persian (sponsored) tyranny to be contrary to their own democratic system of government.[172] Plato and Aristotle, as examples, both point to the fall of Athens as justification for the redefined idea of "empire." According to these philosophers, the empire should not expand beyond the city-state or the narrow geographic limits within which a city-state could function.[173] For the Greeks, the Persian empire was tyrannical precisely because of its greedy consumption of land. Without question, the on-going struggle between the Persians the Greeks influenced this perception.

Does the situation in Asia Minor demonstrate that autonomy existed in the empire? W. Vogelsang writes,

> [T]he apparent cultural autonomy of at least certain of the subject lands, although still requiring an explanation, needs further confirmation and cannot directly be used as a basis for the interpretation of the emergence of and longevity of the Achaemenid empire, and certainly not to substantiate the idea of far-reaching political autonomy of the subject lands.[174]

In other words, from a relatively few examples which lack adequate substantiation, one cannot prove that the provinces elsewhere within the empire—or even in Asia Minor—were autonomous. In fact, the empire required satraps to employ imperial scribes who reported to the king concerning the affairs of the satrapy. More covertly, "king's eyes" and 'king's ears' were additional means of monitoring the events within the

169. Austin, "Greek Tyrants," 289.
170. Referring to Herodotus (*Hist.* 4.97; 5.11), Austin ("Greek Tyrants," 304) asserts that Coes asked Darius to be made "ruler" of Mytilene. In other words, what has often been translated as "tyrant" is really "ruler." Herodotus, according to Austin, makes no mention of "tyrant." At the same time, however, Herodotus does mention twelve "tyrannies" in Asia Minor (300).
171. Young, "Consolidation," 68–69.
172. Arnaldo Momigliano, "Persian Empire and Greek Freedom," in *The Idea of Freedom: Essays in Honour of Isaiah Berlin* (ed. A. Ryan; Oxford: Oxford University Press, 1979), 145.
173. M. Hammond makes mention of the arguments given by Plato and by Aristotle ("Ancient Imperialism: Contemporary Justifications," *HSCP* 58 [1948]: 111).
174. W. J. Vogelsang, *The Rise and Organisation of the Achaemenid Empire* (Leiden: Brill, 1992), 4–5.

provinces (cf. *Hist.* 1.114; *Oec.* 4; *Cyr.* 8.6.16).[175] Furthermore, as Darius's deposing of tyrants demonstrates, local elites in Asia Minor lost power during the Persian period.[176]

Idumea

Eph'al argues that the view that Idumea was a distinct province is conjectural and can at best be based only on evidence about the Hellenistic period.[177] However, it is not clear that one needs to restrict the province to the Hellenistic period. Use of the monumental building in Lachish (Tell ed-Duweir), referred to as "the residence,"[178] can be dated to the Persian period and may have been the governor's residence.[179] Thus, the residence can be dated to the imperial government's reorganization of the Cisjordan, during which Yehud was reorganized and Jerusalem rebuilt.

Y. Aharoni, however, dated the residence in Lachish to the first half of the seventh century B.C.E., to the days of either Sennacherib or Esarhaddon.[180] He suggests that after Assyrian rule ended local Jewish administration continued to make use of the structure. He noted that the remains of Stratum II indicate that the building had been partially destroyed. Saved from complete destruction, the building, he suggests, may have been resettled, though in poor condition, during the Persian period.[181]

175. See also the discussions of J. Balcer, "The Athenian Episkopos and the Achaemenid 'King's Eye'," *AJP* 98 (1977): 252–63; idem, *Sparda*, 123; Fried, *Priest and the Great King*, 217; Olmstead, *History of the Persian Empire*, 59; Young, "Consolidation," 90. Balcer describes Athenian imitation of the "king's eyes" office within the Persian administrative system by the Athenians (*episkopos*). He also notes that the general administrative system set up by Darius was very intricate. Fried states that judges appointed by the imperial government also served as "king's eyes" and "king's ears." Olmstead writes that the king's eyes and ears established more effective control.

176. Fried, *Priest and the Great King*, 155.

177. Eph'al, "Syria-Palestine under Achaemenid Rule," 158.

178. Excavated by O. Tufnell and published in *Lachish II: The Iron Age (Tell Ed-Duwei)* (London: Oxford University Press, 1953); idem, *Lachish III: The Iron Age (Tell Ed-Duwei)* (London: Oxford University Press, 1953).

179. W. J. Bennett Jr. and Jeffrey A. Blakely, *Tell El-Hesi: The Persian Period (Stratum V)* (American Schools of Oriental Research; Winona Lake: Eisenbrauns, 1989), 337.

180. Yohanan Aharoni, *Investigations at Lachish: The Sanctuary and the Residency (Lachish V)* (Publications of the Institute of Archaeology 4; Tel Aviv: Gateway, 1975), 36, 40.

181. Ibid., 33. But see also Campbell ("Jewish Shrines," 166), who remains unconvinced by Aharoni's argument.

D. Ussishkin writes that pottery fragments from pit 3017—found together with burnt brick rubble and other debris—date generally to the Persian period, suggesting that the area was occupied during this time before some event of destruction.[182] Tufnell had also previously concluded that pottery found on the floor suggests the residence was built ca. 450 B.C.E. and remained in use until ca. 350.[183] A. Fantalkin and O. Tal, however, date the residence in Lachish, the city's walls and its gate to ca. 400 B.C.E. They suggest that this building activity was based on a Persian preconceived plan and was a response to the empire's loss of Egypt.[184] Their dating—based on a re-examination of the pottery (plain Attic ware and painted Black and Red Figure ware) that underlay the residence—provides an alternative date to Tufnell's proposal.[185] According to them, a few of the sherds from which Tufnell established an anchor for her dating may have been heirlooms of high-ranking Persian officials.[186] As heirlooms, they would not offer a suitable basis for establishing a dating typology.

Stern remains skeptical about the date because, as he suggests, the excavators were not complete in distinguishing the building phases. Because they did not record the elevation of their finds or their location on the floors, their chronological data cannot be rechecked.[187] He concludes that Aharoni's description of the residence as a combination of a Syrian *bit-hilani* and an Assyrian open-court house accurately portrays the essence of the building. "Moreover, the combination of two separate plans in a single building is one of the characteristics of provincial Persian palaces. The Lachish Residence, therefore, seems to have been constructed under Achaemenid influence."[188] Stern suggests that the difference of this building among the other buildings of the Persian period in Palestine can be explained by the fact that this building was undoubtedly a palace.[189] This conclusion fits with that of Bennett and Blakely who suggest that the residence was the governor's residence.[190] Carter extends the conclusion of Bennett and Blakely when he suggests that Lachish was a provincial seat, though he remains ambivalent about

182. David Ussishkin, "Excavations at Tel Lakhish—1973–1977: Preliminary Report," *Tel Aviv* 5 (1978): 31, 41.
183. Tufnell, *Lachish III*, 48, 133.
184. Fantalkin and Tal, "Re-Dating Lachish Level I," 168–71.
185. Ibid., 172–73; Tufnell, *Lachish III*, 58–59.
186. Fantalkin and Tal, "Re-Dating Lachish Level I," 173.
187. Stern, *Archaeology*, 2:449.
188. Ibid., 2:468.
189. Ibid., 2:468–69.
190. Bennett and Blakely, *Tell El-Hesi*, 337.

the specifics. "Lachish was probably the seat of another province, perhaps Idumea."[191]

The temple in Lachish, another building of significance to this investigation because of what it might say regarding the state of Yahwism in Syria-Palestine during the Persian period, was possibly Yahwistic, though the evidence is inconclusive. Aharoni proposed that two temples or shrines existed in Lachish, and that both were Yahwistic but neither was built during the Persian period. The design of the temples and shrines—Temple 106 and Building 10 (Building R/Q/S 15/16)—was parallel to the Iron-Age temple at Arad, whose last stages (Strata VII, VI) are attributed to the seventh century B.C.E.[192] According to him, Temple 106 demonstrates a "superior" construction to Building 10, which he describes as a shrine. Aharoni argued that no trace of a cult was found near the vicinity of Temple 106 that dated to the Persian period. Based in part on an inscribed altar found near Building 10, however, he concluded that a cult did exist in connection with Building 10 during this period, though this was not the period when the building was built.[193] Temple 106, on other hand, was built sometime during the third century.[194] Based on the inscribed incense altar and the likeness of the two temples to that of Iron-Age Arad, Aharoni proposed that a Yahwistic cult was active at Lachish. The altar belonged to an earlier stratum and showed no signs of use during the later Persian period.

He also concluded that the cult at Lachish, like the cult at Elephantine, must have pledged to observe a prohibition from the time of Hezekiah forbidding sacrifice at any location other than the Jerusalem temple by not offering sacrifices.[195] This conclusion is not well-founded. One can easily demonstrate that the cult at Elephantine chose not to offer sacrifices in order to commend themselves to the sensibilities of those who surrounded them.[196] Concluding that the Elephantine cult avoided

191.   Carter, *Emergence of Yehud*, 292.

192.   Aharoni, *Investigations at Lachish*, 9, 11. Stern (*Archaeology*, 2:201–3) suggests that this temple may serve as an example for all other Judean temples and sanctuaries of the "Assyrian period" (732–604 B.C.E.).

193.   Aharoni (*Investigations at Lachish*, 40) argues that initial building activities in Lachish occurred sometime during the seventh century B.C.E. to establish an Assyrian governor-residence.

194.   Ibid., 11.

195.   Ibid., 9.

196.   Chapter 3 addresses this in more detail. See also Ahlström, *The History of Ancient Palestine*, 871; Briant, *From Cyrus to Alexander*, 602–7; Fried, *Priest and the Great King*, 102–3.

sacrifice to align itself with the Jerusalem cult from the days of Hezekiah is speculative and without any substantial basis.

If the residence dates from ca. 450 and reflects social activity during this time, the residence may have been either the governor's seat of a sub-province or district within Idumea, or it was a facility used as an alternate governor's residence at certain times of the year or used by Persian officials touring through the satrapy.[197] Fantalkin and Tal date the temple and residence in Lachish to ca. 400 B.C.E.[198] If, on the other hand, the temple and palace date to 400, they may have been part of establishing Lachish as the capital of a new province. This date coincides with the Egyptian revolt of approximately the same year and may have been part of an imperial refortification policy.[199]

The Persian government can be said to have been present in the entire area surrounding Yehud, as well as being "concerned" over the administration of that wider area.[200] Neither Yehud's supposedly autonomous existence, nor the Jerusalem cult's supposed administrative and judicial control over the province finds a parallel in the current data set. The biblical texts are the only sources that might make this claim, but the degree to which they reflect reality may be questioned. Thus the activity in Lachish could be interpreted as a demonstration of imperial concern for the stability of the broader Palestine area. From an economic standpoint, Lachish was also an important location because it was located near a major trade route between the coastal plain and the Hebron hills.

Udjahorresnet's Role in Lower Egypt
Satraps and governors were not the only appointed offices in the imperial administrative system. Evidence exists to suggest that the imperial government employed ministers of foreign affairs, as shown by the example of Udjahorresnet and perhaps even Ezra.[201] According to his autobiographical inscription, Udjahorresnet was bestowed the titles of chief physician, priest, scribe, and a supervisor of scribes involved in the

197. As suggested in Edelman, *The Origins of the 'Second' Temple*, 274.
198. Fantalkin and Tal, "Re-Dating Lachish Level I," 167–97.
199. Edelman, *The Origins of the 'Second' Temple*, 277.
200. Leith (*Wadi Daliyeh Seal Impressions*, 7–8) also concludes that a *laissez-faire* mentality does not accurately represent the imperial government.
201. J. Blenkinsopp, "The Mission of Udjahorresnet and Those of Ezra and Nehemiah," *JBL* 106 (1987): 409–21. See also J. Bright (*A History of Israel* [2d ed.; Philadelphia: Westminster, 1972], 387) who speaks of Ezra being a minister of foreign affairs, but he does not discuss Udjahorresnet.

administration of the judicial system in Egypt.[202] When Cambyses invaded Egypt, Udjahorresnet actively collaborated with the Persians by initiating Cambyses into Egyptian customs, religious beliefs, and observances.[203] Having already served as a naval commander under the last two pharaohs of the Saitic dynasty, Amasis (570–526) and Psammeticus III (526–525), Udjahorresnet was no doubt aware of the Persian strength and of the mercenary armies it employed. His experience gave Cambyses reason to consider him a valuable asset. While Udjahorresnet's titles reflect a level of influence within the Persian administration, that he was able to prompt Cambyses to restore[204] the cultic and dynastic center at Sais suggests that his administrative role was substantial under Cambyses.[205] When not in Sais, Udjahorresnet served the Persian government in Susa as the government's special advisor on Egyptian affairs.[206] It is likely that in this capacity Darius later sent Udjahorresnet back to Egypt to review the religious and administrative activities of the Houses of Life.[207]

Udjahorresnet's titles are extensive:

> The one honoured by Neith-the-Great, the mother of god, and by the gods of Sais, the prince, count, royal seal-bearer, sole companion, true beloved King's friend, the scribe, inspector of council scribes, chief scribe of the great outer hall, administrator of the palace, commander of the royal navy under the King of Upper and Lower Egypt, *Khenemibre*, commander of the royal navy under the King of Upper and Lower Egypt, *Ankhkare*, Udjahorresne; engendered by the administrator of the castles (of the red

202.   See M. Lichtheim, *Ancient Egyptian Literature*. Vol. 3, *The Late Period* (Berkeley: University of California Press, 1980), 36–41, for a translation of the inscription.

203.   Blenkinsopp, "Mission of Udjahorresnet," 409–10.

204.   Udjahorresnet's restoration program might be paralleled to that portrayed in Ezra–Nehemiah: "The restoration…included the following: expulsion of foreigners from the temple precincts; elimination of all ritual impurities; installation of legitimate cult personnel; reestablishment of traditional religious observances; provision of the necessary support from the Persian government…" (ibid., 410).

205.   Ibid. Yamauchi (*Persia and the Bible*, 91) notes Cambyses provided funds for the temple at Sais in Egypt, and the temple of Amon at Hibis in the Khargah Oasis was rebuilt by the order of Darius.

206.   Briant, *From Cyrus to Alexander*, 57–59.

207.   See also Lichtheim's translation of Udjahorresnet's inscription (*Ancient Egyptian Literature*, 3:36–37). Briant (*From Cyrus to Alexander*, 473) writes that Udjahorresnet restored the teaching of medicine at the House of Life, insuring that the students had all that was necessary for their studies. These actions were not solely for the benefit of the Egyptian satrapy. Egyptian doctors held a high reputation in the imperial court.

crown), chief-of-Pe priest, *rnp*-priest, priest of the Horus Eye, prophet of Neith who presides over the nome of Sais... (Udjahorresnet Inscription §§7–10)[208]

Nevertheless, the Persian government and its satrap maintained control over Egypt and Udjahorresnet's immediate function in Sais ceased with its restoration. He had some influence in the imperial government's decision regarding which temple was restored,[209] but such restoration was not dependent upon political control held by the priests.[210] And even though Udjahorresnet himself may have been given the honorific of priest, he was first and foremost a Persian employee.[211] That is to say, any assignment of priestly status to Udjahorresnet is not confirmation that high priests held political power in Egypt. Udjahorresnet's activities show that the imperial government was very much involved in the local affairs, including religion, of its satrapies and/or provinces. If Ezra's role in Yehud parallels Udjahorresnet's in Egypt, then this evidence weighs in favor of imperial involvement in Yehud.[212]

Conclusion

There seems to be little question that the Persian imperial government governed its empire through an administrative system whose first priority was loyalty to the imperial government. The way that it punished rebellious territories—in part by removing symbols that expressed national, religious, or cultural identity—suggests rather strongly that the imperial government did not tend to grant autonomy to those under its empire. Rather, what we seem to see is a tolerance for local cultures and religions

---

208. Lichtheim, *Ancient Egyptian Literature*, 3:37.

209. See also Lichtheim's introduction to her translation of Udjahorresnet's inscription (ibid., 3:36–37).

210. "It should be remembered," Ahsltröm asserts, "that there were supervisors over the different 'national' temples in the provinces. This was the case at Acco, which was a naval base for the Persians. Such a supervisor was most probably a Persian appointee, as was Ezra" (*The History of Ancient Palestine*, 849–50).

211. Blenkinsopp ("Mission of Udjahorresnet," 412–13) believes it is reasonable to conclude his mission is connected with the measures described in the Demotic Chronicle.

212. Blenkinsopp (ibid., 409 with nn. 4, 14, 17–19) asserts that Ezra's role parallels Udjahorresnet's—i.e. a special advisor to the Persian king on local affairs of a satrapy or province. See also Ezra 7:11. Ahlström (*The History of Ancient Palestine*, 818) states that Cambyses appointed Udjahorresnet high priest of the temple of Neith.

as long as the territory's highest priority remained, or was expressed as, loyalty to the empire. This seems to be confirmed in what appears to be the imperial government's appointing or monitoring of various administrative officials down to even the district levels.

Chapter 3

YAHWISM AND THE QUESTION OF
GOVERNMENT IN YEHUD

As a province within the Persian empire, Yehud required a governing
structure capable of coexisting with imperial control and politics.[1] The

1. Carter (*Emergence of Yehud*, 102, 283–94; idem, "The Province of Yehud
in the Post-Exilic Period: Soundings in Site Distribution and Demography," in
Eskenazi and Richards, eds., *Second Temple Studies*, 2:106–45) defines the area of
Yehud as primarily the Highlands with some portions in the Shephelah and the
Coastal Plain, an area covering roughly 680 square miles. The use of geographic
areas is not simply a matter of convenience, but purposeful. He writes, "[I]t is
unlikely that a governing body with limited resources and limited autonomy, one
that itself may have been undergoing internal conflict, would be able to extend its
influence beyond certain natural topographical boundaries" (*Emergence of Yehud*,
91). Stern (*Archaeology*, 3:431), with significant dependence on Ezra–Nehemiah,
defines the province of Yehud with a northern limit of Tel en-Naṣbeh, an eastern
limit represented by a line extending from Jericho to Ein Gedi, a western limit of
Gezer and Tel Ḥarasim, and a southern limit of Beth-Zur. Stern (3:428–43) links the
place names found in the lists of Ezra and Nehemiah (1 = Ezra 3:21–35; 2 = Neh
7:25–38; 3 = Neh 11:25–35; 4 = Neh 3:1–22; 5 = the list of the singers: Jerusalem,
Netophah, Azmaveth, Beth-ha-gilgal, and the *Kikkar*) with archaeological remains
of the same place names dated to the Persian period. Ahlström (*The History of
Ancient Palestine*, 843) divides Yehud into the following subdistricts: Keilah, Beth-
Zur, Beth-Hakerem, Jerusalem, and Mizpah. He also tentatively adds the area around
Jericho. Drawing on Ezra–Nehemiah (Ezra 2; Neh 3; 7) and archaeological finds, I.
Finkelstein and N. Silberman (*The Bible Unearthed: Archaeology's New Vision of
Ancient Israel and the Origin of Its Sacred Texts* [New York: Free, 2001], 354), with
similarity to Stern, locate the southern border of Yehud just south of Beth-Zur. They
locate the northern border at a position north of Mizpah and Bethel (conforming to
the late seventh-century border of monarchic Judah), the eastern border east of
Jericho, yet they remain uncertain whether to include Lod in the northern Shephelah
within the western border. Edelman (*The Origins of the 'Second' Temple*, 209–80)
defines the borders of Yehud before 400 B.C.E. as the Shephelah in the west, the
Jordan River in the east, Bethel in the north, and the Beersheba Valley in the south.
In Edelman's reconstruction, Idumea was either a sub-district of Yehud until

Persian-period biblical texts define Yehud's government under the rubric of cultic authority, and scholars such as Weinberg have developed theories (e.g. a theocratic state) based on the "evidence" of these texts.[2] However, the legitimacy of a theocracy or a theocratic-like structure has yet to be established on a firm biblical basis or even a Persian imperial basis.[3] An empire remains the ultimate authority despite the manner by which it exercises control. Because provincial governing structures are the local or regional arbiters of imperial jurisprudence, they cannot operate outside the jurisdiction of imperial politics.[4]

---

400 B.C.E. or was newly constituted. Restructuring the area provided imperial benefit; it established a point from which to protect the trade route from Arabia to Gaza as well as to defend the border shared with Egypt. After the Egyptian revolt, a response bringing structural change was needed (see also Hoglund, *Achaemenid Imperial Administration*, 212). With a heightened concern for defense, the Persian imperial government ceded agricultural land including Lachish from Yehud to provide the needed supplies for patrols monitoring the areas.

2. See Weinberg, *Citizen-Temple Community*, passim. Leith ("Israel among the Nations," 407) claims that Yehud was a theocracy by the time of Ezra. Dandamaev and Lukonin (*Culture and Social Institutions*, 105) state that the activities of Ezra and Nehemiah gradually turned Yehud into a theocracy from the fifth century B.C.E. onwards. Leith ("Israel among the Nations," 407) asserts that by the time Ezra was active in Yehud a theocracy was well established. I introduced this tendency in scholarship in Chapter 1. I will address it further in Chapter 4. For brief and further mention here, I cite again the general works of Ahlström, *The History of Ancient Palestine*; de Vaux, *Ancient Israel*; Dyck, *Theocratic Ideology*; Hanson, *Dawn of Apocalyptic*; Plöger, *Theocracy*; Weinberg, *Citizen-Temple Community*; Wellhausen, *Prolegomena*.

3. I am making this statement based on the definition of theocracy that I will give in Chapter 4. While I recognize that a number of ancient Near Eastern societies connected their monarchs or rulers to the divine world in some way—and I do not dispute that—this connection, as I will explain, does not itself legitimate a theocracy. Divine links or connections are not necessarily theocratic but can be political or ideological mythic-devices of rulers or even of those ruled. Describing a ruler as divine (e.g. the pharaoh in ancient Egypt) does not alter a society into a theocracy— a point that I will discuss with more detail in the following chapter. A theocracy is not merely a switch in ideology or perception but a complex social, economic, and political structure.

4. For a helpful survey of the definition and relationship of "politics and culture" and "political culture," see Mabel Berezin, "Politics and Culture: A Less Fissured Terrain," *Annual Reviews in Sociology* 23 (1997): 361–83. R. Swedberg (*Max Weber and the Idea of Economic Sociology* [Princeton: Princeton University Press, 1998], 18–19) argues that Weber's influential arguments are based on a belief that politics aid in the formation of culture and economy. At the same time, however, both culture and economy are producers of political systems.

Social-Economic-Political Integration in Babylonian āl-Yāhūdu,
Samerina, and Elephantine

The archaeological evidence from Babylonian āl-Yāhūdu, Samaria, and
Elephantine offers cross-cultural perspectives of Yahwists scattered
throughout the Persian empire.[5] The evidence from these territories
suggests that in general practice Yahwists/Judeans integrated into their

5. F. Joannès and A. Lemaire ("Trois tablettes cunéiformes à l'onomastique
ouest-sémitique," *Transeu* 17 [1999]: 17–33) and L. Pearce ("New Evidence for
Jews in Babylonia," in Lipschits and Oeming, eds., *Judah and the Judeans in the
Persian Period*, 399–411) have offered initial publications on the finds from Babylonian āl-Yāhūdu. Cross and Porten are leading figures in the reconstructions of the
societies of Samaria and Elephantine, respectively. See Cross, "Discovery of the
Samaria Papyri," 110–21; idem, "Papyri of the Fourth Century," 41–62; idem, "A
Report on the Samaria Papyri," in *Congress Volume: Jerusalem 1986* (ed. John A.
Emerton; VTSup 40: Leiden: Brill, 1988), 17–26; Porten, "Religion of the Jews,"
116–21; idem, "Settlement of the Jews at Elephantine and the Arameans at Syene,"
in Lipschits and Blenkinsopp, eds., *Judah and the Judeans in the Neo-Babylonian
Period*, 451–70; B. Porten with Jonas C. Greenfield, *Jews of Elephantine and
Arameans of Syene: Aramaic Texts with Translation* (Jerusalem: Hebrew University,
1974); B. Porten and H. Z. Szubin, "'Abandoned Property' in Elephantine: A New
Interpretation of Kraeling 3," *JNES* 41 (1982): 123–31. See also the Aramaic
Textbooks published by B. Porten and A. Yardeni: *Textbook of Aramaic Documents
from Ancient Egypt*. Vol. 1. *Letters* (Jerusalem: Hebrew University, 1986); *Textbook
of Aramaic Documents from Ancient Egypt*. Vol. 2, *Contracts* (Jerusalem: Hebrew
University, 1989); *Textbook of Aramaic Documents from Ancient Egypt*. Vol. 3,
Literature, Accounts, Lists (Jerusalem: Hebrew University, 1993); *Textbook of
Aramaic Documents from Ancient Egypt*. Vol. 4, *Ostraca and Assorted Inscriptions*
(Jerusalem: Hebrew University, 1999). Porten ("Aramaic Papyri and Parchments:
A New Look," *BA* 42 [1979]: 74–104) provides a significant history of works pub-
lished on the Aramaic papyri and a subsequent analysis of the texts. See also
Stephen N. Gerson, "Fractional Coins of Judea and Samaria in the Fourth Century
BCE," *NEA* 64 (2001): 106–21; Achim Krekeler, "Excavations and Restoration on
the Elephantine Island," in *The Near East Antiquity* (Amman: Al Kutba, 1992), 69–
83; Lapp and Lapp, *Discoveries in the Wâdi Ed-Dâliyeh*; M. Leith, "Seals and Coins
in Persian Period Samaria," in *The Dead Sea Scrolls Fifty Years after Their
Discovery: Proceedings of the Jerusalem Congress, July 20–25, 1997* (ed. Lawrence
H. Schiffman et al.; Jerusalem: Israel Exploration Society in cooperation with the
Shrine of the Book, Israel Museum, 2000), 691–707; Meshorer and Qedar, *Samarian
Coinage*; Herbert Ricke and Serge Sauneron, *Die Tempel Nektanebos' II in
Elephantine: Inscriptions Romaines au Temple de Khnoum a Elephantine* (Beiträge
zur Ägyptischen Bauforschung und Alterstumkunde 6; Cairo: Schweiz Institut für
ägypt Bauforschung und Alterstumkunde, 1960); Zertal, "Province of Samaria,"
377–412.

host societies and into the operative systems (social, political, and economic) of those locations. The evidence from Babylonian āl-Yāhūdu, an area in the Babylon-Borsippa region, offers a cultural tradition of integration. In addition, Yahwists in Samaria, without apparently imposing Yahwism as the socially dominant religious tradition or dominant set of social-religious principles, functioned within the administrative structure and legal-economic systems of the imperial province. This was done on the terms formulated by a society that was itself broader than a particular religious cult. In Elephantine, for a further example, Yahwists participated in the legal-economic systems as well as the judicial systems set in place by the local political authority, the satrap, and, by extension, the imperial king.

Without question, one must consider some differences when extending these comparisons to the *golah* community in Yehud. The province of Yehud was considered the "homeland" by exiled Judeans while the other locations mentioned may be accurately described as diaspora communities—particularly Babylonian āl-Yāhūdu and Elephantine. It is equally possible that Yahwistic communities in Samaria also considered Yehud their "homeland." For other Yahwists, however, Samaria itself may have been home. Therefore, the social parallel between these communities and the province of Yehud cannot single-handedly discredit the portrayal of the *golah* community in the Persian-period biblical texts. This community, according to the biblical texts, was socially and religiously defined by exclusivist tendencies in religion, culture, and politics. Foreign women were portrayed as the death of religious fidelity in Ezra–Nehemiah (Ezra 10:1–44; Neh 13:3, 23–30);[6] politics were portrayed as the handmaiden of religion, with Neh 5:14–19 describing a provincial governor whose foremost concern was to not offend Yahweh, and Hag 1:1–15 telling of a vision shared with the governor and high priest that encouraged both to build the temple. In Neh 13:15–21, culture and economy were constrained by a *golah*-initiated Yahwistic religious law demanding strict observance of the Sabbath. Even the Tyrians living in the city were not allowed to trade on the Sabbath day (Neh 13:19).

Of what benefit then is a discussion of these communities? By studying Yahwism in its various contexts, we gain insight into the nature of the religion, whether or not it was inherently prone toward a theocratic

---

6. Eskenazi and Judd point out that it is not self-evident in Ezra–Nehemiah who is literally a foreigner and who is labeled "foreign," even though Judean, by the author to exclude them from the *golah* community ("Marriage," 267). As such, this lack of clarity adds weight to the argument that the *golah* community had strict criteria on who could be allowed membership into the group.

context or even capable of sustaining one. However, by understanding the cultural practices of these communities, and by drawing possible parallels among them, it is possible to expand one's understanding of the society in Yehud. While the Persian-period biblical texts portray a dogmatically exclusive religious community, these texts are the product of a minority. One would be incorrect to assume that only the members of this community were Yahwists. Not only so, there is even suggestion within the biblical texts themselves that not all members of the *golah* community shared the same outlook for the province. Ezra–Nehemiah hints that Yahwists continued in a practice of integration. For example, Neh 13:23–25 (NRSV), states, "In those days also I saw Jews who had married women of Ashdod, Ammon, and Moab; and half of their children spoke the language of Ashdod, and they could not speak the language of Judah, but spoke the language of various peoples." Ezra 10:18–44 identifies a large number of priests who had married "foreign women." And Neh 13:28 states that a son of Jehoiada, son of the high priest Eliashib, was a son-in-law of Sanballat the Horonite. Nehemiah 13:15–16, which laments the transgression of the Sabbath law, suggests that even the inhabitants of Jerusalem sought to integrate into the local economic systems. From the tone of the book of Nehemiah, it is only the character of Nehemiah who seems to have a problem with Yahwists taking an inclusive and integrative posture rather than an exclusive one. Thus, it appears that while Sabbath observance was not a foreign idea in Jerusalem, it was not a social or political law—as shown in part by the author's aggressive concern enforcing it as a civic ordinance. Additionally, Nehemiah's control over the market place and city gate during the Sabbath, as shown in Neh 13:21–22, suggests an attempt to establish this religious observance as civic law. And even if we accept that the narrative of the author is accurate, namely that Nehemiah closed the city gates during the Sabbath and that the governor of Yehud was doggedly Yahwistic, the actions noted appear to be effective only for the city of Jerusalem.[7]

---

7. Note also Hoglund, who offers a reason why the text of Nehemiah may not have been motivated by a concern to portray the figure of Nehemiah objectively: "[T]he emphasis on Nehemiah's actions serves a structural purpose in the composition as a whole. This purpose is to focus attention on the formation of a holy community through the process of separating the community from the peoples around it, physically by rebuilding the walls of Jerusalem and religiously by the reinforcement of cultic regulations such as the observance of the Sabbath" (*Achaemenid Imperial Administration*, 208). See also Brevard S. Childs, *Introduction to the Old Testament as Scripture* (Philadelphia: Fortress, 1979), 632–34; Tamara Cohn Eskenazi, *In an Age of Prose: A Literary Approach to Ezra–Nehemiah* (Atlanta: Scholars Press, 1988), 80–81.

Babylonian āl-Yāhūdu

The Babylonian location āl-Yāhūdu, roughly "Judahville,"[8] is a location
wherein the Judeans had their own city, and there is evidence that this
city was in existence even before or during the early part of the Neo-
Babylonian period.[9] L. Pearce writes, for instance,

> While the transformation of the toponym from one that identifies it on the
> basis of its residents' being from somewhere else to a place-name that
> merely recalls their origins might appear to point to a rapid acculturation
> of Judeans into Babylonian life, this assumption would ignore the
> likelihood that the process of acculturation may have begun earlier than
> the destruction of Jerusalem.[10]

The discovered evidence[11] suggests that these Judeans, who lived in the
Babylon-Borsippa region,[12] integrated into their host society. Approximately 80 names from the TAYN (= Texts from āl-Yāhūdu and Našar)
archives contain a form of the Yahwistic theophoric element, which
suggests a significant Jewish presence.[13] The corpus records various economic and administrative activities of Judeans in Babylonia in the forms
of receipts, debt notes, sales, and leases of houses and people.[14] As
Pearce notes, it provides evidence of an administrative fiscal district
populated in large measure by Judeans. Districts like this in Nippur and
its environs were referred to as *ḫaṭru*—a term found almost exclusively
in the Murašû archives.[15]

One orthography from the texts, URU *šá* LÚ *ia-a-ḫu-du-a-a*, which
adds the standard Akkadian gentilic ending (*-a-a*), demonstrates that the
town was likely to have been named for individuals who came from
Judah.[16] Pearce writes,

8. Pearce, "New Evidence," 402.
9. Ibid.
10. Ibid.
11. Because the evidence from Babylonian āl-Yāhūdu is mostly unpublished, this
discussion relies on the works of Joannès and Lemaire ("Trois tablettes cunéiformes," 17–33) and of Pearce ("New Evidence," 399–411).
12. Pearce ("New Evidence," 402) contra Joannès and Lemaire ("Trois tablettes
cunéiformes," 26).
13. Note also Joannès and Lemaire ("Trois tablettes cunéiformes," 17–33). From
these tablets, the cities of Našar and Yāhūdu are presented as home to a number of
individuals of Judean origin. Našar was already known from texts previously published by Waerzeggers (TuM 2/3 91; VS 4 177). See also Pearce, "New Evidence,"
400.
14. Ibid., 405.
15. Stolper, *Entrepreneurs and Empire*, 71–72. See also Pearce's discussion of
the term in Pearce, "New Evidence," 405.
16. See also Pearce, "New Evidence," 400–402.

In addition to firmly establishing the place of origin of the former residents, it is noteworthy that the orthography *āl šá* ᴸᵁ*Yāḫūdāia* appears in the earliest text of the corpus, which dates to Nebuchadnezzar 33 (572 B.C.E.), 15 years after the 587 B.C.E. deportation. The next-oldest tablet dates to Amēl-Marduk 1 (= 561 B.C.E.) and already preserves the orthography ᵁᴿᵁ*ia-a-ḫu-du* for the toponym. All subsequent attestations of the toponym āl-Yāḫūdu also lack the gentilic ending, suggesting that the Judean deportees and their descendants were sufficiently established in the social and economic life of Babylonia that their town could simply be called 'Judah-ville' or the like.[17]

Given what appears to be a quick transition of the toponym, it is obvious that the city was established within a few decades of the first deportation in 597 B.C.E. That is, a duration of three decades (i.e. by 561 B.C.E.) better allows for a "'normal" process of acculturation to occur than does the very cautious assumption of approximately one decade (572–561 B.C.E.)—especially given that the location became referred to as city X containing Judeans but as "Judahville."[18] The participation of the Judeans in the very ordinary economic transactions—in which they are listed as creditors and debtors in loan documents and receipts—demonstrates that they had sufficiently integrated into Babylonian economic society.[19] Their participation is evidenced further in that they also provided a ready supply of labor for the official administration.[20]

This evidence offers some suggestion that integrating, or assimilating, into the culture was the general and traditional practice of the Judeans in Babylonia. If the *golah* community originated from Babylonia, it is possible to suggest that it was with this tradition of assimilation that the *golah* community, or at least some members of it, immigrated into Yehud. It is also possible that some members of the same community reacted to tendencies of assimilation. From a social-scientific standpoint, a background in this diasporic-cultural ideology might partially explain some of the concerns over intermarriage and Sabbath observance that occur in Ezra–Nehemiah (cf. Neh 13:21–22, 23–28; Ezra 10:18–44), and why the text casts the figures of Ezra and Nehemiah as *golah* "reformers."

Samaria (Samerina)

Legal papyri from fourth-century B.C.E. Daliyeh were discovered in 1962,[21] and have since enjoyed a history of published discussions. In

17. Ibid., 402.
18. As suggested in ibid.
19. As noted in ibid.
20. Ibid., 407–8.
21. The bullae and papyri from Samaria have since enjoyed a history of analysis. See, for instance, Cross, "Discovery of the Samaria Papyri," 110–21; ibid., "Report,"

1963, Cross published a preliminary report that was followed by a more detailed analysis in 1969 that included the finds from 1963 and 1964.[22] Of the papyri, the majority (17) record slave sales,[23] which were part of the typical economic activities of the province.[24] The papyri, whose earliest fixable dates are 375 and 335 B.C.E., contain several personal name-types, predominantly Hebrew with the addition of Aramaic, Babylonian, Edomite, Moabite, Persian, and Phoenician names.[25] The presence of Yahwistic-Hebrew names within the name-types—which is the largest percentage of any specific type—demonstrates that Yahwism existed in Samerina, and the range of the name-types itself indicates Yahwism existed in a multi-ethnic, multi-religious context.[26]

From the bullae associated with the papyri, we find that WD 22, published by Cross,[27] indicates that the son of Sanballat was given a name with a Yahwistic theophoric element.[28] The palaeo-Hebrew inscription on this seal reads, "[Belonging to Yešaᶜ]yahu son of [San]ballaṭ, Governor of Samaria." Through "circumstantial" links—discussion following—the individual named on WD 23 may be considered to be the same individual on WD 22.[29] A reconstructed reading of the damaged WD 23 (ring seal) inscription as לישוע, where the *waw*, absent (due perhaps to damage) on the WD 23 inscription, can be included based on space and inscriptions from Samaria Papyrus 14 (that reads, "Yešuaᶜ, son of

17–26; D. Gropp, "The Samaria Papyri from Wadi Ed-Daliyeh: The Slave Sales" (Ph.D. diss., Harvard University, 1986); idem, *Samaria Papyri*; D. Gropp et al., *Wadi Daliyeh II: The Samaria Papyri for Wadi Daliyeh* (in consultation with James VanderKam and Monica Brady; DJD 28; Oxford: Clarendon, 2001); Kaptan, *The Daskyleion Bullae*; Leith, *Wadi Daliyeh Seal Impressions*; idem, "Seals and Coins," 691–707.

22. Cross, "Discovery of the Samaria Papyri," 110–21; idem, "Papyri of the Fourth Century," 41–62. See also Gropp, *Samaria Papyri*, 3; Lapp and Lapp, *Discoveries in the Wâdi Ed-Dâliyeh*, 30–32.

23. F. M. Cross, "Samaria Papyrus 1: An Aramaic Slave Conveyance of 335 B.C.E. Found in the Wâdi Ed-Dâliyeh," *ErIs* 18 (1985): *7. For additional discussion, see Gropp, *Samaria Papyri*, 3–5.

24. See also Kaptan, *The Daskyleion Bullae*, 22.

25. Ibid., 20. Leith ("Israel among the Nations," 374–75, 386) says that the largest percentage of name-types is Yahwistic. The bullae were originally affixed to legal documents. See also Kaptan, *The Daskyleion Bullae*, 13–27; Leith, *Wadi Daliyeh Seal Impressions*, 3.

26. Gropp, *Samaria Papyri*, 6.

27. Cross, "Papyri of the Fourth Century," 47 figs. 34–35.

28. Ibid.; Cross, "Papyri," pl. 61; cf. also p. 18.

29. On these "circumstantial" links, see Leith, *Wadi Daliyeh Seal Impressions*, 185.

Sanballat"), and an additional (unspecified, but noted by Leith[30]) papyrus fragment (that reads, "[before Yeš]uaʿ son of Sanballat [and] Ḥanan the prefect"). There is also the inscription from WD 22 (that reads, "Yešuʿ/ Yešaʿyahu, son of Sanballat, the governor of Samaria"). Papyrus 5 also contains a possibly related inscription (which reads "[Yešaʿ]yahu, son of [San]ballat, governor of Samaria").[31] It is possible, therefore, to argue that Yahwists were administrative officials in the province of Samaria.[32] At the same time, however, the amount of bullae and seals notably not Judean in style also may suggest that within the social context of the province Yahwism was not dominant religiously or culturally.[33] With specific reference to the style, the Greek style in the bullae and seals outnumbers any more local Near Eastern style by nearly 2 to 1.[34] Statistically speaking, the Hebrew inscriptions (e.g. WD 22; 23) are negligible in terms of the larger corpus of bullae and seals.[35] Nevertheless, the inscriptions are significant because of the individuals connected to them and because they are part of a larger group of bullae containing divine names that are primarily Yahwistic.

The image on WD 23 shows what might be a boar, especially when compared with the winged boar on WD 45. If the previous reconstruction of bulla WD 23's inscription is correct, then the image is an interesting choice by an individual we might consider a Yahwist (cf. Lev 19:4; 26:1). Until, that is, we take again into consideration the influence of Persian motifs and culture. The boar, which appears on cylinders and stamps in the Persian period, may have been a motif borrowed from a larger portrayal of the Persian king hunting wild animals, therefore holding symbolic value in Persian culture.[36] It may have been adopted by

---

30. Ibid.

31. As reconstructed by ibid.

32. See also Cross, "Papyri of the Fourth Century," 58–63; Leith, *Wadi Daliyeh Seal Impressions*, 10; idem, "Seals and Coins," 700; E. Stern, "The Persian Empire and the Political and Social History of Palestine in the Persian Period," in *The Cambridge History of Judaism*. Vol. 1, *Introduction; the Persian Period* (ed. W. D. Davies and Louis Finkelstein; Cambridge: Cambridge University Press, 1984), 81.

33. Leith, *Wadi Daliyeh Seal Impressions*, 11. See also M. C. Root ("From the Heart: Powerful Persianisms in the Art of the Western Empire," *Achaemenid History* 6 [1991]: 1–29) who argues that the imperial government used the art of local territories as a means of establishing hierarchical order and imperial harmony.

34. For reference, of all the Greek- and Persian-style bullae, the largest category consists of lone-standing youths/warriors in various states of dress/undress. See Leith, *Wadi Daliyeh Seal Impressions*, 30.

35. As noted in ibid., 21.

36. Compare Stern, *Archaeology*, 2:537–39, 540–43.

imperial employees to show their loyalty.[37] If WD 23 is the seal of a Yahwist, then it appears permissible, especially give the administrator's position, for a Yahwist to be culturally inclusive, integrating into the surrounding society without fear of reprisal from a religious authority. It could also show that the Yahwism of Samaria did not at this point fully adopt or clearly define the aniconic tradition (cf. Lev 19:4; 26:1; Num 33:53; Deut 7:25).

While the evidence does not permit a detailed analysis into religious beliefs, it provides an initial introduction regarding the spread, variety, and influence of Yahwism throughout the Persian empire. In addition, the bullae with Greek imagery of lounging nude or semi-nude warriors and youths found in Samaria reflect an appreciation for things foreign and may have been indications of status.[38] Furthermore, the likely internationalist or pluralistic atmosphere of the Persian period may have influenced the seal owner's choice of seal and seal type.[39] As Leith notes,

> Behind the remarkably varied Greek and Persian imagery displayed on the seals of these wealthy Samarians and their non-Samarian business partners there were no doubt the subtly compelling factors of prestige and/or 'cultural receptivity'. Evidence both from Persepolis and from the western Persian Empire indicates that high satrapal officials and influential underlings such as local dynasts or large landowners shared a liking for Greek art.[40]

Samaria Papyrus 1 supplies an example of fourth-century sealing practices,[41] which also partially describes legal and economic practices in the province. Seven clay bullae (WD 11A–11G), fairly evenly spaced, still adhered to the papyrus at the time of its purchase in 1962.[42] Since only half of the papyrus was intact, Leith proposes that it is possible that seven more seals adorned the once complete papyrus.[43] Leith notes:

---

37. Ibid., 2:187.

38. Leith (*Wadi Daliyeh Seal Impressions*, 31) describes them as being in a Yahwistic context—one would not expect such celebration of the human body; that is, of course, unless Greek culture had already made significant inroads into the society.

39. According to Leith (ibid., 11), the variety of imagery and seal types in Wadi ed-Daliyeh, for example, may suggest Phoenicia was a cultural mediator between Samaria and the outside world.

40. Ibid., 10.

41. Note also Cross, "Samaria Papyrus 1," pl. 2; Gropp, *Samaria Papyri*, 3, 36–37.

42. As noted by Leith, *Wadi Daliyeh Seal Impressions*, 18–19.

43. Ibid.

The principals to the transaction would of course have sealed the recording document, but the vast majority of the sealings on the Samaria Papyri
must have been produced by witnesses whose listing in the papyri con-
ventionally began with the Governor and ended with the Prefect.[44]

In short, the witnesses to legal documents were often imperial administrative officials. While it is possible that a publicly recognized class of
witnesses, who were regularly called upon, existed,[45] the scarcity of dupli-
cate sealings seems to diminish the possibility.[46] Either way, however,
we can observe, based on the offices of the witnesses, that economic
transactions within the province involved a process that was approved by
the imperially authorized political authorities.

The Wadi ed-Daliyeh papyri were written sometime during 375–334
B.C.E., between the reigns of Artaxerxes II and Darius III.[47] The majority
of the documents were written during the reign of Artaxerxes III (358–
337 B.C.E.).[48] They were written, in other words, during a time when
Persian imperial power was probably waning. If the religious institution
of Yahwism was prone to or contained the administrative apparatus for
controlling its surrounding social-political context, then we would be
permitted to speculate that the governor of the province of Samaria,
being a Yahwist, might have shared at this transitional period the exclusivist tendencies similar to those portrayed in Ezra–Nehemiah. Yet the
evidence from Samaria demonstrates that like the Judeans in Babylonian
āl-Yāhūdu, Yahwists integrated into the society. Even those in authority
followed the local norms or the imperial norms where necessary.[49]

Yahwistic names found on fourth-century coins[50] include the names
Ḥananyah (*ḥnnyh*),[51] Jehoʿanah (*yhwʿnh*), Bodyah (*bdyh*; a name that
appears on four different coin types [cf. Ezra 10:35 *bēdhāh*]), *dl*, possibly short for *dlyh*, or Delaiah, *šl*, possibly short for *šlmyh*, or Shelemiah,
and *wny*, possibly short for *wnyh*.[52] The presence of Yahwistic names on

---

44. Ibid., 18. See also Gropp, *Samaria Papyri*, 37.
45. Cross, "Samaria Papyrus 1," 15* and n. 56.
46. Leith, *Wadi Daliyeh Seal Impressions*, 18.
47. Cf. Kaptan, *The Daskyleion Bullae*, 20.
48. Leith, *Wadi Daliyeh Seal Impressions*, 5–6.
49. Ibid., 17.
50. Meshorer and Qedar, *Samarian Coinage*, 20–28.
51. This might be the same Hananyah who appears as governor in the Samarian
papyri (cf. 7.17; 9.14). See also Gropp, *Samaria Papyri*, 80–85, 93–96.
52. As cited by Gary N. Knoppers, "Revisiting the Samaritan Question in the
Persian Period," in Lipschits and Oeming, eds., *Judah and the Judeans in the
Persian Period*, 276.

economic symbols such as coins further demonstrates that Yahwists had integrated into the economic and political systems of the province of Samaria.

Elephantine

The Jewish colony at Elephantine already existed, by its own testimony (*TAD* A.4.7/A.4.8 [= AP 30/31]), when the Persians conquered Egypt in 525 B.C.E.[53] While a variety of peoples served in the military garrison, it was composed primarily of Jewish settlers who had served there as early as the Saite pharaohs and who were later enlisted by the Persian empire.[54] Elephantine contained a Persian military outpost, or *birah*—a contingent that the area satrap, Arshama, had immediate control over. The temple of Yahu at Elephantine served members of the military and their families, in keeping with the imperial policy that allowed construction of temples in military outposts.[55]

   Does AP 21 (= *TAD* A.4.1), a letter from Hananiah to Yedanyah and his associates at the Jewish garrison,[56] provide evidence that the imperial king personally decided questions of a religious nature?[57] As restored, the letter describes God and King Darius as decreeing the proper procedure for observing the Passover celebration. While the papyrus is very fragmentary, it has been restored based on parallels in several biblical prescriptions:[58]

> Now, this year, the fifth year of king Darius, it has been sent from the king to Arsa[mes the prince, saying, "*Keep away from the Jew*]*ish* [*garrison.*"] Now, do you count four[teen days from the first day of Nisan and the Passover ke]ep. From the 15th day until the 21st day of [Nisan keep the Festival of Unleavened Bread... You] be pure and take heed.

---

53. Porten posits three periods before the Persian conquest of Egypt when Judean mercenaries might have settled in Egypt: (1) the 35-year period from the Syro-Ephraimitisch War of 735 B.C.E. until the siege of Jerusalem in 701; (2) the middle of the seventh century when Manasseh aligned with Egypt against Assyria; (3) the almost 30-year period between the accession of Jehoiakim in 609 and the flight to Egypt after the murder of the Babylonian governor, Gedaliah (*Archives from Elephantine: The Life of an Ancient Jewish Military Colony* [Berkeley: University of California Press, 1968], 8–16).

54. Cf. Dandamaev and Lukonin, *Culture and Social Institutions*, 230–31.

55. For example, Fried (*Priest and the Great King*, 154–55) notes that temples to King Kaunios and Zeus Labraunda in the satrapy of Karia were built in part for the military garrisons.

56. See Porten's reconstruction of "[...Je]wish [garrison]" below.

57. Cf. ibid., 88–89; Hornblower, *Mausolus*, 148.

58. Reconstructed in Porten, *Archives from Elephantine*, 128.

Work do no[t perform on the 15th day or on the 21st day. Beer do no]t drink and anything of leaven do no[t eat. Eat unleavened bread from the 14th day of Nisan at] sunset until the 21st of Nisa[n at sunset. And anything of leaven br]ing into your chambers and seal (it) up during [these d]ays. [*By order of the God of heaven and by order of the ki*]*ng.*[59]

To a certain extent, any conclusion based on this papyrus remains conjectural—especially because of its fragmentary nature. Whether or not this papyrus represents an official decree to observe the Sabbath festival is uncertain. Based on an ostracon (Ostraca Berlin P 10679; Bodleian Aramaic Inscription 7) containing the term, *pashāʾ*, Bezalel Porten suggests that the Passover festival was already celebrated before the letter was written.[60] The Bodleian Aramaic Inscription, for instance, can be dated to ca. 475 B.C.E., while *TAD* A.4.1 can be dated to ca. 419 B.C.E.[61] Thus, for Porten, the papyrus probably does not represent an initial command to observe the festival—which itself is not specifically mentioned in the fragmented text (though he refers to the text as a decree from Darius II[62]). The form of the address is not that of a superior to a subordinate.[63] In line 2 and line 11, for example, Hananiah refers to Yedanyah and his colleagues in the Jewish garrison as "brothers." "The letter, then," Porten writes, "would not be introducing any new festival or new rites—it is too brief for that—but simply reminding the Elephantine Jewish soldiers of the festival practices."[64] What can be said about the letter is that someone bearing a Yahwistic name and in an administrative position was concerned that the Yahwists in Elephantine continued to observe the Festival of Unleavened Bread. One wonders if this concern might mimic Nehemiah's concern over Sabbath observance (Neh 13:15–22), though the text is written in a more amiable and egalitarian style.[65]

Together, AP 30/31, 32, 33 (= *TAD* A.4.7/4.8, A.4.9, A.4.10) document communications between the Elephantine community and Jerusalem, Samaria, and the Egyptian satrap concerning the destruction of the

59. Translation (of TAD A.4.1. [= AP 21:3–10]) in ibid., 129. Portions of Porten's translation also appear in *COS* 3:117.
60. Ibid., 130–31. See also the discussion in Lindenberger, *Ancient Aramaic and Hebrew Letters*, 54.
61. Cf. ibid., 44, 56.
62. Porten, *Archives from Elephantine*, 286.
63. As noted by ibid., 130.
64. Ibid., 133.
65. "Amiable and egalitarian" as denoted by the tone of the letter that is less assertive than Neh 13:15–22 and Hananiah's addressing his letter's recipients as brothers.

temple of Yahu and Yedanyah and colleagues' request for aid for the destroyed temple. His petition was probably for monetary aid and for outside authorities to exercise influence on the local political authorities to allow the cult to rebuild the temple. The appeal directed outside Elephantine's immediate provincial and judicial system suggests that the destruction itself may not have been against the local law, perhaps also that it was possibly a response for a "transgression" on the part of the Yahwistic community.[66] AP 33:9–14—in which Yedanyah and his associates promise not to make any animal (sheep, cattle, or goats) burnt offerings at the temple—strengthens this possibility. According to AP 27 (*TAD* A.4.5), the priests of Khnum bribed Vidranga, who was *fratarka* in Elephantine, to allow them to build a wall through the fortress in Elephantine, part of the construction of a "divine chapel" and a "divine way."[67] In this process, they stopped up a well used for drinking water in the garrison and may have intruded on the boundaries of territories maintained by members of the Jewish community. AP 30/31 (*TAD* A.4.7/4.8) states that these building activities included the partial or complete destruction of the temple of Yahu.[68] The temple of Yahu neighbored the "divine way" and "divine chapel" and, as Porten suggests, it is possible that the sacrifices common to Yahwism may have been a source of strife between the worshipers of Khnum and the worshipers of Yahweh.[69]

According to the letter from Yedanyah and his colleagues the priests (AP 30/31 [= *TAD* A.4.7/4.8]), Vidranga, the Elephantine region's civil-military governor,[70] encouraged the destruction of the temple by members of the Syene community.[71] The commander of the fort at Syene was the

66. Perhaps it was because certain administrative members were implicated in the temple's destruction. AP 30:4–12 (|| 31:4–11) suggests that the local authorities (Vidranga [פרתרכא] and Naphaina [רבחילא; garrison commander—i.e. in Syene]) were responsible for the temple's destruction. Yet it is also important to note that AP 30:16 suggests that Vidranga was punished. In addition, Kraeling (*Brooklyn Museum Papyri*, 114) states that BP 13:7 suggests that Vidranga was demoted from פרתרכא (in AP 30:5) to רב חילא—presumably as punishment. (Regarding Vidranga's position, Porten [*Archives from Elephantine*, 44] states that *frataraka* was a combined civil-military position above the commander of an area.) In addition, Porten (*Archives from Elephantine*, 288–89) states that Vidranga's property was confiscated and he suggests that Vidranga was executed for allowing the disturbance in Elephantine.

67. Porten, *Archives from Elephantine*, 285–86.

68. See also ibid., 284–89.

69. Ibid., 286.

70. Cf. ibid., 44–45.

71. Both communities at Syene and Elephantine exerted influence upon the other, an influence encouraged through intermarriage (Porten, "Religion of the Jews," 118–21).

governor's son, Nafaina, and this might explain why Vidranga permitted the destruction of the Jewish temple. But concluding that the destruction was done for religious reasons requires one to demonstrate why one group in a context marked by religious diversity would react in this manner.[72] There is an alternative possibility, that the temple's destruction had something to do with the military stationed there.[73] The Persian government often destroyed/damaged temples in response to rebellions.[74] Yet the evidence at hand does not really support a rebellion and the possibility remains speculative.[75] What can be said, however, is that the Jewish worshipers promised not to offer burnt offerings (AP 33:10). In recognizing that the Elephantine Yahwistic community had no direct recourse against Vidranga, Yedanyah and colleagues sought aid from individuals or patrons in Yehud and Samerina. The temple, that "even Cambyses found already standing," needed repair, something the priests and nobles of the Jewish communities in Jerusalem and other areas should understand and be sympathetic to.

It is also noteworthy that the letter exonerates from blame Arshama, satrap of Egypt, because "he did not know of the events" (AP 30:30; 31:29). His alleged unawareness suggests he that he may have been absent, perhaps in Susa for his imperial visit, as satraps were expected to do.[76] Should he have been present in the satrapy, he most likely would have been informed. His exoneration was undoubtedly a political move by Yedanyah and colleagues—a move that was intended to avoid conflict with the satrapal authority and to avoid losing any future possibility of restoring the temple.

72. The Hermopolis papyri, Porten (ibid., 120) asserts, clearly show the presence of an Aramean community at Syene whose deities consisted of Nabu, the Queen of Heaven, Bethel, Anathbethel, Eshembethel, and Herembethel. He writes, "In assessing the impact of these Aramean cults on the Elephantine Jews a distinction should be drawn between individuals and the community. Individual Arameans wrote to Jews and greeted or blessed them in the name of pagan deities or of YHH and a pagan deity. Yarho wrote to Haggai invoking Bel, Nabu, Shamash, and Nergal. The tailor Gedal wrote to Micaiah blessing him by YHH and *Hn* (= Han?, Khnum?). Individual Jews invoked the name of Herembethel (C 7) or AnathYHW (C 44) in judicial situations" (120).

73. Cf. Porten (*Archives from Elephantine*, 278–98), who discusses this and related issues at length. He concludes (287–88) that the possibility remains speculative.

74. See also the section "Rebellions Within the Empire: Stopping Pursuits of Self-Governance" in Chapter 2 (p. 34).

75. Again, see Porten, *Archives from Elephantine*, 287–88.

76. See also Fried, *Priest and the Great King*, 183; James C. VanderKam, *From Joshua to Caiaphas: High Priests after the Exile* (Minneapolis: Fortress, 2004), 56.

According to AP 30/31(:19–22), Yedanyah and his colleagues mourned and fasted, refrained from drinking wine and from having intercourse with their wives. They sent petitions to Bagohi (מראן), governor of Yehud, Yehohanan the high priest (יהוחנן כהנא רבא), and his colleagues the priests in Jerusalem (כנותה כהניא), to Ostanes, brother of Anani (אוסתן אחוהי זי ענני),[77] and to the Judean nobles (חרי יהוד חרי יהודיא). None, according to AP 30:18–19/31:17–18, replied.

Approximately three years later, another appeal was made to Bagohi, and to Delaiah and Shelemiah, the latter two being sons of Sanballat, the governor of Samaria.[78] Bagohi, governor of Yehud, and Delaiah, who may have been acting-governor in Samaria, replied jointly, according to the memorandum, AP 32 (= *TAD* A.4.9). In this memorandum, Yedanyah and his colleagues were given permission to rebuild the temple with restrictions regarding offerings.

The cited letter (AP 30:18–19) to the governor and to the high priest and his priestly colleagues in Jerusalem was but one in a series of letters sent to the priests, Ostanes and certain Judean nobles.[79] While one can interpret the high priest's silence as a rejection of the Elephantine cult based on religious grounds, as Briant does, this does not explain the lack of response from the other recipients.[80] He states that the high priest in

77. Lindenberger (in *Ancient Aramaic and Hebrew Letters*, 65), writes ^·^ at the end of אחוה to illustrate a supralinear addition by an ancient scribe.

78. F. M. Cross ("Aspects of Samaritan and Jewish History in Late Persian and Hellenistic Times," *HTR* 59 [1966]: 201–11) suggests that Delaiah became governor ca. 410 B.C.E., acting for his aged father, Sanballat I, and that possibly Shelemyah co-reigned with him. VanderKam, a student of Cross, also concludes that the sons were the active powers and that Sanballat "is almost certainly the man whom Nehemiah calls 'Sanballat the Horonite'…" (*From Joshua to Caiaphas*, 48).

79. Josephus writes that Yehohanan murdered his brother Yeshua in the temple (*Ant.* 11.7.1). In response, Bagoses (Bagoas), the general of Artaxerxes' army, "punished" the Jews for seven years. Regarding the office of high priest, Josephus's account suggests that the authority of the high priest did not supersede that of the Persian-appointed governor.

80. Briant suggests that the high priest did not reply to the letter because the community had broken the law of Moses (*From Cyrus to Alexander*, 586). But this is speculative, and is based upon the presumed official status of the law portrayed in the biblical texts as well as upon the presumed authority of the Jerusalem temple cult and its ability to enforce that law. It is also based on the assumption of a non-letter, i.e. an assumption that Yehohanan did not reply based on the absence of a letter containing the reply. Furthermore, the high priest is not the only party, nor necessarily the first to whom Yedanyah wrote. Why would the other parties fail to reply? Even if one could prove transgression is the reason for the high priest's silence, the governor's reply in spite of the said silence demonstrates the high priest had no jurisdiction over the governor.

3. *Yahwism and the Question of Government*   83

Jerusalem was the arbiter of Yahwistic religious affairs throughout the empire, and that it is only natural to assume that Yedanyah, a Yahwist, would have written to Jerusalem for this reason.[81]

In terms of the cultural environment, the Elephantine Yahwists coexisted with Egyptians and worshipers of Khnum. They appear, according to the Hermopolis letters, as Porten describes, to have intermarried with Egyptians and Arameans from Syene.[82] While one might conclude that this practice, possibly joined with other 'questionable' or forbidden religious practices, led to a rejection of the Elephantine cult by the high priests in Jerusalem, there is no evidence to confirm that conclusion. In addition, the conclusion is based on an unsubstantiated claim that the Jerusalem cult was the authority over all Yahwism.[83] It is significant that there is no evidence explicitly showing that the Jerusalem cult held authority over other Yahwistic cults. It is perhaps even more significant that even the biblical texts do not claim such authority existed.

While the joint reply of AP 32 indicates that a relationship existed between the (acting?) governor of Samerina and the governor of Yehud, the specifics of such a relationship remain unknown.[84] Though the time is earlier, the text of Nehemiah, in comparison, claims that only antagonism existed between Jerusalem and Samaria, especially between Nehemiah, Sanballat, and Tobiah (of Transjordan; regarding the antagonism, cf. Neh 4:1–7; 6:1–3).[85] Either this antagonism lessened or disappeared entirely (though the text of Nehemiah suggests it was deep-rooted), or the biblical text misrepresented the relationship between Yehud and Samerina for ideological gain.

AP 33 (= *TAD* A.4.10), a draft of a letter from Yedanyah (son of Gemaryah), Mauzi (son of Nat[h]an), Shemayah (son of Haggai), Hosea (son of Jathom), and Hosea (son of Nattun)—all of whom legally held property in Elephantine—was apparently intended for "our" lord (the identity of whom is unclear but who could have been the governor or Arshama, the satrap). The "divine chapel" appears to have adjoined

---

81. Ibid.

82. As noted by Porten, "Religion of the Jews," 121.

83. Cf. Briant, *From Cyrus to Alexander*, 586.

84. Leith ("Israel among the Nations," 386) conjectures that the Zadokite priestly family of Jerusalem and the leading Samarian families were allied by diplomatic marriages (see also, Neh 13:28; *Ant.* 11.8.2).

85. Briant (*From Cyrus to Alexander*, 588) states that the antagonism between leaders of provinces can be compared to that of the satraps Sardes and Daskyleion in Asia Minor who disputed any permanence of the control over the frontier territories held by the other.

Yedanyah's house (BM 9:6; 10:5) and may have been additional reason
for concern regarding the building activities of the Khnum priests.[86] This
letter presents itself as a bribe[87] and promises that the religious community will offer no sheep, oxen, or goats as burnt offerings, and it will
make a donation of silver and barley to the lord's household. The reference to burnt offering might suggest that the destruction of the temple in
410 B.C.E. was due in part to offended sensibilities of the Syene community, who in response convinced Vidranga to act or to allow the Egyptian
community to retaliate. On the other hand, the reference may be only an
appeal to the lord's religious sensibilities, to insure a favorable reply. In
the end, Vidranga's (possible) punishment and the success of rebuilding
the temple were possible through the judicial and administrative systems
of the province. Moreover, Yahwistic religious law was not the measure
against which individuals and judicial or political decisions were
weighed; nor was it according to Yahwistic religious law that sales of
property were mediated or disputes regarding property settled.

Other Extra-Biblical Archaeological and Textual Information

Coins, bullae and seals allow one to analyze the political and possibly
also religious authorities in Yehud from an additional perspective.[88]
While bullae and seals may be produced somewhat independently, minting coins was often the responsibility of a civic authority.[89] Therefore, to

86. Porten, *Archives from Elephantine*, 286.
87. Ibid., 53, also n. 97.
88. J. Betlyon ("The Provincial Government of Persian Period Judea and the
Yehud Coins," *JBL* 105 [1986]: 633–42) is confident about the contribution of coins
to studies of the provincial government in Persian-period Yehud. He also states that
the coins substantiate the argument of L. Mildenberg ("Yehud: A Preliminary Study
of the Provincial Coinage of Judaea," in *Greek Numismatics and Archaeology:
Essays in Honor of Margaret Thompson* [ed. Otto Mørkholm and Nancy M.
Waggoner; Wetteren: NR, 1979], 183–96) that Yehud took part in revolts against the
empire. Gerson ("Fractional Coins," 106–21) is likewise confident.
89. *A brief word on money in the Persian empire*: Dandamaev and Lukonin
(*Culture and Social Institutions*, 206) suggest that establishing an "imperial money"
was not entirely successful and that subsequently a money economy played only a
minor role in the imperial economy. According to Briant (*From Cyrus to Alexander*,
70–71), tributes appear to be paid in weight, not coin/money-type. He also suggests
(409) that establishing an imperial money system may not have been a pressing
concern for the Persian empire. Darius' creation of the *daric* (gold coin so named by
the Greeks), for instance, was less for economic reasons and more for symbolic, "elle
vise moins à solder ses dépenses qu'à illustrer son pouvoir et à grandir son pres-

appreciate their relevance one must ask two questions: What might the images and inscriptions of the coins represent, along with the inherent social meanings and values?[90] And secondly, who had the authority to mint coins for a particular context?

Chronology and Coins
The numismatic evidence for Yehud dates mostly after the Persian period, to the Macedonian, Ptolemaic, and later periods. The relative scarcity of Persian-period coins and the designs of the coins do not provide us with an unquestionable portrayal of the political and economic situations in Persian-period Yehud. The coins, which are mostly of small denomination, may have been minted to provide for local economic needs, such as providing day wages to soldiers and other workers.[91] To facilitate this, the governor may have permitted local authorities to produce mints of small denomination. L. Mildenberg categorizes the coins into imperial, provincial, and local issues. Of the latter two categories, he states that local coinage appeared—presumably with the permission of the imperial government—before the coinage minted by provincial governments. Provincial coinage began appearing in the provinces of

tige...faire de son règne un moment fondateur" (Briant, *Histoire de l'Empire perse*, 421). Cook (*Persian Empire*, 69–71) states that the Lydian and Greek practice of minting coins whose weight was guaranteed by a stamp of the ruler or civic authority continued under the early Achaemenids. Bar-ingots and cut-silver remained the standard currency throughout the empire, however. He writes, "The Persian royal issues could almost be regarded as coinage of the Greek world, and so too, on a rather broader front, the silver minted by satraps and commanders in the West for their military needs from the late fifth century on" (71). In light of the fact that money continues to be weighed, rather than the weight accepted by virtue of a seal, I do not see a reason why the Persian authorities would be overly concerned with the practice of minting in local provinces.

90. Leith claims that the images on coins should not necessarily be interpreted in religious terms. Provincial mints copied foreign issues. "The coinage of Judah and Samaria in the fourth century includes devices in imitation of Greek coins. But the adoption of Greek images such as the Attic owl or the head of the goddess Athena need not be interpreted religiously" ("Israel among the Nations," 369).

91. As suggested by Peter Machinist, "The First Coins of Judah and Samaria: Numismatics and History in the Achaemenid and Early Hellenistic Periods," in *Achaemenid History*. Vol. 8, *Continuity and Change* (ed. Heleen Sancisi-Weerdenburg et al.; Leiden: Nederlands Instituut voor Nabije Oosten, 1994), 373. He writes, "[T]here must have been numbers of soldiers moving through Palestine in the fourth and early third centuries, and the need to deal with them, and the traders and others associated with them, must have been a considerable stimulus to monetary production" (ibid.).

Samaria and Yehud in around 360 B.C.E., while local coinage dated from
450 to 332 B.C.E.[92]

The bulk of the *yhd[h]* coins were found in an area south of Jerusalem's city limits, at Beth-Zur, and at Tel Gamma.[93] Mildenberg cited 28
types and variants that can be divided chronologically to the Persian,
Macedonian, and Ptolemaic periods.[94] The coins depicting birds, falcons,
lilies, or a portrait of the Persian king (including the *yḥzqyh hpḥh* coin
depicting both a head and an owl) and inscribed *yhd* date to the Persian
period. Those coins depicting a head on the obverse and what appears to
be a winged lion on the reverse and inscribed with *yḥzqyh* alone date to
the Macedonian period. And the coins inscribed with *yhd* or *yhdh* and
depicting youthful male heads or a portrait of Ptolemy I and the Ptolemaic eagle date to the Ptolemaic period. While Mildenberg dates the style
of coin depicting a bird standing and looking backward and inscribed
with *yhwdh* to the Persian period, Meshorer concludes that the coin style
belongs instead in the Ptolemaic period, based on the extended orthography representing the full spelling of the name Judaea (*yhwdh*). Before

92. L. Mildenberg, "On the Money Circulation in Palestine from Artaxerxes II
Till Ptolemy I: Preliminary Studies of Local Coinage in the Fifth Persian Satrapy.
Part 5," *Transeu* 7 (1994): 64 n. 5, 67–68. See also Carter's discussion in *Emergence
of Yehud*, 268–70. Compare U. Rappaport's view ("The First Judean Coinage," *JJS*
32 [1981]: 14) that it was the duty of the *pḥh* to provide coins as small change.

93. Yaʾakov Meshorer, *Ancient Jewish Coinage*. Vol. 1, *Persian Period through
Hasmoneans* (Dix Hills: Amphora, 1982), 17, 30–31. The *yhd[h]* coins were origi-
nally classified with the "Philisto-Arabian" coins presumed to be struck in Gaza.
(See, for instance, D. Jeselsohn, "A New Coin Type with Hebrew Inscription," *IEJ*
24 [1977]: 77–78; A. Kindler, "Silver Coins Bearing the Name of Judaea from the
Early Hellenistic Period," *IEJ* 24 [1974]: 73–76; Y. Meshorer, *Jewish Coins of the
Second Temple Period* [Tel Aviv: Am Hassefer and Massada, 1967]; L. Y. Rahmani,
"Silver Coins of the Fourth Century BC from Tel Gamma," *IEJ* 21 [1971]: 158–60.)
Mildenberg ("Yehud," 183–90) argues that the coins were originally grouped with
the "Philisto-Arabian" coins because they bore the image of an owl, an image common in Gaza. Betlyon ("Provincial Government," 636) conjectures that Phoenician
and Philisto-Arabian coins probably accounted for the bulk of the currency used in
Judah (Yehud) supplementing the smaller denominations minted in Judah with the
larger issues from mints outside of Judah. Meshorer (*Ancient Jewish Coinage*, 27)
connects the minting of the Philisto-Arabian coins that depict the letters ב or בי with
the governorship of Bagoas. On the ratio of the use of the Semitic inscriptions, for
example, he notes that five coins from the Abu Shusheh hoard depict the ב while one
is inscribed בי.

94. Mildenberg, "Yehud," 183–96. Meshorer (*Ancient Jewish Coinage*, 21) adds
that the majority of the designs on the *yhd[h]* coins are copied from international
currency and that it is unlikely that the symbols acquired any new Jewish symbolic
value.

the Macedonian conquest, one of the most characteristic features of the coinage was a shorter spelling: *yhd*.[95] The more complete spelling of Judaea (*yh[w]dh*) was a development under the Ptolemaic period.[96]

Based on two excavated sites, Ḥorvat Zimri and the City of David, Carter provides a data set comparing the number of coins dating to the Persian period with those from later periods.[97] From the 74 coins excavated at Ḥorvat Zimri, 3 per cent of the coins date to the Persian period, 66 per cent date to the Hellenistic period, and 31 per cent date to the Roman through the Byzantine periods.[98] From the 227 coins excavated at the City of David (from Strata 9 through 1), 0.4 per cent date to the Persian period; 9.6 per cent date to the early Hellenistic period; 49.7 per cent date to the Hasmonean period; 31.7 per cent date to the early Roman period; 4.4 per cent date to the Byzantine period; and 3.9 per cent date to the Islamic and later periods. If the increase of coins demonstrates an increasingly autonomous Judean polity, then the negligible percentages of coins dating to the Persian period may indicate that this autonomy had not yet been attained, and that the coins were minted for local purposes under the permission of the imperial authorities. It is equally possible that these negligible percentages are due simply to aspects of archaeology (i.e. that a complete sample has not been discovered, that access to some areas is more restricted, etc.)—a possibility that is made even more poignant since Persian-period sites and the Persian-period strata were traditionally of less interest to excavators.[99]

Avigad dates the small, silver *yḥzqyh* coins to ca. 330 B.C.E., roughly within the year following Darius III's defeat to Alexander at Gaugamela.[100] He suggests that Yeḥezkiyah was the last governor of Persian-period Yehud. He associates the name Yeḥezkiyah with the 66-year-old priest mentioned by Josephus (*C. Ap.* 1.187–89), and who conferred with Ptolemy I in 312 B.C.E.[101] This association, however, is unparalleled as

95. Meshorer, *Ancient Jewish Coinage*, 15.

96. Ibid., 17. Rappaport ("Judean Coinage," 10) adds that it is possible the dropped final *h* on the so-called Aramaic coins may have simply been due to room and aesthetics. Attic coins, for example, designate AΘE for Aθεναι. J. Naveh ("Dated Coins of Alexander Janneus," *IEJ* 18 [1968]: 20–26) discusses a similar issue regarding the transliteration of "Alexander the King" on a Hasmonean coin into Aramaic.

97. Carter, *Emergence of Yehud*, 270–71.

98. Ibid., 270.

99. Cf. Briant, *From Cyrus to Alexander*, 1–5; Carter, *Emergence of Yehud*, 31–39.

100. Avigad, *Bullae and Seals*, 35.

101. Ibid., 29. See also Dandamaev and Lukonin, *Culture and Social Institutions*, 198. Note Cross ("Judaean Stamps," in *Leaves from an Epigrapher's*

the Persians did not give the offices of the governor and of the high priest to the same person.[102] More importantly, the (high) priest during this time was not Hezekiah but Onias (cf. *Ant.* 11.347).[103] One must conclude, therefore, that the Yeḥezkiyah mentioned on the coins was not, contra Josephus and Avigad, the individual named in *C. Ap.* 1.187–89.

Mildenberg dates the *yḥzqyh* coins inscribed with *hpḥh* to the Persian period while those without the designative term he dates to the Macedonian period. Meshorer, however, compares the coins to ones found in Samaria inscribed with the name *yrbʿm* that date between 350–333 B.C.E., during the time the temple at Mt. Gerizim was being constructed.[104] Meshorer states:

> But the Jereboam [*sic*] coins from Samaria also lack the title, and they are surely from the Persian period. Thus Mildenberg's theory cannot be accepted. Moreover, the close relationship between the coins carrying the title and those which do not is supported by the finds from the Tel Gamma hoard, where both types of Yeḥezkiyah coins were found together.[105]

Based on the parallel to the Jeroboam coins, Meshorer's argument is convincing. Since coins may have been weighed for monetary value,[106] it may not have been necessary to follow an exact formula for inscriptions or imagery. In addition, if multiple individuals were employed by a single minting location, there exists the possibility, based on skill and equipment, for variances in the inscriptions to occur.

Finally, J. Betlyon concludes that coins minted in Yehud after 370 B.C.E. and before the Macedonian period were products of Yehud's participation in a revolt led by the Sidonian king, Abdaštart I, along with

Notebook: Collected Papers in Hebrew and West Semitic Palaeography and Epigraphy [HSS 51; Winona Lake: Eisenbrauns, 2003], 143), who writes, "The 'Hezekiah' inscribed in Palaeo-Hebrew on the coin has been identified as Εζεκιας, a chief priest who accompanied Ptolemy Soter (305–283/82 B.C.E.) to Egypt in the early third century. This identification is doubtful; we should expect *the* high priest's name on the coin. Hezekiah was not in the succession."

102.   Cf. Rappaport, "Judean Coinage," 16; VanderKam, *From Joshua to Caiaphas*, 118.

103.   See also VanderKam, *From Joshua to Caiaphas*, 124, 491–92.

104.   Cross, "Aspects," 201–11; Meshorer, *Ancient Jewish Coinage*, 32–33. Note Meshorer further: "One issue depicting the name 'Jeroboam' reinforces the importance of the temple. The design on the coin contains two figures standing in a building which may represent the new edifice on Mount Gerizim" (34). Regarding the construction of the temple at Mt Gerizim, see also Josephus (*Ant.* 11.306–10).

105.   Meshorer, *Ancient Jewish Coinage*, 34.

106.   Cf. the discussion of the gradual rise of a monied economy in Carter, *Emergence of Yehud*, 259–73.

sympathetic kings of Cyprus; the coins are similar to the silver and bronze issues produced by the Sidonians during the revolt.[107] According to him, Sidon and Cyprus pressured the province to mint coins with an image of Yehud's own leaders, encouraging the Jewish officials to place their images on the coin—a highly unusual practice.[108] He states that the high priest in Jerusalem took part in the revolt.[109] Moreover, he concludes that the silver drachm should be dated to the period following the revolt, ca. 362–358 B.C.E., and that it finds an analogy with the coinage struck by Mazday, the satrap in Sidon during this time period.[110] The satrap minted coins to fill a gap created by a lack of a minting authority.[111]

As Carter notes, the support of Yehud for the revolt of Tachos (ca. 370–362 B.C.E.) or the Tennes Rebellion (ca. 352–347 B.C.E.) is unproven.[112] Only one of the sites that Betlyon draws upon for archaeological evidence of destruction in the mid-fifth century (i.e. Hazor, Megiddo, ʿAtlit, Lachish and Jericho) was part of the province of Yehud. "And there is, in fact, no evidence of a Persian period destruction at Jericho; rather the site seems to have been abandoned sometime in the late Persian period."[113] He dates the *ywḥnn* coin to sometime during 335–330 B.C.E.[114]

Even if Yehud did not participate in the Tennes Rebellion, it is possible that Yohanan,[115] to fill a gap left between the Persian and Greek

107. Betlyon, "Provincial Government," 637.

108. Ibid.

109. For his evidence, Betlyon (ibid.) cites Stern's discussion of sites in the Shephelah and the Negev (*Material Culture of the Land of the Bible in the Persian Period, 538–332 B.C* [Warminster: Aris & Phillips, 1982], 254–55).

110. J. Betlyon, *The Coinage and Mints of Phoenicia: The Pre-Alexandrian Period* (HSM 26; Chico, Calif.: Scholars Press, 1980), 14–16; idem, "Provincial Government," 637–38. Regarding the silver drachm, he states ("Provincial Government," 637 n. 19) that the drachm is not Jewish in character and must represent some foreign influence during its period of minting. See also D. Barag ("Some Notes on a Silver Coin of Johanan the High Priest," *BA* 48 [1985]: 166–68; idem, "A Silver Coin of Yohanan the High Priest and the Coinage of Judea in the Fourth Century B.C.," *INJ* 9 [1986]: 4–21) for further analysis of the coin.

111. Betlyon, *Coinage*, 15.

112. Carter, *Emergence of Yehud*, 277–79. But for further reference, compare Cross ("Judaean Stamps," 143) who speculates that Yehud's involvement in the Tennes Rebellion led to the production of "an autonomous currency." Cross's speculation is based on an argument given by D. Barag in 1966 ("The Effects of the Tennes Rebellion on Palestine," *BASOR* 183 [1966]: 6–12).

113. Ibid., 279, see also 160–62.

114. Ibid., 279.

115. On Yohanan's struggle with foreign authority, see also Josephus, *Ant.* 11.7.297–301.

authorities, issued silver coinage,[116] and the silver coin inscribed with *ywḥnn hkhn* would fit this context.[117] Considering the possible waning power of the Persian empire, it is possible that the temple treasury took on additional minting duties to fill a gap left by a preoccupied imperial government.

Bullae and Seals

In 1976, Avigad published seals and seal impressions found on bullae and jar handles that were inscribed with either or both *yhd* and *pḥh*. He dated these findings to sometime between 538 and 433 B.C.E.[118] Stern writes, "[I]n the assemblage of the sixty-five Persian-period bullae from Judah published by N. Avigad, stamped from twelve different seals, *all* were inscribed, some with the name of the provincial official and his title, but most with personal name alone…"[119] Together, the seals and the coins mention four governors: Elnathan, Yehoʿezer, Aḥzai, and Yeḥezqiyah.[120] The biblical texts mention Sheshbazzar, Zerubbabel, and Nehemiah. The Elephantine papyri mention Bagohi.

Table 2. *Possible List of Governors in the Persian Period*[121]

Dates	Governors	References
538–	Sheshbazzar	Ezra 5:14 (*pḥh*)
520–510?	Zerubbabel	Hag 1:1, 14 (*pḥt yhwdh*)
510–490?	Elnathan	bulla and seal (*pḥwʾ*)
490–470?	Yehoʿezer	jar impression (*pḥwʾ*)
470–	Ahzai	jar impression (*pḥwʾ*)
445–433	Nehemiah	Neh 5:14; 12:26 (*pḥh*)
ca. 407	Bagohi	papyrus, AP 30/31 (*pḥh*)
ca. 330	Yehezqiyau	silver coins (*pḥh*)

116.   Barag ("Some Notes," 168) concludes—based on Cross's papponymy theory—that this Yohanan was not the same individual mentioned in the Elephantine papyri, but most likely his grandson.

117.   So also ibid.

118.   Avigad, *Bullae and Seals*.

119.   Stern, *Archaeology*, 2:545. Stern also states (2:548) that Aramaic *yhd* seal impressions were found at Gezer, Mozah, Nebî Samaîl, Tell en-Naṣbeh, Tell el-Fûl, Jerusalem, Ramat Raḥel, Ḥusan, Bethany, Jericho, En-Gedi, and in the archive published by Avigad.

120.   Ibid., 2:550.

121.   Portions taken from Avigad, *Bullae and Seals*, 35; Meyers and Meyers, *Haggai, Zechariah 1–8*, 14.

The seal inscribed [וא]חפ ןתנלא תמא תימלשל belonged to Shelomith, the wife of Elnathan.[122] N. Avigad published the inscription on the seal as, "Belonging to Shelomith, maidservant of Elnathan, the governor."[123] However, because אמת also denotes "wife," Meyers and Meyers conclude that the inscription indicates that Shelomith was Elnathan's wife.[124] Moreover, according to 1 Chr 3:19, she was the daughter of Zerubbabel and therefore a Davidide, and for the Jewish community this gave a certain legitimacy to the governorship of her husband, Elnathan, who was not a Davidide.[125] For these reasons, given Shelomith's family, and therefore political, connections, it seems best to conclude that Shelomith was the wife of Elnathan.

The Biblical Texts and Theories of Government

One must ask two initial questions regarding the government in Yehud: (1) What is the significance of the title "governor" given to Sheshbazzar (פחה = Ezra 5:14; ἐπάρχῳ = 1 Esd 6:18 [on the uses of the latter term, compare *Hist.* 3.70, 126; 4.166; *Ana.* 4.4.4; *Hel.* 6.1.2, 3; also, Thuc. 1.126; *Hist.* 6.106]) and Zerubbabel (פחת יהודה = Hag 1:1, 14; 2:2, 21); and (2) What new governing structure, if any, did Nehemiah set in place?

The answer to the second question—what new governing structure did Nehemiah set in place—depends in part on the answer to the first. If Sheshbazzar and Zerubbabel were governors, then a history of governors prior to Nehemiah exists and Nehemiah did not establish the priests as political authorities in his absence—as many of the interpretations addressed in this investigation seem to imply.

If Persian-appointed governors led the government of Yehud, other issues become important as well: What was the relationship between Joshua and Zerubbabel? The texts of Haggai and Ezra speak of them as the servants of Yahweh acting in one accord (Ezra 3:2, 8; 4:3; 5:2; Hag 1:1, 12, 14; 2:2, 4).[126] Should this be understood as confirmation that a

---

122.   Cf. E. Meyers, "The Shelomit Seal and the Judean Restoration: Some Additional Considerations," *ErIs* 18 (1985): 33*–38*; idem, "The Persian Period and the Judean Restoration: From Zerubbabel to Nehemiah," in *Ancient Israelite Religion: Essays in Honor of Frank Moore Cross* (ed. Paul D. Hanson et al.; Philadelphia: Fortress, 1987), 509–21.

123.   Avigad, *Bullae and Seals*, 11–13. Avigad suggests (11) that אמת corresponds to אבד.

124.   Meyers and Meyers, *Haggai, Zechariah 1–8*, 14.

125.   Carter, *Emergence of Yehud*, 52; Meyers, "The Shelomit Seal," 33*–38*; ibid., "The Persian Period," 509–21.

126.   One could also include Neh 12:1 and 1 Esd 5:8, 48, 56, 68, 70; 6:2.

diarchy existed? Rebuilding the temple is the primary reason they are
mentioned together (cf. Ezra 3:2; 4:3; 5:2; Hag 1:1, 12, 14; 2:2, 4).
Meyers and Meyers suggest that Zerubbabel aroused great hopes in the
people that they would be politically independent in the future (cf. Hag
2:20–23). In this respect, it is interesting that Haggai always refers to
Zerubbabel as governor, but Zechariah does not refer to Zerubbabel as
governor.[127] On Zechariah's part, this may have been a polemical or
propagandistic device used to bolster the ideological agenda in the text—
a point that will be discussed below.

     If Sheshbazzar and Zerubbabel were governors, and one accepts the
added testimony of the extra-biblical evidence (of the bullae and seals
[cf. Table 2, p. 90]), then a history of government in Yehud exists prior
to Nehemiah.[128] As a result, arguments for a theocratic development in
Yehud after Nehemiah must explain the social and political evolution of
an imperial province into a theocracy (or theocratic-like structure).
Subsequently, this explanation must answer the following rather skeptical question: If in fact a theocracy existed and in light of the history of
governors in Yehud,[129] what changed the social, political, and economic
systems of Yehud, an imperial province, into those characteristic of a
theocracy?

Discussions of Government in Yehud
According to the Persian-period biblical texts, Sheshbazzar, Zerubbabel
and Nehemiah were governors of Yehud. Apart from these individuals,
the texts say nothing about the presence of governors in Yehud. To
explain the situation, the tendency in modern scholarship thus far has
been to grant power to the priesthood after Nehemiah's term.[130] Doing so,

127.   Meyers and Meyers, *Haggai, Zechariah 1–8*, xxxiv.
128.   Contra Alt (cf. "Die Rolle Samarias bei der Entstehung des Judentums," in
Festschrift Otto Procksch zum Sechzigsten Geburtstag [ed. Albrecht Alt; Leipzig: A.
Deichert and J. C. Hinrichs, 1934], 5–28; idem, "Die Landnahme der Israeliten in
Palästina," in *Kleine Schriften zur Geschichte des Volkes Israel* [ed. Albrecht Alt;
Munich: Beck, 1953], 89–125).
129.   In addition to the bullae and seals referred to above, note AP 30/31, which
refers to Bagohi, and the silver coins that refer to Yehezqiyah (see Table 2, p. 90).
130.   Dyck, *Theocratic Ideology*, passim; Eph'al, "Syria-Palestine under Achaemenid Rule," 152; Leith, "Israel among the Nations," 367–68; Plöger, *Theocracy*,
passim; Weinberg, *Citizen-Temple Community*, 118–26. Weinberg insufficiently
judges the *yhwd* stamps. The change from *yhd* to *yršlm* on the stamps, he argues,
signaled the rising significance of Jerusalem and the high priests. (But note Carter
[*Emergence of Yehud*, 301], who correctly shows that the *yršlm* seals are not Persian period.) Weinberg writes further (*Citizen-Temple Community*, 125), "The epigraphic material proves that in the second half of the fourth century BCE the local

however, ignores the testimony of the extra-biblical evidence, noted above (cf. Table 2, p. 90), that governors continued to function in the province after Nehemiah through almost the entirety of the Persian period.

Sheshbazzar, the Governor. According to Ezra 1:8, 11, Sheshbazzar[131] headed the so-called return to Yehud sometime after 539 B.C.E. Coupled

administration of the province of Yehud was apparently transferred to the head of the citizen-temple community. Two further arguments could be cited in this regard: (1) the coin from Beth-zur with the legend *ḥzkyw*, and (2) the view of Cross: 'It is not improbable that Hezekiah was a high priest during the fourth century' [F. M. Cross, "Judean Stamps," *ErIs* 9 (1969): 23] who, as *peḥâ*, also had the authority to mint coins." Weinberg's dependence upon Cross's theory as convincing evidence is dubious. (Cross can only speculate as to the possibility.) The *ḥzkyw* coin mentions only that Hezekiah was governor and says nothing about him possibly being a high priest. If, as Weinberg proposes, Jerusalem had become a citizen-temple community by this time, and the high priest was the political authority, then certainly that inscription would have found its way onto the coin (compare the coin minted by Yohanan the high priest during the rebellion of that time [as discussed in Barag, "Some Notes," 166–68; see also the section, "Coins," above].) Regarding Cross's theory as a whole, see also VanderKam (*From Joshua to Caiaphas*, 97), who states that Cross's reconstruction of high priests lacks compelling evidence.

131.   Clines (*Ezra, Nehemiah and Esther*, 40–41) notes that several scholars argue Sheshbazzar was another name for Zerubbabel. See also Johannes Gabriel, *Zorobabel: Ein Beitrag zur Geschichte der Juden in der ersten Zeit nach dem Exil* (Vienna: Mayer & Co., 1927), 48–79; Bruno M. Pelaia, *Esdra e Neemia* (Rome: Marietti, 1960), 39. Some arguments for the two names referring to the same person are based on 1 Esd 6:18 and on an omission of the "and" conjunction before Zerubbabel. In addition, Josephus writes, "Cyrus also sent back to them the vessels of God which king Nebuchadnezzar had pillaged out of the temple, and carried to Babylon. So he committed these things to Mithridates, the treasurer, to be sent away, with an order to give them to Sanabassar, that he might keep them till the temple was built…" (*Ant.* 11.1.3). In the same section Josephus provides a copy of the letter of Cyrus to the governors in Syria, which states: "I have also sent the vessels which king Nebuchadnezzar pillaged out of the temple, and have given them to Mithridates the treasurer, and to Zorobabel the governor of the Jews, that they might have them carried to Jerusalem…" Clines (*Ezra, Nehemiah and Esther*, 41) notes, however, that most have given up trying to associate the two names with one individual. "The major difficulty with it is that in ch. 5, set in the time of Zerubbabel, Sheshbazzar seems to be referred to as a governor of a former time (5:14, 15, *q.v.*). A further objection is that one person is not likely to have had two Babylonian names (Daniel, for example, had a Hebrew name and a Babylonian name)…" In light of this, Clines notes that some have attempted to trace a Hebrew origin for the name Zerubbabel (possibly a joining of זרע and בבל). He also indicates that the Chronicler makes a faulty identification of Zerubbabel with Sheshbazzar (65, 88–89). VanderKam (*From Joshua to Caiaphas*, 6–8) also addresses Sheshbazzar's two possible names,

with the responsibility of leading a group of settlers, Sheshbazzar, the text quickly points out, carried with his person the Jerusalem temple's accessories.[132] If we accept the claim in Ezra, these accessories anticipated his role in restoring the temple, which enjoys a central place in the narratives of the Persian-period biblical texts.

Ezra and 1 Esdras identify Sheshbazzar as a governor, ruler, and prince (Ezra 5:14 [פֶּחָה]; 1 Esd 2:12 [προστάτη]; 6:18 [ἐπάρχῳ]; Ezra 1:8 [נָשִׂיא]).[133] Ezra 5 claims that Sheshbazzar was a governor commissioned by Cyrus, but apparently commissioned for a specific mission only: to "return" the temple utensils and rebuild the Jerusalem temple (vv. 14–15). Verse 16, however, suggests that while Sheshbazzar laid the foundation, the temple was not rebuilt.[134] The use of the perfect tense to describe the actions of Sheshbazzar in this verse suggests completeness; with this final verse, Ezra departs from the text and the text switches its focus to Zerubbabel.

concluding the identification of Sheshbazzar and Shenazzar is an attractive possibility. P. Sacchi (*The History of the Second Temple Period* [JSOTSup 285; Sheffield: Sheffield Academic Press, 2000], 60–61) says that Sheshbazzar was Shenazzar and a vassal king of Judah when Cyrus conquered Babylon. Regarding the Chronicler and the story of the return, C. Torrey (*The Chronicler's History of Israel: Chronicles–Ezra–Nehemiah Restored to Its Original Form* [1954; Port Washington: Kennikat Press, 1973], xxvii) argues that the entire account is fictional. Leith ("Israel among the Nations," 380) dismisses Sheshbazzar's role, claiming that no notable return occurred before 520 B.C.E. and the activities of Zerubbabel and Joshua.

132.   Ezra suggests Cyrus proclaimed the edict so Sheshbazzar might personally restore the temple (cf. Ezra 1:1–2). Ezra 1:7–8 romantically claims Cyrus himself brought out the temple utensils.

133.   In 1 Esdras, Σαναβασσάρῳ, a Babylonian name, is used. Lester L. Grabbe (*Ezra–Nehemiah* [New York: Routledge, 1998], 76) indicates that while some manuscripts read "Zerubbabel who is Sanabassaros," standard interpretation maintains the identification of Sanabassaros with Sheshbazzar. Clines (*Ezra, Nehemiah and Esther*, 40–41, 89) agrees that Sanabassaros is a form of Sheshbazzar. He suggests that linking Zerubbabel and Sheshbazzar as the same person is dubious.

134.   While Sheshbazzar is credited with laying the foundations of the temple in Ezra 5:16, Ezra 3:1–13 (note esp. v. 6) indicates the event occurred some years later. It seems clear that Ezra 5:16 and 3:6 are not in chronological order. So what can be made of these two statements concerning the foundation? Bringing Haggai and Zech 1–8 into the discussion, VanderKam (*From Joshua to Caiaphas*, 9) states that Sheshbazzar built the lowest part of the temple foundations and Zerubbabel resumed the task. In addition, he observes that Ezra divides the building of the temple into two stages. The first stage involved "building the altar in the seventh month of an unspecified year in Cyrus's reign." Stage two was set in Darius' second year (521 or 520 B.C.E.). In the second stage Zerubbabel and Joshua build the temple (12–14, quote from p. 12).

Although it is not the only possible conclusion, it seems possible that Ezra–Nehemiah abandons Sheshbazzar because he no longer fit the author's agenda, which was the "restoration" of the Jerusalem temple and the religious community attached to it. Several names on the list in Ezra 2:2 are the names of prominent individuals in Yehud, but Sheshbazzar's name is missing.[135]

It might be possible to recover Sheshbazzar from the list. To begin with, Blenkinsopp parallels the זכרון ספר of Mal 3:16–18 with the genealogical listing that took place during Nehemiah's administration (cf. Neh 9:38–10:1 [10:1–2 MT]).[136] The names of those who are chosen or "spared" will be written in the Book of Remembrance. This Book may have served the same purpose as the genealogical listing of Ezra 2: "these are the captive exiles." While Sheshbazzar is not named specifically among the leaders in Ezra 2, it is possible that he appears under the title "the governor" in v. 63.[137] Nevertheless, it is still possible, given the nameless governor, that Sheshbazzar's absence from this list reflects the author's or redactor's general dismissal of him from the narrative. One thing should be clear, however: it is not obvious that his absence in the narrative demands his dismissal from the role of governor.[138] Ezra only mentions him *when his activities involve the temple*. Therefore, it is possible that Sheshbazzar fulfilled his term while the texts avoid further mention because his activities no longer involved the temple.[139] Another possibility, of course, is that Sheshbazzar died.

Zerubbabel and Joshua: A Diarchy? Discussions of Zerubbabel and Joshua—and of the government in place during their activities—often focus on an interpretation of the crown(s), as possible symbols of political authority, in Zech 6:9–15.[140] The MT and LXX refer to "crowns"

135. Ezra 2:1–2 states: "Now these were the people of the province who came from those captive exiles whom King Nebuchadnezzar of Babylon had carried captive to Babylonia; they returned to Jerusalem and Judah, all to their own towns. They came with Zerubbabel, Jeshua, Nehemiah, Seraiah, Reelaiah, Mordecai, Bilshan, Mispar, Bigvai, Rehum, and Baanah. The number of the Israelite people…"
136. Blenkinsopp, *History of Prophecy*, 210.
137. VanderKam, *From Joshua to Caiaphas*, 11.
138. Note also Briant, *From Cyrus to Alexander*, 46–47.
139. Ezra moves quickly from Sheshbazzar to Zerubbabel. Sheshbazzar's activities overshadow his person. The text only mentions him when the author/editor can relate his activities to the temple (Ezra 1:8, 11; 5:14, 16). By way of comparison, the Deuteronomist employs a similar strategy in his assessment of various Israelite and Judean kings (cf. 2 Kgs 15–16).
140. For example, see Paul L. Redditt, "Zerubbabel, Joshua, and the Night Visions of Zechariah," *CBQ* 54 (1992): 251–52. Both the LXX and MT have crowns,

(Zech 6:11–12), but there seems to be but one (functional?) crown—at least as emphasized within the narrative (one crown is for זכרון, according to Zech 6:14).[141] The crown(s)' recipient(s) include Joshua the high priest (cf. Zech 6:11) and perhaps others (e.g. the unnamed צמח; compare Zech 3:8 and 6:12) who remain unspecified.

Nehemiah mentions Zerubbabel three times: twice as a leader (one among others) of returnees (Neh 7:7; 12:1), and once as acting like the later Nehemiah (thus, a governor) who ensured that the people provided for the Levites (12:47). Haggai mentions Zerubbabel and Joshua together five times, each instance bound by a consistent theme, the building of the

plural, while the NRSV translation makes reference to a singular crown made of gold and silver.

141.   Scholarly conclusions regarding the crowns are numerous. P. Ackroyd (*Exile and Restoration: A Study of Hebrew Thought of the Sixth Century B.C.* [OTL; Philadelphia: Westminster, 1968], 198) argues that the crowns were intended for Joshua and Zerubbabel, respectively. Contra Ackroyd, Meyers and Meyers (*Haggai, Zechariah 1–8*, 353) state that the suggestion that both Zerubbabel and Joshua were crowned presents more problems than it solves. They read Zech 6:9–15 as a discussion of two crowns (336–37, 349–64), one of which is placed on the head of Joshua while the other stands as a reminder in the temple. They add (352–53) that Zech 1–8 contain implications of a diarchy between Zerubbabel and Joshua. Beyond this, however, their conclusions are unclear. R. Carroll ("Ancient Israelite Prophecy and Dissonance Theory," *Numen* 24 [1977]: 146) suggests that the crowns were likely made for Zerubbabel alone. D. Petersen (*Haggai and Zechariah 1–8: A Commentary* [OTL; Philadelphia: Westminster, 1984], 275), alternatively, suggests that more than one crown was made for Joshua, but that the crowns do not signify kingship. Blenkinsopp (*History of Prophecy*, 207–8) posits that the crown placed upon Joshua's head is quite clearly intended for Zerubbabel. Regarding Joshua's role he writes, "The substitution of the high priest Joshua for the Davidite Zerubbabel, and the insistence on the high status of the priest that follows, are understandable in view of the enhanced role of the temple clergy after Zerubbabel had disappeared from the scene" (208). But what about the reference to צמח in Zech 6:12? The term seems usually to refer to the Davidic line (Jer 23:5; 33:15; Zech 3:8 [and 6:12]). According to Zech 3:8, Joshua is not צמח. Cross ("Reconstruction," 9–10) asserts that Zerubbabel and Joshua are linked, presumably with respect to authority; he argues that in Haggai and Zechariah the king and the high priest constitute a diarchy. Moreover, he finds (11–14) the work of Chr₁ (original Chronicler = 1 Chr 10–2 Chr 34) to be a parallel to Haggai and Zechariah and concludes Chr₁ was written to support a restoration program for a kingdom under Zerubbabel. VanderKam (*From Joshua to Caiaphas*, 38–42) also states that the passage refers to two crowns (and two thrones): one for Joshua and one to be held for the future Davidic branch. He concludes this based on the study of Uffenheimer, who argued צמח never refers to an individual in the present moment but always to one who exists in the future. See VanderKam, *From Joshua to Caiaphas*, 31, and B. Uffenheimer, *The Visions of Zechariah: From Prophecy to Apocalyptic* (Jerusalem: Kiryat Sepher, 1961).

temple (Hag 1:1, 12, 14; 2:2, 4).[142] Haggai always mentions Joshua after Zerubbabel until the closing oracle;[143] there, Zerubbabel is mentioned alone in Hag 2:21–23 and is referred to as the signet ring of Yahweh. In Zech 4:6–10, Zerubbabel seems to be mentioned alone as Yahweh's chosen, the one who laid the foundations of the temple.[144] Each time Ezra mentions Zerubbabel and Joshua together it is in the context of the construction of the temple (Ezra 3:2, 8; 4:2–3; 5:2).[145] 1 Chronicles mentions Zerubbabel once in a list of Davidic descendants (3:19).

When discussing the figures of Zerubbabel and Joshua, Zechariah, as Cook notes, never viewed his "messianic hopes" for a diarchy as being realized.[146] Zerubbabel was a candidate who ultimately did not meet the job description.[147] In addition, Zechariah does not overtly support the high priest operating beyond the traditional high-priestly role; the text looks instead toward the restoration of the Davidic king.[148] This important fact demands attention because, as R. Wilson states, Zechariah operated within the "temple-cult circles."[149] If Zechariah were a product of a priestly circle, the text's yearning for the restoration of a Davidic ruler suggests that at least one circle of priests was not aware of or supportive of the high priest holding political power on his own apart from a Davidic ruler.[150]

142.   Blenkinsopp (*History of Prophecy*, 201) posits that Haggai belongs to the optimistic prophecy tradition as modeled by Hananiah, which is associated with the state cult. He writes, "The prediction addressed to the Davidite Zerubbabel of an imminent end to the contemporary political order, meaning concretely the breakup of the Persian empire (Hag 2:6–9, 20–23), is not different in essence from Hananiah's prophecy of emancipation from the Babylonian empire, a prophecy delivered in the temple (Jer 28:1–4)."

143.   As pointed out by VanderKam, *From Joshua to Caiaphas*, 21.

144.   VanderKam asserts that the passage definitely connects Zerubbabel with building the sanctuary. Ibid., 35–36.

145.   That is, apart from Ezra 2:2 which is merely a list of those who led returns.

146.   Cook, *Prophecy and Apocalypticism*, 131. Cook's larger argument is the development of proto-apocalypticism based on center and periphery in Yehud.

147.   Ibid., 132.

148.   Childs, *Introduction*, 479; Cook, *Prophecy and Apocalypticism*, 136; Meyers and Meyers, *Haggai, Zechariah 1–8*, 226–27.

149.   Robert R. Wilson, *Prophecy and Society in Ancient Israel* (Philadelphia: Fortress, 1980), 289. Note also D. Petersen ("Zerubbabel and Jerusalem Temple Reconstruction," *CBQ* 36 [1974]: 368), who suggests that Zechariah has either a pro-Priestly or Chronistic redaction.

150.   Hanson (*Dawn*, 227, 243, 247, 261) links Zechariah with the Zadokites. Yet compare Cook (*Prophecy and Apocalypticism*, 123). Blenkinsopp (*History of Prophecy*, 204), who links Zech 1–8 with the Deuteronomists, notes that a

When the imperial government permitted the rebuilding of the Jerusalem temple, it did so as a measure of enhancing stability and control in the region.[151] Zechariah interpreted the event as divine assurance that the temple would be functional again and would be the location of the divinely appointed authority. Even though the prophet's audience may have accepted this interpretation to a greater or lesser degree, it does not change the imperial agenda behind the events—it is more or less this same imperial concern that motivates the missions of Ezra and Nehemiah. The imperial government's concern was for greater stability and control in and over its territories.[152]

Haggai, Zechariah's contemporary, claims that the people must rebuild the temple before Yahweh can manifest his glory and, as Blenkinsopp states, show his hand in the political arena (cf. Hag 1:2–11).[153] In this claim and its related discussion, Haggai presents a possible path to political authority being centralized in the Jerusalem temple administration.[154] Until Yahweh and the intended community realized this prophetic vision, however, any desires of political authority centralized in the temple remain illusory. The calendric framework in the text of Haggai, as Meyers and Meyers observe, constituted a prophetic countdown to the rededication of the Jerusalem temple.[155] Yet this political power, centralized in the temple, may have been considered only temporary. The intermittent eschatological outbursts in Haggai (cf. Hag 2:21–23; compare also Zech 4:6–10) suggest that the diarchic rule would give way to an eventual revival of monarchic rule.[156]

It appears, however, that members of the society did not share Haggai's vision of restoration. Haggai 1:4, 9 explains that the people were more concerned about their own houses than they were about the

---

Zechariah, son of Iddo, is listed in Neh 12:16 and it is possibly the same person. Yet he also notes that Zechariah and Iddo are common names. Also note the comment by Meyers and Meyers (*Haggai, Zechariah 1–8*, xli) that Zechariah's vision of the flying scroll (Zech 5:1–11) alludes to Yehud's self-rule. This conclusion, as I argue, is only possible as an idealized alternative reality for which the prophet longs, and not as an actual reality.

151. Meyers and Meyers, *Haggai, Zechariah 1–8*, 335.

152. See also the extended discussion in Hoglund, *Achaemenid Imperial Administration*, 207–40.

153. Blenkinsopp, *History of Prophecy*, 202.

154. See also the discussion of the passage in Meyers and Meyers, *Haggai, Zechariah 1–8*, 37–43.

155. Ibid., 38.

156. As noted by ibid., 39.

temple.[157] As VanderKam points out, "the adjective חרב [used to describe the temple in Hag 1:4] refers, not to a building that is in the process of reconstruction, but to one that has been destroyed with only the debris remaining from it."[158] What has happened since the time Sheshbazzar returned with the temple utensils? Haggai and Zechariah point out that the people have built their own houses but the temple remains in ruin. It is possible to conclude, as Kessler does, that "ideological convictions" led the people to protest the building of the temple, saying "it was not yet time."[159] Thus, some of the people concluded that reconstruction would bring more harm than benefit.[160] However, this assumes that the sum, or a majority—enough at least to influence the social and political policies of the imperial government—of the society in Yehud shared the same ideological conviction. The apparent disagreements over intermarriage and Sabbath observance (examples discussed above) seem to imply that not all members of society, or even all members of the *golah* community, agreed with the religious ideological claims of Haggai, and more generally, the Persian-period biblical texts.

Zechariah, as a prophetic work, and as a pro-Davidide and possibly messianic work,[161] describes an existence hoped for, not one based in reality.[162] Within the prophetic framework, the crowns (even the flowing

157. The collapse of religious enthusiasm in the community and priesthood described within Malachi a half-century or more following the dedication of the temple does not depict a context governed by the cult (Blenkinsopp, *History of Prophecy*, 209–10).

158. VanderKam (*From Joshua to Caiaphas*, 15–16) claims the term חרב in Hag 1:4 indicates no foundation was laid at the time. And further, "Taken in this sense, Haggai's statement about the condition of the temple in the sixth month of Darius's second year would conflict with information in Ezra, which pictures work on the temple as continuing—or rather stopping and starting—from the time of Cyrus to Darius's second year (and beyond)." See also Francis I. Andersen, "Who Built the Second Temple?," *ABR* 6 (1958): 22–26; Otto Kaiser, "חרב", *TDOT* 5:150–54.

159. J. Kessler, "Building the Second Temple: Questions of Time, Text, and History in Haggai 1.1–15," *JSOT* 27 (2002): 250–51.

160. Kessler (*The Book of Haggai: Prophecy and Society in Early Persian Yehud* [VTSup 91; Leiden: Brill, 2002], 245) adds that the people's ideological convictions may very well have been driven by certain theological agendas.

161. Cf. Cook, *Prophecy and Apocalypticism*, 134.

162. The present is interpreted in light of what the prophet perceives the results to be in the future (see also Carroll, "Ancient Israelite Prophecy," 141; VanderKam, *From Joshua to Caiaphas*, 22–42). On the other hand, prophecy often failed in several respects, creating dissonant situations with regard to identity and belief (see Carroll, "Ancient Israelite Prophecy," 135; idem, *When Prophecy Failed*; Leon

oil in Zech 4) symbolize not an established fact but a possible and desired future.[163] Cook is probably correct when he observes that there is a messianic thrust in the first section (i.e. Zech 1–8, esp. 4–6) of the prophetic text.[164] Zechariah was written to illustrate a desired direction or an ideal that the author had for the community. The text looks to the restoration of Davidic rule, apparently redefined as a shared rule with the high priest (cf. Zech 4:6–10).[165] If Zechariah was a Zadokite,[166] the completion of the temple and the prophecy connecting Zerubbabel and Joshua to it reflect an attempt to secure priestly authority in the "restored nation," or at least in validating Zerubbabel's rule.[167] The author(s) or redactor(s) include priestly authority in the prophetic oracle, though it is initially tempered somewhat (esp. in Zech 3) by the continued, expressed

Festinger, Henry W. Riecken, and Stanley Schachter, *When Prophecy Fails* [Minneapolis: University of Minnesota Press, 1956]). Along these lines, Blenkinsopp (*History of Prophecy*, 207) suggests that the accuser (i.e. the satan) prosecutes Joshua, the high priest, and his colleagues for the people's lapse into apostasy. Joshua and his entourage are saved because the prophet views them as leading the people into a new messianic age (cf. Zech 3:1–10).

163.   Cook, for example, argues that the hopes for a diarchy portrayed in Zechariah were never realized during the author(s) time (*Prophecy and Apocalypticism*, 131–33).

164.   Ibid., 134–36.

165.   Cook (ibid., 135) notes that Zechariah stops short of elevating the contemporary figure, Zerubbabel, or even Joshua, choosing instead to focus on an ideal figure, a future Davidide, the Branch.

166.   Ibid., 123; also, J. Wellhausen, *Die kleinen Propheten übersetzt und erklärt* (Berlin: Georg Reimer, 1898), 185.

167.   The possibility of a restored nation as understood by the Zadokites assumes, even if only on the part of the Zadokites, that the Yahwism of the Zadokites was practiced by "all Israel." O. Margalith ("The Political Background of Zerubbabel's Mission and the Samaritan Schism," *VT* 41 [1991]: 316) suggests the population of Yehud had a strong polytheistic-syncretistic consciousness like that in Elephantine. He bases this on a very difficult assumption that only 5 per cent of the Judahites were exiled—Judah prior to the exiles (597, 586 B.C.E.) was polytheistic-syncretistic in nature—and the remaining 95 per cent of the people, who remained in the land, continued to practice religion as they had always done (314–17). Blenkinsopp (*History of Prophecy*, 201) asserts that the community in Jerusalem was concerned that whatever cult that had been carried out since the destruction of the Jerusalem temple became polluted and rendered the cult unacceptable. According to Blenkinsopp, the critique of pollution—found in similar prophetic denunciations—was most likely directed at cultic centers other than Jerusalem. As a result, he concludes it to be clear that Haggai and Zechariah were central cult prophets in close relationship with the priests. Weinberg (*Citizen-Temple Community*, 109–10), on the other hand, argues that Haggai and Zechariah expected a diarchy.

hope for the future rule of a Davidide.[168] In ch. 4, however, the Davidic Branch and the high priest may share this future rule. The focus on the Branch in ch. 3, which changes to a focus on a diarchy in ch. 4, was to be a reminder to the prophet's audience that the high priesthood alone could not lead the people into the coming age.[169] Together, Haggai and Zechariah describe an ideal nation, but one that did not exist at the time.[170]

Nehemiah and Ezra: A Governor and an Enigma. Ezra–Nehemiah begins with an (alleged) imperial decree from Cyrus that the people of Yahweh may return to Jerusalem and rebuild the temple (Ezra 1:3). In turn, the text describes Ezra and Nehemiah as the vanguards of the Yahwistic faith—even commissioned as such by the imperial government. One cannot escape the unabashed agenda of the text. Imperial actions intended to enhance the administrative system of the empire—more specifically, the province of Yehud—were interpreted as actions undertaken for the benefit of the *golah* community. The religious ideologies of this group, which seem to motivate the author(s)/redactor(s), limit the recipients of imperial benevolence to those members of *golah* community who are described as the only legitimate people of Yahweh.[171] With this

168. See also Cook, *Prophecy and Apocalypticism*, 136.
169. As noted in ibid., 136, also 136 n. 52.
170. Carroll ("Ancient Israelite Prophecy," 146) suggests that attempts to combat dissonance can be found in Haggai and Zechariah. The expectations of Zerubbabel as a ruling Davidide held by the group/party writing the texts failed to be realized. This does mean, to be sure, that Zerubbabel no longer governed. The expectations of Zerubbabel were unofficial, in terms of politics, beliefs of a specific party or group. J. Morgenstern ("Jerusalem—485 BC [Concluded]," *HUCA* 31 [1960]: 4–5) says that Haggai and Zechariah perceived Zerubbabel to be the restoration of the Davidic monarchy. He interprets the silence of the texts concerning Zerubbabel—after Zerubbabel is mentioned a few times—to be the result of a failed rebellion that Zerubbabel was said to have headed. As Hoglund (*Achaemenid Imperial Administration*, 55–56) has pointed out, however, Morgenstern's broader reconstruction of Persian-period Judean history fails on several points. His analysis of the catastrophe in 485 B.C.E. following the rebellion makes only selective and inadequate use of the biblical evidence for the economic conditions prior to 485. Morgenstern misinterprets several key passages from Ezra. Moreover, his thesis fails to correlate with archaeological evidence that has emerged subsequent to the early 1970s. For further reference on the unfulfilled prophecy of Zechariah, see Cook (*Prophecy and Apocalypticism*, 123–65), who concludes that Zech 1–8 is proto-apocalyptic—a literary genre defined by its outlook toward a future divine restoration of a group or people.
171. See also Blenkinsopp, *Isaiah 56–66*, 49; Janzen, "'Mission' of Ezra," 619–43; Kessler, "Persia's Loyal Yahwists," 91–121; D. Smith-Christopher, "The Mixed

conclusion, Hoglund's observation that the walls of Jerusalem in Ezra–Nehemiah held a weighty role in the narrative as symbols representing the separation of the righteous community from the profane (cf. Neh 11:1) makes perfect sense.[172]

Briant's conclusion regarding Nehemiah and the importance of Yehud finds an important place here and is worth noting in its entirety:

> It thus appears that from Cyrus to Artaxerxes there was considerable consistency in royal policy, though we are not able to say that the Great King took special interest in this small region. The importance of Judah is only an 'optical illusion' created by the uneven distribution of evidence. In particular, there is nothing to prove that Susa or Persepolis considered Judah a bulwark of Persian dominion against fickle and unruly Egypt. More likely, from the Persian point of view, Nehemiah's mission was to establish a new basis for assessing tribute and guaranteeing regular payment: mutatis mutandis, and keeping in mind their purposes, his reforms can be compared with those carried out by Artaphernes in 493 in the cities of Ionia that had been ravaged by war and social tension.[173]

It is possible, as Smith-Christopher proposes, that the stern tone in Ezra–Nehemiah's address of intermarriage reflects significant lines of stress between social groups in Yehud. This stress may have been the result of an unequal distribution of power between the landed aristocracy and leaders from or affiliated with the *golah* community.[174] This certainly provides a social explanation for Ezra–Nehemiah's prohibition

Marriage Crisis in Ezra 9–10 and Nehemiah 13: A Study of the Sociology of the Post-Exilic Judaean Community," in Eskenazi and Richards, eds., *Second Temple Studies*, 2:243–65; idem, *Biblical Theology*; Smith, *Religion of the Landless*; idem, "The Politics of Ezra: Sociological Indicators of Postexilic Judaean Society," in Davies, ed., *Second Temple Studies*, 1:72–97. Also note my discussion of Smith in the section, "The 'Social Infrastructure' in Yehud" in Chapter 1 (p. 19).

172. Hoglund, *Achaemenid Imperial Administration*, 210.

173. Briant, *From Cyrus to Alexander*, 585–86, see also 603, and also 476–88. Nehemiah's mission was to establish a new basis for tribute and guaranteeing regular payment (cf. ibid., 586). The arguments of Hoglund (*Achaemenid Imperial Administration*) and Berquist (*Judaism in Persia's Shadow*) coincide with Briant's. Lipschits ("Achaemenid Imperial Policy," 38–39) rejects Hoglund's argument in particular, stating he does not see how Yehud could have held any military-strategic purposes for the Persian empire. Yet neither Hoglund nor Berquist argue that Yehud was itself a rampart against Egypt. They argue that the imperial garrisons set up in Yehud were intended to control their general areas, offer strategic military points in a buffer zone when necessary, and to safeguard the financial flow throughout their localities (Berquist especially on the last).

174. Smith-Christopher, "Mixed Marriage," 243.

of intermarriage, making it primarily social and secondarily religious.[175] That is, if Ezra's and Nehemiah's attempts to control intermarriage were attempts to control access to political and economic power, then that this prohibition was enforced was not due primarily to a concern for creating a religious community but for using religion as a social-religious justification for the prohibition (though the two are clearly related).

Nehemiah demonstrated the authority of the governor over the religious administration when he counterbalanced the priestly pursuit of power (contained primarily within the Jerusalem temple) by securing the positions and incomes of the Levites within the temple (cf. Neh 13:10) and other various posts in Jerusalem (Neh 7:1; 13:13, 30).[176] It was a political move: he solidified power by placing Levites who were loyal to him in positions of authority where they could keep high priestly pursuit of power in check.[177]

Nehemiah's role as governor, his documented actions, and his claim that other governors existed before him (Neh 5:15) show that Yehud was under the political authority of governors, at least through the time of Nehemiah, ca. 433 B.C.E.[178] The Elephantine papyri, coins, seals, and bullae (as discussed above) witness to the presence and continued activity of governors within Yehud even after Nehemiah. These types of evidence call into question the view expressed in Ezra–Nehemiah that the *golah* community enjoyed the special support of the imperial government. In light of this and other evidence, the missions of Ezra and Nehemiah should be interpreted as part of the imperial government's enhancement of territorial integration within the imperial administrative system.[179]

---

175. Tamara Cohn Eskenazi (*Ezra–Nehemiah* [ed. Carol A. Newsom and Sharon H. Ringe; Expanded ed. with Apocrypha; Women's Bible Commentary; Louisville: Westminster John Knox, 1998], 124–26) suggests that the concern over intermarriage expressed in Ezra–Nehemiah was primarily a concern over property rights. See also Hoglund (*Achaemenid Imperial Administration*, 232–40) who includes a similar concern over land property rights within a larger issue of social and political control over the Levantine area sought by the imperial government.

176. As noted by Smith, *Palestinian Parties*, 102.

177. A modern parallel exists. Ayatollah Khomeini placed, within Iran's post-revolutionary government, disagreeing individuals in posts of equal rank and status to counterbalance any unilateral claim to ultimate authority. See the discussion of Khomeini in Mehran Kamrava, *The Political History of Modern Iran: From Tribalism to Theocracy* (Westport: Praeger, 1992), 96–97.

178. Briant, *From Cyrus to Alexander*, 585.

179. Cf. Hoglund, *Achaemenid Imperial Administration*, 207–40.

The figure of Ezra, who was not identified as a governor, remains unclear.[180] H. Schaeder argued, drawing from Ezra 7:12, that Ezra was an official in charge of Jewish affairs within the Persian empire.[181] H. G. M. Williamson states that the imperial government created an official position specifically for Ezra before he went to Jerusalem to give his mission a higher sense of authority.[182] Hoglund, however, claims that parallel examples, in which an individual took charge of imperial interests for any religious or nationalistic group, are wanting.[183] S. Mowinckel, before him, made the same critique while emphasizing the insignificance of Yehud within the larger imperial sphere.[184]

While Ezra is never identified as a governor, his putative imperial commission, as reported by Ezra–Nehemiah, supported actions that affected the political administration and the related situation in Yehud.[185] If Ezra's mission parallels that of Udjahorresnet in Egypt under Darius I, then his activities represent those of liaison of Judean affairs to the imperial government.[186] These included putting the administration of the local judicial system on a firm basis.[187] Given that, Ezra filled an imperial role that was already established.

According to an alleged copy of the imperial letter contained in Ezra 7:11–26, the Persian king commissioned Ezra, "the priest," to be a scribe in Yehud.[188] In Ezra 7:25–26, the king gave Ezra power to appoint

180.   Lester L. Grabbe (*Judaism from Cyrus to Hadrian* [Minneapolis: Fortress, 1992], 136) argues that the figure and mission of Ezra are problematic. Briant (*From Cyrus to Alexander*, 584) argues that Ezra's mission was to establish royal order within the area of Yehud. Still, the question remains: With what authority did Ezra, if he existed, act?

181.   Hans H. Schaeder, *Esra der Schreiber* (Beiträge zur Historischen Theologie 5; Tübingen: J. C. B. Mohr, 1930), 48–57.

182.   H. G. M. Williamson, *Ezra, Nehemiah* (WBC 16; Waco: Word, 1985), 100.

183.   Hoglund, *Achaemenid Imperial Administration*, 228.

184.   Sigmund Mowinckel, *Studien zu dem Buche Ezra–Nehemiah, I–III* (Skrifter Utgitt Au Det Norske Videnskaps-Adademi I. Oslo II. Hist.-Filos. Klasse, Nu Serie, 3, 5 and 7; Oslo: Universitetsforlaget, 1964), 117–24.

185.   See also Briant, *From Cyrus to Alexander*, 585; Grabbe, *Judaism*, 136.

186.   On Udjahorresnet, see the section "Udjahorresnet's Role in Lower Egypt" in Chapter 2 (p. 63). See also Blenkinsopp, "Mission of Udjahorresnet," 409–21.

187.   So also J. Blenkinsopp, *Ezra–Nehemiah* (OTL; Philadelphia: Fortress, 1988), 147.

188.   There remains much debate concerning the authenticity of the "official" letter found in Ezra 7:11–16. See Clines, *Ezra, Nehemiah and Esther*, 10–16; Hoglund, *Achaemenid Imperial Administration*, 226–27; Jacob Myers, *Ezra, Nehemiah* (AB 14; Garden City: Doubleday, 1965), 57–63; Rudolph, *Esra und Nehemia*, 73–77; Williamson, *Ezra, Nehemiah*, 97–105.

magistrates and judges according to the "law of your god and the law of the king."[189] The Aramaic phrase, דתא די־אלהך ודתא די מלכא, implies that this law must meet the imperial requirements that would also qualify the law as the law of the king.[190] A related phrase in Ezra 7:14, "the law of your god, which is in your hand," does not imply that Ezra brought the law with him. It is clear from v. 25 that the law should already have been known in the province;[191] Ezra's law was not a new creation or the product of the *golah* community; securing the judicial and administrative systems of its provinces was not an arbitrary act by the Persian government but part of a larger process of organization.[192] Note the informed observation of Berquist:

> The establishment of law codes greatly enhanced the standardization of imperial administration, as did the creation of regional governmental structures. An efficient bureaucracy minimized the need for the emperor's personal attention to local situations, while still maintaining control over every corner of the empire.[193]

Despite what can be considered an important administrative role, the text of Ezra virtually ignores the judges and magistrates that Ezra was commissioned to appoint. Who were they and how did they function? For the author(s)/redactor(s) they are not important; they and the details of their appointments do not fit the agenda of the text.[194] Instead, the text states

189.   Satraps and governors could appoint judges, but Ezra was neither a satrap nor a governor. This ascribed power seems, instead, to be a later addition written during a time when giving Ezra satrap-like powers would not be perceived threatening.
190.   While the "King's Law," as first imposed by Darius, was not necessarily a singular law for the entire empire, it did require standardization. See Berquist, *Judaism in Persia's Shadow*, 55; Briant, *From Cyrus to Alexander*, 511; Fried, *Priest and the Great King*, 213–17; idem, "The *ʿAm Hāʾāreṣ* in Ezra 4:4," in Lipschits and Oeming, eds., *Judah and the Judeans in the Persian Period*, 138; Hoglund, *Achaemenid Imperial Administration*, 230.
191.   As also noted in Blenkinsopp, *Ezra–Nehemiah*, 148.
192.   See also *Hist.* 3.31; *Ana.* 1.6.4–5.
193.   Berquist, *Judaism in Persia's Shadow*, 55.
194.   While one may safely assume that the agendas manifest within the texts are conscious endeavors, they may be unconscious as well. M. Kundera, for example, says that remembering is a form of forgetting (*Testaments Betrayed* [New York: Harper Collins, 1995], 128). The authors of the texts remember certain events through which they proscribe meaning and continuity for their perspective. At the same time, they are "forgetting" other events that, while they may have had a stronger social impact upon the whole of society, do not embody meaning within the authorial perspective. An unconscious tendency to "forget" certain events, however, is often

that the (*golah*) Yahwistic religious law was the law of Yehud, and that
Yahweh preserved both the "holy seed" and its claim to the land (cf. Ezra
9:1–15). In so doing, the book of Ezra links the collective self-identity of
Yehud's citizens, selectively defined, to the traditions of the Abrahamic
and Mosaic covenants (compare also Neh 9). Note also Hoglund:

> [I]t is the writer of the biblical narratives who, with skill and imagina-
> tion, has tied…political concerns to a profoundly theological under-
> standing of the community and its role in the world. The writer also has
> moved the figures of the reformers from mere imperial collaborators
> to individuals of considerable importance to the writer's own day. For
> example, by seeking to identify Ezra's reforms with the contents of
> a completed Pentateuch, the author opened the way for Ezra to be
> enshrined in later tradition as the paradigm of the teacher of Torah to the
> community.[195]

Garbini has put forth an alternative proposal regarding Ezra. He concludes that the book of Ezra—which he argues took its material from
1 Esdras and can therefore only be dated afterwards (cf. 159 B.C.E.)[196]—
describes Ezra as a friend of Artaxerxes I given full administrative,
political, and religious powers—which he used to give "the community
of those who had returned from Babylonian exile" a new face.[197] As
Garbini notes, a figure of such stature would most likely have left traces
in biblical books after the fifth century B.C.E.[198] These traces, however,
are absent from all Jewish sources, such as Ben Sira, before the work of
Josephus (*Ant.* 11.5.1–5).[199] This leads him to conclude that Ezra was a

---

the result of a motivating ideology or agenda. E. Ochs and L. Capps ("Narrating the
Self," *Annual Reviews in Anthropology* 25 [1996]: 22) write, "Each telling of a narrative situated in time and space engages only facets of a narrator's or listener/reader's
selfhood in that it evokes only certain memories, concerns, and expectations."

195.   Hoglund, *Achaemenid Imperial Administration*, 246.

196.   G. Garbini, *Myth and History in the Bible* (trans. Chiara Peri; JSOTSup
362; Sheffield: Sheffield Academic Press, 2003), 102.

197.   Garbini, *History and Ideology*, 151–52.

198.   Therefore, Garbini (ibid., 166) does not accept that the tradition was linked
to a person; instead, he argues that Ezra is a hypocoristicon meaning, "He (i.e. God)
is help." עזרא, he asserts, means "inner court of the temple" in Ezek 40–48, Chronicles, Ben Sira, and in rabbinic Judaism. In doing so, however, he is perhaps unfairly
reading a later concept back into Ezra–Nehemiah.

199.   Ibid., 152–53. Garbini (*Myth and History*, 103) also points out that Ezra,
who was supposed to be a central figure in "post-exilic" Judaism, was not cited by
Ben Sira, who wrote a series of portraits on the most important figures from Jewish
history (chs. 44–50). To be clear, however, many (historical) individuals are not
mentioned in Ben Sira's account.

literary creation and not a historical figure.[200] An "objective evaluation" of the evidence, he claims, leads to no other conclusion but that the person of Ezra in the fifth century B.C.E., as well the social and religious reforms attributed to him, did not exist historically.[201] He states, instead, that the book was written to justify the Jerusalem temple over the temple at Gerizim—which was constructed by Alexander the Great near the end of the fourth century B.C.E.[202] He suggests that the text of Ezra appears to be a collection of letters from Persian kings intended to give the writing a historiographic appearance. "In fact the narrative is a political pamphlet, built on invented letters, where a completely incredible reconstruction of the events of the first postexilic years is depicted."[203] Garbini's rather extreme thesis has failed to gather much support. It is not clear how his dating of the text effectively supports the social-historical context to which he appropriates it. Moreover, one need not dismiss the person of Ezra entirely to explain the apparent agenda of the text. That being said, however, his argument importantly highlights the presence of a dominating concern for the Jerusalem temple in Ezra.

Of the three generally proposed dates for Ezra—before Nehemiah, in the interval between Nehemiah's activities, and after Nehemiah—Smith says that one can eliminate Ezra's activity during the interval between Nehemiah's activities.[204] While, as noted above, some propose Ezra's activities in Yehud took place after Nehemiah's, ca. 398 B.C.E., the date is inconclusive.[205] This proposal—namely, the interval between Ezra's activities—contradicts the dates in the text. If, for example, the length of

200. He follows the works of G. Hölscher, *Geschichte der Israelitischen und Jüdischen Religion* (Giessen: J. Ricker, 1903); Ernst Renan, *Histoire du peuple d'Israël*, vol. 4 (Paris, 1893); C. Torrey, *The Composition and Historical Value of Ezra–Nehemiah* (BZAW 2; Giessen: J. Ricker, 1896); Maurice Vernes, *Précis d'histoire Juive depuis les origines jusqu'à l'époque Persane* (Paris: Hachette, 1889).

201. Garbini, *History and Ideology*, 155. He was not the first to come to this conclusion; see also C. Torrey, "The Chronicler as Editor and as Independent Narrator," in *Ezra Studies* (New York: Ktav, 1970), 208–51; idem, "The Exile and Restoration," 285–335.

202. Garbini, *Myth and History*, 101.

203. Ibid.

204. Smith, *Palestinian Parties*, 91. According to Carter (*Emergence of Yehud*, 52), Nehemiah's presence in Yehud extended from 445–433 B.C.E. Cook (*Persian Empire*, 32–33) places the mission of Ezra in 538 B.C.E. as preparation for Cyrus's attack upon Egypt, which Cambyses carried out. Both Ezra and 1 Esdras, however, date Ezra's activities to the reign of Artaxerxes I (cf. Ezra 7:1–6; 1 Esd 8:1–4). All of this, however, continues to be debated.

205. For an informed discussion of the dating of Ezra, see Clines, *Ezra, Nehemiah and Esther*, 16–24.

Nehemiah's interval period was only about two to three years (cf. Neh 1:1; 2:1; 5:14; 13:6), then explaining the number of foreign marriages he finds upon his return is difficult if Ezra, who was also concerned with intermarriage (cf. Ezra 10:2–44), was in Yehud during Nehemiah's absence.[206] While one might claim that the Persian government recalled Ezra because of the trouble he instigated—a possibility that is purely speculative—Nehemiah's actions toward mixed marriages pose a problem. Why would the Persian government send someone who was likely to instigate the same troubles that led to Ezra's recall? Therefore, one cannot date Ezra's activities to the time of Nehemiah's temporary absence.[207]

Alternatively, one might date Ezra's activities in Yehud to sometime around 460 B.C.E., as part of an imperial response to a Greek intrusion into the Egyptian revolt.[208] This proposal makes sense as part of an imperial concern to enhance the imperial governments control over the administrative systems of local territories. By codifying laws at this time, the administrative and judicial systems were placed under a firmer control, as local laws were organized so that they would support and not contradict the king's law.[209]

If Ezra's role parallels Udjahorresnet's,[210] his role was as an imperial functionary to a province, not to a single group. The lack of other substantiating evidence, however, creates problems for drawing any conclusions on who Ezra was and what he did. Nevertheless, drawing a parallel between Ezra's role and the role of Udjahorresnet better explains Ezra's function than any explanation proposing that Ezra's was a unique and unprecedented role created by the imperial government for the small province of Yehud. If this Ezra codified the laws of the province (Ezra 7:6–10; Neh 8:1–18), he presumably codified them within the general imperial framework dictated by the "law of the king" (cf. Ezra 7:26).[211] This latter phrase, as Fried observes, refers not only the edicts of the imperial king but to the imperially delegated judicial system.[212] Finally, she notes further:

---

206.   Smith, *Palestinian Parties*, 91. See also, Otto Eissfeldt, *The Old Testament: An Introduction* (Oxford: Oxford University Press, 1965), 553; Ulrich Kellermann, "Erwägungen zum Problem der Esradatierung," *ZAW* 80 (1968): 75–87.

207.   Smith, *Palestinian Parties*, 91.

208.   Hoglund, *Achaemenid Imperial Administration*, 226.

209.   See also Berquist, *Judaism in Persia's Shadow*, 53–55.

210.   See the section on "Udjahorresnet's Role in Lower Egypt" in Chapter 2 (p. 63).

211.   So also Fried, *Priest and the Great King*, 212–27.

212.   Ibid., 217.

Artaxerxes' Letter puts the behavior of the local leadership (ראשי
האבות זקנים) and the local assembly (קהל) in perspective. The sanctions
listed in the edict (i.e., the ability to confiscate land and property, to
threaten with death, flogging, and imprisonment) were not given to a קהל
or to the local leadership. Artaxerxes assigned these powers to Persian
officials—to the royal judges and magistrates that Ezra appointed. He
did not authorize local leaders or local assemblies to formulate law or to
enforce it. As was true throughout the Persian Empire, local leaders and
assemblies met only to hear the law imposed upon them by satrap or
governor. Persian judges and officials executed that law. There was no
self-rule in Judah, as there was none in any province in the empire.[213]

Proposed Governing Structure(s) after Nehemiah. To facilitate the discussion in this section, I use two theories as foils for this analysis: Weinberg's *Bürger-Tempel-Gemeinde*, and Smith's theory, which I call the
(Religious) Group Struggle. Both ultimately place the cult in power after
Nehemiah, though they arrive at this conclusion from two different
perspectives. Both seem to ignore the importance of the extra-biblical
evidence for imperial governors, such as Bagohi, and focus instead on
the presumed religious power and parties in Yehud.

J. Weinberg's Bürger-Tempel-Gemeinde. According to Weinberg, the
economies of the communal-private and state sectors in Yehud merged
and the leaders of the Jerusalem cult gained control over the hybrid
economy.[214] This structure, he proposes, was not unique to Yehud; he
draws from the well-known historian, I. Diakanoff, to suggest that one
can trace a similar development of both sectors at various locations in the
ancient Near East.[215] The economy, according to Weinberg, was primarily a commodity-based market economy, containing both an intensification of trade and an active urbanization process that marked its social
development.[216]

Because the economies of both sectors, communal-private and state,
were similar, their respective representatives "converged," resulting in
even fewer social differences between them. When the temple merged

213.   Ibid., 220.
214.   Weinberg, *Citizen-Temple Community*, 92–93.
215.   Ibid., 92. He cites Igor M. Diakonoff, *The Main Features of Ancient
Society [Russian]: 'The Problems of Pre-Capitalist Societies in Eastern Countries*
(Moscow, n.p., 1971), 132–33.
216.   Weinberg, *Citizen-Temple Community*, 92. However, see also Carter
(*Emergence of Yehud*, 294–96) for a critique of Weinberg's use and understanding
of urbanization.

with the community, a new structure was formed, the *Bürger-Tempel-Gemeinde*.²¹⁷ "This citizen-temple community," Weinberg writes, "gave to its members an organizational unity and a collective self-administration, and took care of political and economic mutual aid."²¹⁸ Weinberg posits the "post-exilic community of Palestine" to be the "best documented example" of a citizen-temple community during the Persian period. This community, therefore, became his model by which he reconstructed the "agricultural relations" and the relationship between central and local administrations.²¹⁹ It is an accessible social model, Weinberg maintains, for economic development throughout the ancient Near East.

Several problems exist. Weinberg sees only one community existing in Yehud,²²⁰ or in the very least, he sees the economic, political, and social contexts of Yehud defined by one community. While social-group ideology can influence an economy, economies themselves do not merely operate within a communal structure; they dominate and define the structure.²²¹ It is difficult to see, based on the biblical texts, how effective a single community could be on the economic system of the province of Yehud. It is extremely difficult to substantiate a social model based on the limited perception of the biblical texts—texts that cannot substantiate any presentation of their portrayal of reality as objective social reality.²²²

In addition, how similar in social-economic development were societies elsewhere in this period—those of, to name a few, Armenia, Babylonia, Bactria, Maka, Parthia, Sardis, Scythia and Sogdiana? Weinberg argues that the similarities manifest themselves in urbanization,²²³ a process he believes to be common throughout the ancient Near East:

---

217.   Weinberg, *Citizen-Temple Community*, 92.

218.   Ibid., 92–93.

219.   Ibid., 93, 106.

220.   Even Weinberg (ibid., 100–103) notes that the community to which he refers makes up only part of Achaemenid Judah, yet he continues to speak of it as a whole society.

221.   Weber, *Protestant Ethic*, 54–55.

222.   Carter (*Emergence of Yehud*, 297) makes a similar observation.

223.   Lester L. Grabbe notes that biblical scholars are often remiss in their overestimation of the extent of urbanization and their misconstruction of the consequences of urbanization in Israel and Judah ("Sup-Urbs or Only Hyp-Urbs? Prophets and Populations in Ancient Israel and Socio-Historical Method," in *'Every City Shall Be Forsaken': Urbanism and Prophecy in Ancient Israel and the Near East* [ed. Lester L. Grabbe and Robert D. Haak; JSOTSup 330; Sheffield: Sheffield Academic Press, 2001], 96). Carter states that the term urbanization is anachronistic and more appropriately describes developments in pre-Industrial Age Western culture.

The important features of this time are noticeable intensification and diversification; individualization and democratization of economic activity; an intensive process of urbanization together with the formation of a specific urban psychology, characterized by a physical and psychic mobility; a sceptical attitude toward tradition and predisposition to innovations; an overcoming of particularistic closedness and a strengthening of universalistic openness; an active and wide-ranging migration, in the main voluntary, which embraced larger masses of people and wide territories and stimulated the rapprochement and interaction of different cultures; a noticeable complication of the social structure in connection with an appearance of many marginal social groups; an intensive process of individualization and autonomization of humanity together with a dissemination, even revival, of large agnatic and/or territorial units; a formation of vast empires accompanied by the inevitable emergence and dissemination of autonomous, self-governing cities, whose one form was the citizen-temple community in places such as Mesopotamia, Syria, Asia Minor, Armenia; and finally there was the formation of an autonomous intelligentsia, to some degree independent from temple and state, which was the main agent of the gradual transition from the mythological king of thinking to the scientific-rational one.[224]

Weinberg's conclusions for the social setting in Yehud seem based on a fundamental belief that the social institutions, structures, systems, and so on, were designated by the *Bürger-Tempel-Gemeinde*. He maintains that the *bet abot* structure was a vehicle preserving Judean identity,[225] a particular idea that is generally accepted, and that its unity strengthened the *Bürger-Tempel-Gemeinde*.[226] The *golah* community inhabited the city of Jerusalem, he claims, and became an imperially recognized citizen-temple community. He conjectures that Nehemiah, therefore, was not the פחה of Yehud but of Jerusalem,[227] and that the "edicts" of Cyrus,

Moreover, while urban centers existed in horticultural and agrarian cultures as early as the Bronze Age, this was different from "urbanization" (*Emergence of Yehud*, 295 n. 101).

224.   Weinberg, *Citizen-Temple Community*, 128–29.

225.   Weinberg, "Das Bēit ʾAḇōt."

226.   Ibid., 400–401. For an additional discussion on Weinberg's use of *bet abot*, see Cataldo, "Persian Policy," 247–48.

227.   Weinberg, *Citizen-Temple Community*, 118–19. If Nehemiah was governor over the city of Jerusalem alone, why do the writers not use a term more akin to *ḥazannu* (Assyrian, "city governor" [cf. ABL 91:12; ADD 160:8; 166:2; 169:2; HSS 5 67:57]) or פרתרכא (Aramaic, "civil-military leader" [cf. AP 30:5; *TAD* B.2.9]) rather than *piḥatu*? For a discussion of the terms, see R. A. Henshaw, "The Office of Šaknu in Neo-Assyrian Times I," *JAOS* 87 (1967): 517–25; idem, "The Office of Šaknu in Neo-Assyrian Times II," *JAOS* 88 (1968): 461–83; Zertal, "Province of

Darius I and of Artaxerxes I in Ezra–Nehemiah recognized Jerusalem as an autonomous citizen-temple community. Yet certainly such a civil-military position (cf. Neh 2:7–9), if Nehemiah was the authority of Jerusalem only, was more likely to have been known as something closer to a parallel with Vidranga, who was identified as פרתרכא (cf. AP 30/31), civil-military leader, than to פחה. That פחה refers to a provincial governor is demonstrated in bullae and seals, coins, and papyri (see also Table 2, p. 90). In addition, the authenticity these "edicts" contained or alluded to in the biblical traditions is questionable, and the evidence supporting the imperial recognition of an autonomous community is lacking. Weinberg tries to argue that the city's autonomy was not a problem for the empire, and that the empire saw in the city's or community's autonomous existence a means of maintaining social order in the area of Yehud.[228] Yet this too is dubious and lacks any supporting evidence.

According to Weinberg, the relationship between the central imperial-bureaucratic organization and its local organs and administrations was "particularly complicated and multifaceted."[229] This proposed complicated and multifaceted nature of this relationship is his means of arguing that a diversity of autonomous governing structures coexisted with the Persian imperial presence.[230] However, his consideration of this system remains problematic and at points insufficient;[231] Weinberg argues that one must consider the entire system of this relationship when discussing

Samaria," 381–84. In addition, Weinberg's proposal requires that the Persian government allowed and even established such narrowly defined city-states.

228.   For Weinberg's discussion of the edicts, see *Citizen-Temple Community*, 110–20. Regarding his belief in the benefit of the community to the empire, see ibid., 131–32.

229.   Ibid., 105–6.

230.   Ibid., 106.

231.   Fried (*Priest and the Great King*, 184 n. 180, 187–88) points out that Weinberg's argument is based in part on his dismissal of Sheshbazzar and Zerubbabel as governors, and that Yehud was part of Samerina until Nehemiah established it as a separate province. As Fried shows, however, there is evidence that shows Sheshbazzar and Zerubbabel were governors. Moreover, Alt's theory that Yehud was initially part of Samerina—from which Weinberg borrows—is now generally considered to be wrong (cf. P. Bedford, "On Models and Texts: A Response to Blenkinsopp and Peterson," in Davies, ed., *Second Temple Studies*, 1:154–62; Hoglund, *Achaemenid Imperial Administration*, 69–71; H. G. M. Williamson, "Judah and the Jews," in *Studies in Persian History: Essays in Memory of David M. Lewis* [ed. Maria Brosius and Amélie Kuhrt; Leiden: Nederlands Instituut von Het Nabije Oosten, 1998], 156–58), though the theory still retains some supporters, including S. McEvenue ("The Political Structure in Judah from Cyrus to Nehemiah," *CBQ* 43 [1981]: 353–64).

the genesis of the citizen-temple community. This genesis included the central and local administrative interactions, chronological and geographically variable attitudes of the empire to different citizen-temple communities (of which Jerusalem was the best example), and the subjective aspirations of the communities themselves.[232] This last complex element is the manner through which Weinberg explains a community whose ultimate loyalty is not to the Persian empire but to its own religious ideologies. In other words, according to Weinberg, the *golah* community defined its own bureaucracy according to its own desires—desires that the group's religious-political aspirations fueled.

Yet even in its autonomy, the citizen-temple community in Jerusalem, Weinberg argues, required support from the central administration because it could not stand up against the Samarians and Ammonites.[233] The Persian government approved the reconstruction of the Jerusalem temple to show its support.[234] He writes, "The building of the temple was initiated by the central administration and served as a gathering point as well as a point of solidarity for the *bēt ʾābôt*. The temple was a symbol which revealed the favour of Yahweh and the good-wishes of Cyrus."[235] While the citizen-temple organism was developing, the Persian government avoided administrative changes promoting the development of any individual power. It was not, according to Weinberg, until the edict of Artaxerxes I that the empire officially granted autonomy and separated the citizen-temple community from the surrounding social-political structure(s).

With the relationship between the Persian empire and the citizen-temple community firmly established, Weinberg concludes that political authority was transferred to the high priest in the fourth century B.C.E. This process not only shifted the power structure but also was part of a larger restructuring that helped create the province of Yehud.[236]

232. Weinberg, *Citizen-Temple Community*, 106–7.
233. Ibid., 111.
234. Ibid., 117, says that Ezra 9:9 shows imperial support was indisputable.
235. Ibid., 111–12.
236. Ibid., 125. He argues that the postexilic community was not a defined citizen-temple community until 458/457 B.C.E. and that until this time, Yehud was annexed to Samerina. Nehemiah was the first administrative leader over the defined community, while Sheshbazzar and Zerubbabel were not governors in the official sense, but leaders of the group/community and temple construction (only Zerubbabel on this last; see ibid., 114–15). It was only after the contributions of Nehemiah that the community was able to become a fully defined citizen-temple community capable of governing all of Yehud. See also Bedford ("Models and Texts," 154–62) and Williamson (Judah and the Jews," 156–58) who raise a substantial critique on

In their individual studies of settlement patterns in Syria-Palestine (covering the Neo-Babylonian period to the Persian period), Hoglund, Carter, Lipschits, and Edelman each have countered claims of urbanization in Persian-period Yehud. They argue that there was, instead, a trend toward ruralization in small farmsteads.[237] Weinberg's conclusions are based in part on the occurrence of urbanization; they require an urbanization process to centralize power in the city and ultimately the temple.[238] This process, he argues, was also necessary to centralize private property in the hands of the high priests of Jerusalem. Yet, from the cited studies, it would seem that agricultural production[239] drove the economy, not trade and the buying and selling of private property, as Weinberg argues. While evidence of trade exists, it appears during this time to have been only a minor part of an increasing commercialism within a society rooted in agrarianism.[240] It was not a primary economic factor defining the society.[241]

Weinberg's theory does not withstand the criticisms discussed in this section. If Yehud is his best example of a citizen-temple community in the Persian realm, it is possible that no citizen-temple communities existed under Persian rule.[242] Sufficient evidence to prove that the

Weinberg's proposal of what essentially amounts to two governors, a political governor and a religious governor. See also Carter, *Emergence of Yehud*, 302–4.

237.   Carter, *Emergence of Yehud*, 172–248; Edelman, *The Origins of the 'Second' Temple*, 292–310, 332–51; Hoglund, "The Achaemenid Context," 54–72; O. Lipschits, "Demographic Changes in Judah between the Seventh and the Fifth Centuries B.C.E," in Lipschits and Blenkinsopp, eds., *Judah and the Judeans in the Neo-Babylonian Period*, 323–76; idem, "Achaemenid Imperial Policy," 24.

238.   Weinberg's understanding of the impact of the *golah* community is obviously influenced by his large numbers of persons exiled and the total number of persons in the land after the return of the exiles. Carter (*Emergence of Yehud*, 297–99) offers a substantial critique of Weinberg's numbers and of Weinberg's reliance upon the accuracy of the Golah Lists.

239.   Grain seems to have been a significant agricultural contribution (cf. Neh 13:5, 10, 12, 15). See also Carter (ibid., 103–4, 121–22, 250) for a discussion of grain silos in Yehud.

240.   See also Hoglund, "The Achaemenid Context," 60–62.

241.   See also Carter, *Emergence of Yehud*, 249–59.

242.   Dandamaev and Lukonin assert that semi-autonomous temples communities also existed in Asia Minor (*Culture and Social Institutions*, 106). They provide as an example the Mylasan community from the fifth century B.C.E. on, headed by priests who were the rulers of the Hekatominids' clan. To this point, I have found no corroborating evidence. According to Hornblower (*Mausolus*, 34–51), the Hekatomnids were a ruling dynasty, not a priesthood. He notes further (52–53) that Mausolus's policy toward the coastal cities in Asia Minor was to promote an oligarchy,

temple-cult of Jerusalem governed the imperial province of Yehud does not exist.

M. Smith's (Religious) Group Struggle for Power. It was, according to Smith, a struggle for power among religious groups that characterized the nature of the government within Yehud after Nehemiah's departure.[243] Religious parties—the composition of which Smith gathers from Nehemiah's "memoirs"—pitted themselves against each other as they vied for power. The Separatists, to whom Smith asserted Nehemiah belonged, paired off against the Assimilationists.[244] The first group consisted of a few priests, most of the Levites,[245] most of the Jerusalem plebs, and allied itself with the Yahweh-alone party. The latter group was composed of most of the priests, most of the gentry of Jerusalem and Judea, and allied itself with the Yahwistic gentry of the territories surrounding Judea.[246]

If Smith's suggestion that one of these parties controlled the sociopolitical environment of Yehud is correct, then what divided and defined Yehud was not economy, social class, or even political loyalties.[247] What

---

while the inland Karian cities began a process of coexisting κοινα, with πόλεις. The Hekatomnids, he suggests, were probably considered tyrants in Karia (71).

243.   Smith (*Palestinian Parties*, 108–9) concludes that Nehemiah is best described as a tyrant in the Persian empire. Hoglund (*Achaemenid Imperial Administration*, 216–23) substantially criticizes the view of Nehemiah as a tyrant because it provides Nehemiah with a great deal of political independence from the Persian government. In addition, I would point out that examples of tyrants within the Persian empire are usually only from Greek localities. For tyrants in the Persian empire, see Austin, "Greek Tyrants," 289–306; Briant, *Histoire de l'Empire perse*, 62–63, 76, 94–95, 150–51, 154, 156–68, 359–62, 510–13, 706–8, 837, 852, 875, 877; Young, "Consolidation," 53–112. M. Douglas ("Responding to Ezra: The Priests and the Foreign Wives," *BibInt* 10 [2002]: 1–23), on the other hand, argues that the best way to understand the priestly editor of Ezra is to understand that the editor was responding to political tyrants. However, as noted, there is not evidence that the priests governed Yehud or that the system of governance was that of a tyranny.

244.   Though he does not quote Morgenstern often, Smith's divisions appear quite similar to Morgenstern's "nationalist" and "Universalist." See J. Morgenstern, "Jerusalem—485 BC," *HUCA* 27 (1956): 101–79; "Jerusalem—485 BC (Continued)," *HUCA* 28 (1957): 15–47; "Jerusalem—485 BC (Concluded)," 1–29.

245.   The Levites sided initially with the priests, or Assimilationist party, according to Smith, while Nehemiah won over the Jerusalem bourgeoisie, or Separatists (*Palestinian Parties*, 118–19).

246.   Ibid., 117–18.

247.   For instance, "Nehemiah's break with the high priest Eliashib had ended the priesthood's mediations between the Yahweh-alone group and the old Judaean

divided and defined Yehud was whether or not the individual believed worshiping Yahweh alone was pure worship. The defining value and fundamental structure of the society, Smith seems to be suggesting, was the religious institution.

According to Smith, the Persian-period biblical texts detail not only a continuing struggle between the main social-religious divisions, but simultaneously a process of Judaizing that brought the groups closer.[248] He quickly points out, however, that though the groups may have developed closer theologies, the two primary divisions (Separatist and Assimilationist) remained distinct and antagonistic even into the time of Antiochus Epiphanes. Both groups struggled against the other for power, and both saw control of the Jerusalem temple as essential for the attainment of political power.[249]

Smith argues that either the Separatist or the Assimilationist divisions governed post-Nehemiah Yehud, and society functioned as a religiously defined context. Yet his proposal can only be correct if every group in Yehud depended upon Jerusalem for identity and definition, thus depending on it also for structure, value, and meaning.[250] Furthermore, he has not fully substantiated his reliance upon certain biblical texts as accurate portrayals of party or division ideology, and his belief that the texts accurately reflect the culture of *the* society in Yehud is problematic. No substantial evidence exists to support his suggestion that the position

---

families. Now the bulk of the priesthood and the gentry were united by opposition to the separatists" (ibid., 118). VanderKam (*From Joshua to Caiaphas*, 51–52), however, notes that Eliashib may not have been high priest: "Is this Eliashib the high priest? He may seem to be the same man because he is an important figure in the temple—so important he could displace fundamental elements of the sacrificial cult for the convenience of Tobiah the Ammonite (see Neh 2:10 where Tobiah is pictured as on opponent of Nehemiah). It is a fact, nevertheless, that this Eliashib is styled only 'the priest,' not 'the high priest.' It is also possible that by this time Eliashib's son Joiada had become the pontiff (if Neh 13:28 is to be read in that way)… It would not be surprising if the Eliashib of Neh 13:4, 7 and the one of Ezra 10:6 proved to be the same man (a temple chamber is under consideration in both places), but he was not the high priest."

248.   Cf. Smith, *Palestinian Parties*, 123–24.

249.   Ibid., 130–46.

250.   In addition, his proposal reduces social identity to religious identity or membership. One might also note here Berquist's concern ("Constructions of Identity," 58) that theories of identity practiced by scholars have tended to be top-down and emphasize objective group membership. Top-down theories fail to account for those forces of identity that operate externally—as external, observable reality—to the group or individual as well as those forces that operate internally—as personal reality.

and function of governor ceased to exist after Nehemiah. Actually, the Elephantine papyri (407 B.C.E.) show that the role of governor continued. They name Bagohi as a governor (AP 30–32) who was in by 410 B.C.E. And other governors are known from the seals, bullae, and coins.[251] Smith is not unaware of the Elephantine papyri, yet he views the papyri suspiciously and uses them very sparingly.[252] Extra-biblical evidence, however, should not be considered only secondarily important. Instead, this evidence offers a perspective on the ancient context that is not necessarily caught up in the inner-group quibblings of the biblical texts.

Summary and Conclusions. The papyri discovered at Elephantine, known for over a century, demonstrate that the position of governor continued after Nehemiah to at least 407 B.C.E. The biblical texts themselves, however, are silent about the continued roles of governors. They offer no clear evidence of a progression from governor to priest and any attempt to confirm priestly power based on the biblical texts alone is not without significant problem. Furthermore, the coins that contain possible priestly names do not, as previously discussed, clearly indicate that priests took over the function of political control. From extra-biblical evidence, it is clear that governors existed in Yehud throughout almost the entire Persian period. There is no evidence proving that the cult governed the province or even that the empire granted the city of Jerusalem autonomy.

Because of the Persian empire's tense relationships with Babylonia and Egypt, the Persian government sought to maintain control over its provinces. This does not mean that one is required to assume that the stability of the Persian empire was contingent upon Yehud as its linchpin of border control.[253] Yet one should also not reject the role of Yehud's part in the empire's broader concern for defense, stability, and control.[254] By controlling its provinces, the empire controlled the possibility of additional rebellions.

251. As discussed in "Other Extra-Biblical Archaeological and Textual Information" in Chapter 3 (p. 83).
252. He is extremely doubtful of the conclusions given by A. Cowley (*Aramaic Papyri of the Fifth Century B.C.* [Oxford: Oxford University Press, 1923], 21, 38) and Porten (*Archives from Elephantine*, 130, 149, 280).
253. See also Briant, *From Cyrus to Alexander*, 91.
254. As noted by Lisbeth S. Fried, "The Political Struggle of the Fifth-Century Judah," *Transeu* 24 (2002): 61–73; Hoglund, *Achaemenid Imperial Administration*, 210; Meyers, "The Persian Period," 516.

Chapter 4

CONCEPTS OF THEOCRACY

Introduction

Because very few scholars have offered a careful definition of theocracy, usage of the term is imprecise.[1] Yet, as C. Geertz explains, "[Definitions] do, if they are carefully constructed, provide a useful orientation, or reorientation, of thought, such that an extended unpacking of them can be an effective way of developing and controlling a novel line of inquiry."[2] This chapter therefore focuses on some of the various uses of the term "theocracy," looking for commonalities that will aid in the development of a more clearly articulated definition.

In his article evaluating the use of the term "theocracy" by anthropologists and archaeologists to describe the social-political context of ancient Maya, D. Webster notes: "A difficulty with the concept 'theocratic' social organization is that this ill-defined term has always carried a freight of variable, implied, or expressed connotations in addition to that of priestly leadership."[3] These "connotations" are often not expressed or articulated by those who employ the concept of theocracy, and many have given little systematic thought to the definition of a theocracy or what its implications are for a society.[4] Webster notes further:

> [The term theocracy] has been applied to various stages of virtually all pristine states. It has been used to designate a *type* of sociopolitical organization found among complex societies. It has denoted a *stage* of sociopolitical evolution preceding 'secular' states. It has been applied to societies on various evolutionary levels, including chiefdoms, states, and intermediate

---

1. Wellhausen (*Prolegomena*, 411) noted this tendency in the works of others from his own time.

2. Clifford Geertz, *The Interpretation of Cultures* (New York: Basic, 1973), 90.

3. Webster, "On Theocracies," 814. He notes further (813) that even the definitions from dictionaries are usually not very helpful. Definitions there are often "minimal and ambiguous."

4. Cf. ibid., 812.

transformational forms. It has carried a wide range of connotations concerning the hierarchical structures of complex societies, and their relationship to other cultural processes or institutions.[5]

It seems often to be the case that the ceremonial facades of a society (temple architecture, rich tombs, and symbolism and iconography) found in various archaeological investigations, rather than the basic institutions underlying those remains, are used by investigators to justify a context as being theocratic.[6] Investigators typically contrast such remains with what is known about later "secular" states, which has led to unwarranted conclusions producing many misconceptions of overemphasis.[7] For Yehud specifically, the religious texts of the *golah* community are so used.

Texts and carvings that represent concerns for death and worship cannot alone qualify a context as theocratic. As Webster argues, "[T]he impressive ceremonial façade of sociopolitical organization in theocracies should not draw us into the conclusion that ceremonialism exists only to serve itself, or that other social conditions and institutions characteristic of known processes of state formation are absent."[8] If we take into consideration the processes and end-results of state formation and we initially follow Webster's leanings, then we may hypothesize that in a theocracy, the (legitimated) authority of a society's dominant religion controls a society's politics and economy.[9] In addition, there may be no clear distinction between a "religious" and a political or civic law. In the process of state formation, this might occur as the dominant religious institution contains or absorbs the political order[10] and enforces religious ideologies (even agendas) through what one might term "jurisprudence."[11] When a society legitimates[12] a theocracy, the religious

5. Ibid.

6. As noted by Webster (ibid., 815) of archaeologists and anthropologists generally.

7. Ibid.

8. Ibid., 816.

9. I am referring now to a control that has been collectively legitimated by the governed society. I am not making the argument that a theocratic government is totalitarian, a connection that T. Todorov (*The Morals of History* [trans. Alyson Waters; Minneapolis: University of Minnesota Press, 1995], 193) observes is sometimes made by critics of theocracies.

10. It also controls the social and economic infrastructures of a society, as will be discussed below. The focus here is upon law within the political sphere.

11. For reference, note Ibn Khaldun's definition of jurisprudence (*The Muqaddimah: An Introduction to History* [trans. Franz Rosenthal; 3 vols.; New York: Pantheon, 1958], 3:3).

12. Cf. Bourdieu's observation of legitimation (*In Other Words: Essays toward a Reflexive Sociology* [trans. Matthew Adamson; Stanford: Stanford University Press,

institution (or an administrative body over which it exercises authority), following Webster's proposal, becomes the centralized decision-making social-political institution:

> In all successful complex societies policies of centralized decision-making must be effectively translated into social action, and there is no question that this aim is facilitated if those in positions of power and authority can claim a moral or supernatural justification for their actions. Unfortunately many writers go no further than this, and leave one with the impression that ceremonialism is the *source* of political and economic leadership and differentials of early states. I maintain, rather, that it is a way of validating and consolidating leadership positions based, ultimately, on other sorts of *pre-existing* differentials (e.g., monopolization of basic capital resources), thus buttressing them or augmenting them, and on adaptive stresses most easily met by increasing centralized and specialized decision making.[13]

Discussions of "Theocracies" in Ancient Near Eastern Contexts

I have chosen the scholars whose views are included in this section as a representative sampling of scholarly discussions of various contexts in the ancient Near East that have been identified as theocracies. These represent the variety in the use of the term "theocracy." Where their inclusion proved fruitful is in the differences contained in their uses and expressed understandings of the term.

The first part of this chapter is dedicated to historical discussion; not only will this section analyze the definitions of theocracy used by the included scholars, but it will also discuss the historical contexts to which the definitions were applied. The later section includes case studies that will focus on a comparative sociological analysis whose purpose is to reveal the "family resemblances" of theocracies in various societies, or why societies once described as theocracies were incorrectly labeled as such. The latter portion of this chapter looks for common elements, or "family resemblances,"[14] that might help configure a structural model for

---

1990], 135). Legitimation, he posits, results when agents apply to the objective structures of the social world structures of perception and appreciation that have emerged from and because of the objective structures and the conscious and unconscious interactions that agents have with them.
    13. Webster, "On Theocracies," 815 (emphasis in original).
    14. On "family resemblances," see Cook, *Prophecy and Apocalypticism*, 21–22. Cook borrows the initial concept from Ludwig Wittgenstein, *Philosophical Investigations* (trans. G. Anscombe; New York: Macmillan, 1968), 32.

the working definition. These elements must have social-scientific value and be capable of being applied cross-culturally as part of a social model. Negative results and positive results are equally beneficial here. These parts together comprise a brief macrosociological analysis. In practice, macrosociology analyzes large-scale and long-term social processes.[15] It provides an interpretative framework that allows one to abstract social patterns and behaviors and to identity common and distinctive elements in various societies.[16] In the following chapter, I will apply the working definition of theocracy developed from this analysis to Yehud.

Josephus's "Theocracy"
Josephus, as far as can be determined, was the first to use in writing the term "theocracy." He writes,

> Now there are innumerable differences in the particular customs and laws that are among all mankind, which a man may briefly reduce under the following heads: Some legislators have permitted their governments to be under monarchies, others put them under oligarchies, and others under a republican form; but our legislator had no regard to any of these forms, but he ordained our government to be what, by *a strained expression*, may be termed a Theocracy, by ascribing the authority and the power to God, and by persuading all the people to have a regard to him, as the author of all the good things that were enjoyed either in common by all mankind, or by each one in particular, and of all that they themselves obtained by praying to him in their greatest difficulties. (*C. Ap.* 2.164–66; emphasis mine)[17]

This passage marks the documented-historical origin of the term "theocracy."[18] It is also important because Josephus used this term here to

15. Randall Collins, "On the Microfoundations of Macrosociology," *AJS* 86 (1981): 984; Gerhard Lenski and Jean Lenski, *Human Societies: An Introduction to Macrosociology* (New York: McGraw–Hill, 1987), 3–4.

16. As noted in C. Carter, "A Discipline in Transition," in *Community, Identity, and Ideology: Social Science Approaches to the Hebrew Bible* (ed. Charles E. Carter and Carol L. Meyers; Sources for Biblical and Theological Study 6; Winona Lake: Eisenbrauns, 1996), 8.

17. Note also the relevant Greek text: ὁ δ' ἡμέτερος νομοθέτης εἰς μὲν τουτων οὐδοτιουν ἀπειδεν, ὡς δ' ἄν τις εἴποι βιασάμενος τὸν λόγον θεοκρατίαν ἀπέδειξε τὸ πολίτευμα θεῷ τὴν ἀρχὴν καὶ τὸ κράτος ἀναθείς (*C. Ap.* 2.165–66).

18. According to the Liddell–Scott–Jones Greek–English Lexicon (hereafter LSJ), there is only one recorded use of θεοκρατια, which is by Josephus. A search through the Classical Greek texts on Perseus Digital Library (http://www.perseus. tufts.edu) confirms this. The closest term etymologically seems to be θεόκραντος, which contests no immediate derivation from θεοκρατία and is defined by LSJ as "something accomplished or wrought by the gods." An example can be found in Aeschylus, *Agamemnon* (*Ag.* 1481): τί γὰρ βροτοῖς ἄνευ Διὸς τελεῖται [:] τί τῶνδ'

describe not only the Jewish community in Roman Palestine, but also the entire biblical history of Israel since the time of Moses.[19] Theocracy, as he uses the term,[20] appears able to coexist with other forms of government (e.g. monarchy, aristocracy, etc.).[21]

Josephus considered Israel, and the later Jewish communities, to be theocracies because Moses first established the ancestral society by ascribing the authority and the power to God, and by persuading all the people to enter into a (covenantal) relationship with God (cf. *C. Ap.* 2.164–65). Since that time, the Jewish people, according to Josephus, continued to live under these laws. Yet his use of other terms to describe ancient Israel in its various stages leads to some confusion about how he may be defining a theocracy as a system of government.

Elsewhere, he describes Israel as a monarchy, an aristocracy, and an aristocracy oligarchy (cf. *Ant.* 11.109–13). As a result, Josephus's labeling of Israel from the time of Moses as a theocracy (*C. Ap.* 2.164–65) is puzzling. He defines "aristocracy" as a context wherein the (high) priests were at the head of affairs (*Ant.* 11.109–13; 14.89–91).[22] In *Ant.* 11.109–13, Josephus defines Persian-period Yehud as a combination of aristocracy and oligarchy. He states that not only did the high priests lead the people in the religious celebration of Passover,[23] after their release

ου θεόκραντόν έστιν; ("What has been fulfilled for man except for that by the will of Zeus? What of these has god not accomplished?").

19. I find Josephus's definition of theocracy problematic in that he tries to justify its coexistence within a dominant culture that does not validate a theocracy. So also Hubert Cancik, "Theokratie und Priesterherrschaft: Die mosaische Verfassung bei Flavius Josephus, c. Apionem 2, 157–198," in *Theokratie* (ed. Jacob Taubes; Munich: W. Fink/F. Schöningh, 1987), 72–73. Cancik goes so far as to say that Josephus's priestly utopia was never realized.

20. J. McLaren ("Theocracy, Temple and Tax: Ingredients for the Jewish-Roman War of 66–70 CE" [paper presented at the Society of Biblical Literature, National Meeting, Atlanta, Ga., November 21, 2004], 22) describes Josephus's use of theocracy in the following way: "According to Josephus a theocracy was the best form of government. God stood at the head, with the priesthood, under the direction of the high-priest, acting as instruments of divine control (*C. Ap.* 2.184–185). This form of administration parallels what Josephus identifies as an aristocratic one (*Ant.* 4.223, 11.111, 20.251), in which the Jews are under the leadership of the priests." However, it is not clear that Josephus fully admits that a theocracy was a system of government.

21. He highlights four primary types of government: monarchy, oligarchy, aristocracy, and republic (*C. Ap.* 2.164–65). While a theocracy may be considered a fifth type, Josephus often seems often to blend theocracy with aristocracy.

22. See also Cancik's discussion ("Theokratie und Priesterherrschaft," 72–76).

23. Ezra 6:17–22 states that only the "returned exiles" kept the Passover. To accept Josephus's claim of a priestly government in light of passages such as this,

from Babylonia, they also governed the affairs of the people until the Hasmoneans set up a "kingly government." Yet there is substantial evidence to show that Yehud was under the authority of imperial governors, not under the authority of the priests, which his aristocracy seems to require.[24]

In *Contra Apionem*, Josephus responded to Apion, who had claimed the Jews had no laws (cf. *C. Ap.* 2.125), by claiming that Jewish laws could be traced back to Moses, the great legislator. Note also,

> And where shall we find a better or more righteous constitution than ours, while this makes us esteem God to be the governor of the universe, and permits the priests in general to be the administrators of principle affairs, and withal intrusts the government over the other priests to the chief high priest himself. (*C. Ap.* 2.184–87)

For Josephus, the priestly leadership, under God, formed the governmental structure.

Yet Josephus also acknowledges that the Jewish communities were often under the political authority of foreign leaders.[25] And it seems at many points that his purpose in *Contra Apionem* was apologetic, defending the sanctity, nobility, and intellectual prowess of Judaism against the criticism of Apion.[26] He extolled the virtues of Judaism and its link to Moses when he argued that the laws by which the Jews lived were older even than the laws of the Greek and Roman empires.[27]

one must define Yehud as the *golah* community and accept that the leaders of this community came from the priestly members of the *golah*. Yet there is evidence enough—in the form of bullae, seals, and papyri—to show that the governing leaders of Yehud were not priests or necessarily members of the *golah* community.

24. For further reference, see Table 2 (p. 90).

25. V. Tcherikover (*Hellenistic Civilization and the Jews* [New York: Atheneum, 1970], 45) adds that Josephus's account of Alexander's visit with Jaddua in Jerusalem (*Ant.* 11.8.4–5), an event some interpret to imply the high priest held political authority, was historical myth intended for local consumption.

26. For example, see the role and message Josephus gives Agrippa II in *J. W.* 2.342–404. See also McLaren, "Theocracy." J. Barclay ("The Politics of Contempt: Judeans and Egyptians in Josephus's *Against Apion*," in *Negotiating Diaspora Jewish Strategies in the Roman Empire* [ed. John M. G. Barclay; Library of Second Temple Studies; London: T&T Clark International, 2004], 123), argues that Josephus was concerned with presenting Judean religion as consonant with the highest philosophy; it was upon that concern that he structure his apology. See also *C. Ap.* 1.175; 2.168, 239, 255–57, 281.

27. Josephus writes, "No I venture to say, that our legislator is the most ancient of all the legislators whom we have anywhere heard of…but for our legislator, who was of so much greater antiquity than the rest (as even those that speak against us

Josephus referred to Apion's negative description of the Jews when Josephus wrote, "That there is a plain mark among us, that we neither have just laws, nor worship God as we ought to do, because we are not governors, *but are rather in subjection to the Gentiles*, sometimes to one nation, and sometimes to another…" (*C. Ap.* 2.121–24, emphasis mine), thereby also admitting that the Jews were subject to foreign political authority. As I understand, Apion criticized the Jewish community as 'insignificance' and 'ignorance,' claiming it had no valid laws or religion, lacked political autonomy and was therefore subject to Gentile authorities.[28] He clearly believed the Jews were an insignificant and disloyal lot (cf. *C. Ap.* 2.50), incapable of an intellectually based religion and lifestyle.[29] (He likens them to the Egyptians, whose religion he perceived to be banal and inferior to Greek religion.[30]) On a fundamental level, then, Josephus seems to have argued that the Jewish community was a "theocracy" in part because that classification defended the integrity and sanctity of the people and their religion.

He admits to the dependence of the Jews on laws foreign to Yahwistic religion: "But, as for the [distinct] political laws by which we are governed, I have delivered them accurately in my books of Antiquities…" (*C. Ap.* 2.287). Following the fall of the monarchy, the Jews, except for perhaps the Hasmonean and Maccabean periods, were under the authority of an occupying empire; the Jews in Roman Palestine, for example, were under the jurisdiction of a Roman governor and ultimately the caesar. They were, in other words, governed by political laws that were not their own.

By his definition, the Jewish community was a theocracy when it governed itself according to the Mosaic law, or Torah, although someone or something else may have governed it politically. Religious law existed, not for political purposes, but to teach religious piety (*C. Ap.* 2.291). Yet according to his statement in *C. Ap.* 2.164–65, Josephus argued that a theocracy was a social order governed religiously and politically by the laws of God. This apparent conflict in definition seems to demonstrate

---

upon all occasions do always confess), he exhibited himself to the people as their best governor and counsellor, and included in his legislation the entire conduct of their lives, and prevailed with them to receive it, and brought it so to pass, that those that were made acquainted with his laws did most carefully observe them" (*C. Ap.* 2.151–56).

28. At this point in his writing Josephus is arguing with Apion on whether or not the Jews can be considered citizens of Alexandria.

29. Barclay, "Politics of Contempt," 119.

30. As noted by ibid., 112.

that even Josephus had trouble with his own definition and concept—a difficulty he clearly recognizes when he describes it as a "strained expression."

If one accepts Josephus's definition of theocracy, then each society that believed in divine guidance through history, as Cancik notes, must also be considered a theocracy.[31] This criticism, one should notice, is not only appropriate for Josephus's definition of the term, but for many of its subsequent uses in scholarship.[32] Josephus's theocracy, he observes, "Sie braucht kein Militär. Die Priesterschaft ist eine Aristokratie—nach Josephus überhaupt die beste Verfassung" (cf. *Ant.* 4.233; 14.41, 78, 143).[33]

When Josephus described a theocracy, he spoke more of a religious phenomenon than he did a political structure, focusing primarily on the phenomena binding together (religious) tradition and social identity for the Jews.[34] The Jews remained, even after the Jewish–Roman War, under the political authority of the Romans.

Cancik's description of Josephus's definition is an appropriate conclusion:

> Er konkurriert mit den Bestrebungen der Schriftgelehrten und Rabbinen, die das neue Judentum nicht priesterlich begründen, nicht um Opfer und Tempel, sondern auf Schrift, Gesetz, Synagoge. Als *religiöse* Idee ist die jüdische Theokratie mit der ,flavischen Kaisermystik' unvereinbar. Als *politisches* Konstrukt einer Priesteraristokratie jedoch ist die Theokratie des Josephus auf den römischen Staat, seine Polizei und Außenpolitik angewiesen.[35]

J. Wellhausen: Theocracy, the Un-Political Institution

Wellhausen rejected the idea that the nation of Israel, even in its nascent stage under Moses, was a theocracy or theocratic institution.[36] "In ancient

31. Cancik, "Theokratie und Priesterherrschaft," 72.
32. Examples will be discussed in more detail below.
33. Cancik, "Theokratie und Priesterherrschaft," 72.
34. Cf. *C. Ap.* 2.82–84, 291–92. Cancik (ibid., 75) suggests that Josephus's use of theocracy was directed against messianic-monarchic tendencies in Judaism. His definition of theocracy contained no king and no military. This makes sense in light of the rebellious relationship that some of the Jews had with the Roman authorities (e.g. the Jewish–Roman War in 66–70 CE). Josephus's intent, in light of Cancik's remarks, would have been to present Judaism in a favorable light by emphasizing that the fundamental root of all action by the Jews was to live according to the laws proscribed by Moses.
35. Ibid.
36. Wellhausen, *Prolegomena*, 422.

Israel the theocracy never existed in fact as a form of constitution. The rule of Jehovah is here an ideal representation; only after the exile was it attempted to realise it in the shape of a Rule of the Holy with outward means."[37] The law codes of the theocracy—those laws found in the Priestly Code especially—and the structure of the theocratic institution as specified in this code, Wellhausen states, could not have existed during the time of Moses.[38] The cultic festivals, religious tithes, even centralized worship required the existence of the very thing that Moses was supposed to bring about—namely, the state.[39]

Thus, for Wellhausen, it would have been impossible for the monarchic Israelite state to have been patterned after a Mosaic theocracy. The central, executive power that was necessary for a theocracy did not exist beforehand.[40] The monarchy was, instead, a new and "natural" creation brought on by the military prowess, charisma, and centralizing tendencies of Saul and David.[41]

Not until after the exile of 586 B.C.E. (specifically Persia's conquest of Babylon, which was followed by a return of the diaspora) did the Jewish community take on a shape that could conceivably be perceived as a theocracy.[42] Wellhausen writes,

> The cultus of Israel is essentially distinguished from all others by its *form*, the distinctive and constitutive mark of the holy community. With it the theocracy begins, and it with the theocracy; the latter is nothing more than the institution for the purpose of carrying on the cultus after the

37. Ibid., 411.
38. He writes further (ibid., 411–12), "Of the sacred organisation supposed to have existed from the earliest times, there is no trace in the time of the judges and the kings. It is thought to have been a sort of pedagogic strait-waistcoat, to subdue the ungovernable obstinacy of the Hebrews and to guard them from evil influences without. But even should it be conceded that a constitution could come into existence in ancient times which was so utterly out of relation to the peculiar life and temper of the people, the history of the ancient Israelites shows us nothing so distinctly as the uncommon freshness and naturalness of their impulses."
39. Ibid., 412–13.
40. Ibid.
41. Ibid., 413–14. He notes, "David was in the eyes of later generations inseparable from the idea of Israel: he was the king par excellence: Saul was thrown into the shade, but both together are the founders of the kingdom, and have thus a much wider importance than any of their successors. It was they who drew the life of the people together at a centre, and gave it aim; to them the nation is indebted for its historical self-consciousness. All the order of aftertimes is built up on the monarchy; it is the soil out of which all the other institutions of Israel grow up" (ibid.).
42. Ibid., 411.

manner ordained by God. For this reason also, the ritual, which appears to concern the priests only, finds its place in a law-book intended for the whole community; in order to participate in the life of the theocracy, all must, of course, have clear knowledge of its essential nature, and in this the theory of sacrifice holds a first place... It is not from the atmosphere of the old kingdom, but from that of the church of the second temple, that the Priestly Code draws its breath. It is in accordance with this that the sacrificial ordinances as regards their positive contents are no less completely ignored by antiquity than they are scrupulously followed by the post-exilian time.[43]

The incarnation of the theocracy required the completion of the cult weaving itself into the consciousness of the people—a process, according to Wellhausen, whose initial stages required the shelter of the monarchy.[44] Yet it was only after a time in which prophecy was no longer tied to history, or supported by it, that the prophets began to elevate Yahweh as the head of their theocracy.[45] This process began ca. 722 B.C.E. and continued through the Persian period. Thus, according to Wellhausen, a theocracy did not exist during the period of the Israelite monarchy because the cult was itself still in the process of becoming self-aware of its role as a burgeoning national cult. This process would not find its completion until shortly before the destruction of the Jerusalem temple in 586 B.C.E.[46] Moreover, a theocracy was due in part to a change in the prophetic institution. Before the "post-exilic" period, the prophets saw any possible religious or theocratic institution as being inseparable from the monarchic state. Afterwards, they imagined a "world empire" governed by Yahweh and unattached to the human states from history.[47]

Wellhausen admits that his definition of theocracy was not intended to be political.[48] A theocracy as symbolized by the Mosaic ideal, for Wellhausen, was a 'un-political' product, whose counterpart was often, historically, foreign rule.[49] Nevertheless, his definition finds difficulty when he claims that over time the cult took the place of the weakening monarchy. This would seem to suggest that the cult took on some of the monarchy's political functions.

43. Ibid., 53, 82.
44. Ibid., 420.
45. Ibid., 414–19.
46. Ibid., 413–21.
47. Ibid., 414–19.
48. For example, see ibid., 190.
49. Ibid., 422. See also Berquist's discussion of Wellhausen on this point (*Judaism in Persia's Shadow*, 5).

In Wellhausen's definition, one must separate the political and religious spheres, including their respective laws, to justify using the theocratic label. However, in most ancient Near Eastern societies, religion and politics were closely bound to the culture. In the case of imperial rule, subjugated peoples, who often retained their local cults, were still obligated to follow the political laws of the empire.

J. Dyck: Theocracy as Ideology

Dyck defines theocracy in the following manner:

> The word 'theocracy'—literally 'rule by God'—was invented by Josephus to describe the blending of religion and politics which characterized the Jewish nation in the Second Temple period and set it apart from other forms of government... Insofar as 'rule by God' meant in effect 'rule by priests' Judah was a theocracy for most of the Second Temple period. Indeed for much of this period Judah was ruled by the high priest, either in a dyarchy with governors appointed by the Persians or as the sole ruler and representative of the people as was the case under the Ptolemies.[50]

Based perhaps on his misunderstanding of the role of politics in Josephus's definition of theocracy, Dyck's conclusion that the high priest governed Yehud for much of the Second Temple period is incorrect.[51] The "post-exilic community," Dyck proposes, was a theocracy in part because it continued to believe in its own divine selection.[52] And even though the temple, which symbolized this divine selection, was not yet rebuilt, a sense of Yahweh's rule was still present through the shared beliefs of the (religious) community.[53] Dyck states further:

> By speaking of theocracy and ideology I also intend to foreground the socio-political implications of what the Chronicler says. Josephus treats the status of the temple as an accomplished fact or at least as a feat accomplished by Moses in the very distant past. The Chronicler, on the other hand, makes David the founder of the theocratic kingdom of Yahweh. What I aim to demonstrate...is that the theocratic constitution of Judah in the Second Temple period was not so much a 'reality' to be taken for granted as an ideological achievement in which the Chronicler played no small part.[54]

---

50. Dyck, *Theocratic Ideology*, 1–2.
51. This statement is based in part on the conclusions developed throughout Chapters 2 and 3.
52. Dyck, *Theocratic Ideology*, 1–4.
53. Ibid., 44–45.
54. Ibid., 4.

For Dyck, a theocracy developed through the community's shared beliefs at a time when a strong statement of self-identity was necessary in the absence of the national temple (and a monarchy). The cohesiveness of the community provided the "infrastructure" necessary for the deity's rule. Upon this infrastructure and the shared sense of identity or communal cohesiveness, the *golah* community established a society based on the "rule" of Yahweh.[55] Dyck suggests that in Yehud a theocracy represented an ideology intended to maintain the social self-identity of the Jewish community in the Persian period: "I use the word theocracy, not in the specific sense of rule by priests, but in the broader sense of a temple-centered polity or (as Weinberg puts it) a citizen-temple community."[56]

While Dyck has previously stated that Yehud was ruled either by the priests or by a diarchy,[57] he now attempts to include the social-political structure of the *Bürger-Tempel-Gemeinde*. This structure, as was discussed in Chapter 3,[58] is based in part on governance by the leaders of the cult. Dyck relied upon the *Bürger-Tempel-Gemeinde* structure when it was widely accepted.[59] Since that time, however, there has been an increase in the number of scholars who have questioned the validity of Weinberg's model because of his uncritical use of the biblical texts (e.g. the lists of returnees in Ezra 2 and Neh 7), his argument that urbanization shaped the social-economic context of the province (and specifically the *Bürger-Tempel-Gemeinde*), and his argument that two "governors" or leaders of the *Bürger-Tempel-Gemeinde* (a political leader, whose seat was in Samaria, and the leader of the *golah* community) existed in Yehud until after 458/457 B.C.E., the missions of Ezra and Nehemiah.[60]

Dyck also misunderstands Josephus's definition of theocracy and incorrectly describes the "Jewish nation" as a theocracy for most of the Second Temple period. According to him, a theocracy developed through

55. See also ibid.
56. Ibid., 3–4.
57. See his definition above. Note also: "My concern was to demonstrate that the broader definition of Israel on offer in Chronicles, a broader ideology of identity as compared to that presented in Ezra–Nehemiah, was at the same time part of and indeed an essential ingredient in *an ideology which legitimated Jerusalem's claim to hegemony over all Israel*" (ibid., 115 [emphasis mine]).
58. See the section on "J. Weinberg's Bürger-Tempel-Gemeinde" in Chapter 3 (p. 109).
59. Dyck, *Theocratic Ideology*, 3–4.
60. See, for example, Bedford, "Models and Texts," 154–62; Carter, *Emergence of Yehud*, 294–96, 302–4; Williamson, "Judah and the Jews," 156–58. See the section on "J. Weinberg's Bürger-Tempel-Gemeinde" in Chapter 3 (p. 109).

the shared beliefs of the Jewish community. For this reason, a theocracy was not as much a "reality" as it was an ideological achievement.

O. Plöger: Theocracy and Eschatology[61]

Whereas the previous definitions looked toward Israel or Judah's past to explain a "post-exilic" theocracy, Plöger added a future perspective.[62] Plöger posited that restoration eschatology contributed to the unrest within the Persian-period Jewish community by perpetuating suspense and anxiety over the hoped-for restoration of the Israelite nation.[63] Theocracy, then, was a (needed) response to the social and political unrest following the Babylonian exiles.[64] This theocracy, Plöger argued, perceived itself to be incommensurate with the world and interpreted its own existence as the fulfillment of definite promises given by Yahweh through the prophets (e.g. Daniel, First Isaiah, Third Zechariah, and Joel).[65] The leaders of the community believed that the eschatological viewpoint was a necessary supplement to the establishment of an Israelite theocracy.[66] According to Plöger,

> The intensification of the eschatological aspect is only intelligible against the background of an intensification of the more or less latent differences within the Jewish community. This is the beginning of a development which ends in conflict not just between two parts of Israel, but between Israel and Israel; for on both sides there were those who considered themselves members of a theocracy; the eschatological groups also lived by the community principle which had been dominant since the formation of the Jewish community… [T]he result of these conflicts, which gradually increased, and of conventicler-type breakaways, was the gradual transformation of the restoration eschatology—which was essentially still monistic in its appearance and was regarded up to then as a faith-strengthening supplement to the theocracy, and for this purpose could use individual Parseeistic-dualistic ideas in an illustrative capacity—into the dualistic-apocalyptic form of eschatology. This, then, was the second way

61. See also the discussion of Plöger in the section "Religious Groups in Power Struggles" in Chapter 1 (p. 12). This section builds upon the previous one.

62. Plöger expands upon W. Rudolph's theory developed in *Chronikbücher* (HAT 1/21; Tübingen: J. C. B. Mohr, 1955).

63. For reference, Plöger's primary interest in *Theocracy and Eschatology* was eschatology—specifically, older restoration (prophetic) eschatology and the different, dualistic, newer form of apocalyptic eschatology (cf. *Theocracy*, 108). As a side note, it is interesting to observe that the older definitions given by Wellhausen and Plöger all seem to be influenced by a perception of the prophets as culture movers.

64. Ibid., 109.

65. Ibid.

66. Ibid., 111.

in which theocracy and eschatology began to be connected; the theocratic community began to regard itself as a constituent of Yahweh's heavenly kingdom, to emerge in the eschatological revolution as part of the new aeon, when the substance of this world passes away.[67]

Plöger recognized that the priests did not have political autonomy in Yehud, and for this reason, the theocratic struggle under Persian rule was kept hidden, waiting to be revealed at a later time.[68] This need to keep this struggle hidden suggests that theocratic aspirations, as Plöger argues, were against imperial desire:

> [T]he last century of Persian rule may have been occupied by the hidden struggle as to whether a theocracy could be based on eschatological faith and still remain a theocracy, or whether a life *in statu promissionis* must ultimately lead to the dissolution of a theocracy.[69]

The first veiled steps toward a theocracy were taken with the "re-establishment" of the Jewish (or *golah*) community under Ezra and Nehemiah.[70] What the Persian imperial government saw in this act was better administrative control—provided by establishing clearer social-group boundaries—that functioned within the administration of the empire established initially under Darius. Plöger suggests that Ezra and Nehemiah began to consolidate the various eschatological groups (who saw in the prophets of the past witnesses of models and instructors of faith and who pushed for restoration based on the prophetic messages) under a common goal and an identity that saw in the "re-establishment" of the Jewish community the future of a unified, theocratic Israel:[71]

> The political changes which led to the collapse of the Persian Empire meant along with other consequences a revival of eschatological expectations in those groups who were committed to the eschatological faith. It must have been all the more painful when the Samaritan schism, which was connected directly or indirectly with the political changes, provided effectual confirmation of the view of the exclusive theocratic circles that were opposed to them; this view was given a historical-theological rationale not long afterwards in the work of the Chronicler.[72]

Finally, one can say that, according to Plöger, a theocracy was an idea that shaped the social and religious ideologies of a group. Yet it was also a perceivable threat; the theocratic aspirations in Persian-period Yehud

67. Ibid., 112.
68. Ibid., 116.
69. Ibid., 115.
70. Ibid., 111.
71. Ibid., 110–11.
72. Ibid., 112.

had to remain hidden. Plöger focused primarily on theocracy as a religious ideology that provided the basis for the developing apocalyptic eschatology within the Jewish community in Persian-period Yehud.

J. Assmann: Theocratic Government in Ancient Egypt

Assmann defines three categories of theocratic government in ancient Egypt: direct theocracy, co-regency, and representative theocracy. It is this last, as Assmann argues, that was the more common in the first four Egyptian dynasties.[73] He describes the Egyptian state centered in Thebes at the beginning of the Third Intermediate Period (1069–664 B.C.E.) as a direct theocracy, in part because the god Amun reigned at Thebes by oracular proclamation. "This form of direct theocracy was nothing more than the institutionalization of a 'theology of will,' the Ramesside theology that imputed the course of history to divine volition."[74] Further, he notes,

> Though Herihor assumed the title of king, he demoted kingship to a priestly status. He kept his priestly titles and even included the high-priest title as prenomen in his titulary. The title of king was an expression of his standing not vis-à-vis god but vis-à-vis Ramesses XI; it signified his political sovereignty, in the sense of independence from Tanite kingship, not his representative relation to divine power. This important distinction is often blurred in references to the regalia of the Theban high priests. The high priests of the Twenty-first Dynasty represented the rule of god as servants, not as rulers. This is direct theocracy.[75]

In a direct theocracy, as Assmann defines it, the god rules while the "worldly" position of ruler remains unoccupied.[76] For him,

> Direct theocracy turned the theology of will into political reality. Ramses III had already gone a long way in this respect. In his hymns to Amun, he represents himself as a lowly man who has taken god into his heart and serves him faithfully 'on his water.' His prayers to and dialogues with Amun speak the language of personal piety. On the other hand, in his historical inscriptions this same Ramesses III conveys an almost operatic sense of his own divinity. Herihor took an entirely different line. Though he adopted certain of the regalia of the Ramesside vision of the king, he relinquished its bombastic aspects. He remained priest, general, and vizier, while leaving ruling authority to Amun.[77]

73. Jan Assmann, *The Mind of Egypt: History and Meaning in the Time of the Pharaohs* (trans. Andrew Jenkins; New York: Metropolitan, 2002), 299–300.
74. Ibid., 203.
75. Ibid., 300–301.
76. Ibid., 299–300.
77. Ibid., 301.

According to Assmann, there are several ways for a direct theocracy to be manifest: the ruler is not the image of God but is God; high priests acting as servants, not rulers, represent the rule of God; oracular proclamation demonstrates the institutionalization of a "theology of will."[78] "A theology of will," Assmann posits, "requires a procedure for establishing god's intent. To this end, the Egyptian forms of consulting the oracle, already greatly expanded during the Ramesside period, were brought to full perfection."[79] This 'theology of will,' as Assmann uses it, refers to the Ramesside theology that imputes the course of history to divine volition.[80] In other words, this theology maintains that the divine directed history. This is an interesting though perhaps vague definition of the theology as a historical determinant. What society of the ancient Near East, after all, did not believe that history and existential reality were in some way directed by the divine?

Herihor, who ruled from 1080–1073 B.C.E., institutionalized this "theology of will" under Amun, Assmann argues, and created a direct theocracy centered in Thebes:[81]

> The end of the New Kingdom was ushered in by a revolt on the part of the high priest of Thebes. And ultimately it was a general, Herihor…who not only took over the office of high priest but also ascended the throne in that very capacity. The seizure of power by Herihor triggered the collapse of the unity of the state. It marked the end of the New Kingdom and the onset of the Third Intermediate Period. Geographically, the old north–south dualism was restored. Politically, however, the conflict underlying the schism—military versus priesthood, war versus religion—was an entirely new one. In the north, a Libyan dynasty of military leaders ascended the throne—now moved from Avaris to Tanis—and reigned over Lower and Upper Egypt in accordance with the traditional system of pharaonic kingship.[82]

78. Ibid., 203, 299–301.
79. Ibid., 301–2.
80. Ibid., 203.
81. Ibid. Note further: "At the end of the Twentieth Dynasty, a theocracy—a god-state—was established in Thebes ruled over by Amun himself via the medium of the oracle. This shift signaled Egypt's reversion from the model of 'representation' to a model of 'direct' theocracy, but with the roles reversed. In the original version of direct theocracy, the king reigned as god; now god reigned as king. A text from this period expresses the new theology in unequivocal terms: *Mighty in retribution, mightier is he than Sekhmet, like a fire in the storm; high in grace, who provides for him who praises him, who turns round to heal suffering, for he looks on men, there is none that he knows not, and he hearkens to millions of them. Who can resist your wrath, who can divert the fury of your power?* [Hymn on the Banishment Stela, Louvre C 256…]" (*Mind of Egypt*, 245–46).
82. Ibid., 203.

The "theology of will," determined through oracular proclamation, occurred primarily in festivals, in the movements of the gods through a highly restricted code representing "yes" and "no." "Oracular divination was thus associated with religious festivals in the same way as was personal piety, and likewise developed spontaneously as part and parcel of Egyptian religious festival culture. The festival itself was an enactment of the presence of god, of which the oracular performance was a constituent."[83] These divine oracles dictated acts of government.[84] The high priests represented the deity not as rulers but as servants of the deity who ruled through them.[85]

Co-regency was an intermediate step between a direct and a representative theocracy. For Assmann, this model best defines Akhenaten's (and Aten's) reign during the Amarna Period.[86] "As ruler, the pharaoh did not embody the god, but neither did he represent him. God and pharaoh ruled together as father and son."[87] To secure his authority as the divine son, Akhenaten also eliminated the priesthood as a representative institution.[88]

Given that the boundaries between direct and representative theocracies were fluid, Assmann's distinction of this intermediate category is somewhat curious.[89] Even he admits that

> In historical reality, the distinctions between direct and representative theocracy are frequently hard to ascertain: de facto rule is invariably bound up with titular rule. But it remains useful to make the distinction at a theoretical level. In its classical form, pharaonic kingship rested on the principle of representative theocracy.[90]

83. Ibid., 301–2.
84. Ibid., 203. See also van Dijk's discussion in "The Armana Period," 289–90.
85. Assmann, *Mind of Egypt*, 300–301.
86. Van Dijk ("The Armana Period," 311) suggests that both Akhenaten's actions and the ascendancy of Amun-Ra were an attempt to solve the problem of the unity and plurality of the gods. See also L. Žabkar ("The Theocracy of Amarna and the Doctrine of the Ba," *JNES* 13 [1954]: 88) who also states that Amarna was a theocracy. Yet, rather than attempting to solve a "polytheistic problem," as van Dijk states, Žabkar suggests that the pharaoh placed himself in direct relation to Aten to express the intimate nature of "divine filiation." Thus, for Žabkar, the focus was upon articulating the divine–human relationship rather than on trying to fix a "problem."
87. Assmann, *Mind of Egypt*, 300.
88. I would also suggest that he did this as part of his converting of Egypt from a polytheistic society into a henotheistic one. To be successful, he needed to control the priesthoods.
89. J. Assmann, *Herrschaft und Heil: politische Theologie in Altägypten, Israel und Europa* (Munich: Carl Hanser Verlag, 2000), 28.
90. Assmann, *Mind of Egypt*, 299–300.

In a "representative theocracy," he states, the priests function as both rulers and priests.[91] In Egypt, the pharaoh became the representative of God and symbolized the relationship that the divine and earthly kingdom shared.[92] In addition to oracular proclamation, the governing structure of the representative theocracy in Egypt was absorbed by the religious institution through "metaphors and models" of the divine–human relationship, which were commonly present in the religious festivals and accoutrements.[93] For a more specific example, the pharaoh, whose position also represented a divine–human model, was a "unifying reference" figure that pointed the earthly gaze of the religiously faithful to something "higher" and divine.[94] Thus, the pharaoh represented the creator god and ruled over all creation as the god's representative.[95]

According to Assmann, a representative theocracy does not compete with an earthly kingdom but forms the kingdom's condition.[96] In other words, a representative theocracy forms the political institution while simultaneously endeavoring to set the citizens of a kingdom into a direct relationship with the divine.[97] Assmann does not stray far from defining theocracy as an ideology, though he allows that ideology must be "institutionalized" within the social and political orders. At times, however, he seems to accept that this institutionalization may be no more than a superficially redefined set of social values and meanings.

The above definitions have been imprecise and not particularly helpful. The general tendency seems to be reliance upon theocracy as a religious ideology or organization. The definitions fail to address adequately the social, economic, and political elements of a theocracy. An ideology is not a thing in and of itself; it is a reflection or production of a more complex social, economic, and political order and reality.[98] It is, in other words, part of a society's superstructure and cannot exist without a proper infrastructure.[99] What this suggests at this point is that any adequate

91. Ibid.
92. Ibid., 44, 48.
93. Ibid., 110.
94. Ibid., 216.
95. Assmann, *Herrschaft und Heil*, 44.
96. Ibid., 48.
97. Assmann writes, "Das ist das Prinzip der repräsentativen Theokratie. Eine ganz andere Theoligisierung erfährt das Prinzip der vertikalen Solidarität, wenn es den einzelnen Menschen unmittelbar mit der Gottheit in Beziehung setzt, ohne Vermittlung über deren königliche Repräsentation" (ibid., 216).
98. Cf. Bourdieu, *Practical Reason*, 33.
99. Cf. Berger, *Sacred Canopy*, 132–33. Note also Berquist, *Judaism in Persia's Shadow*, 241.

definition must explain how a governing system and its fundamental
ideology are rooted in both a society's infrastructure and its superstructure, which include the social, economic, and political orders.

Case Studies

These case studies expand upon the above analysis of definitions of
theocracy. As previously mentioned, these studies look for similarities
that are common among various societies once or currently presumed
to be theocracies. These studies look for the "genetic" material of a
theocracy in the social, economic, and political spheres of the society.
This will extend the previous analysis of definitions, focusing now on the
infrastructural components of a theocracy. Some of the results will be
negative, and these results contribute by revealing why a theocracy fails
to describe accurately the society. Both the positive and negative results
will work to reveal the common elements of a theocracy as I proceed
toward a working definition of the term.

Maya

I chose the Classic Maya civilization[100] because it was once widely
assumed to be theocratic by its investigators.[101] This initial assumption
was the result of a lack of understanding of not only spatial organization
in the archaeological record but also of Maya texts, which are mostly
monumental and funerary. Webster writes,

> [T]he urban status of Maya centers has long been debated, as has the
> complexity of their economic and political institutions. Before hiero-
> glyphic inscriptions could be adequately read, it was commonly assumed
> that the Classic Maya had a very unique organizational structure and thus
> could not easily be compared with other ancient states. Now that the
> Preclassic archaeological record has been fleshed out we know that the
> first idea is incorrect, and we long ago abandoned the 'vacant ceremonial

100.   As W. Ashmore ("Classic Maya Landscapes and Settlement," in *Meso-
american Archaeology: Theory and Practice* [ed. Julia A. Hendon and Rosemary A.
Joyce; Blackwell Studies in Global Archaeology; Malden, Mass.: Blackwell, 2004],
169) defines it, the boundaries of the Maya area extended south to north from the
Pacific shores of modern-day Guatemala to Yucatan's coast on the Gulf of Mexico.
They extend west to east, from lowland southern Mexico to western Honduras.
101.   As represented in works of J. E. S. Thompson (*The Rise and Fall of Maya
Civilization* [Norman: University of Oklahoma Press, 1954]; idem, "The Maya
Central Area at the Spanish Conquest and Later: A Problem in Demography,"
Proceedings of the Royal Anthropological Institute of Britain and Ireland 97 [1966]:
23–37).

center' and 'priest-peasant' models of Maya society. Even with all the new insights from the inscriptions, however, details of ancient Maya social and political organization are hotly debated, so this issue still lingers.[102]

Nevertheless, as Webster noted, some still argue that Maya was theocratic in nature.[103] Such arguments notwithstanding, the current evidence shows that a "theocratic Maya" is merely the product of investigators reducing a complex society to a primitive society.[104] As they do so, they assume a retardation of political development within the society—an idea that presumes that the goal of every political realm is an evolution into a secular, democratic authority or rule.[105] This study, therefore, is beneficial in that it not only shows what a theocracy is not; it also shows some limitations of the theocratic label.

The obvious presence of religious symbolism and ritual was initially misleading. According to Maya worldview, the world was divided into three domains: the Underworld, the Middle world (earth), and the celestial domain.[106] Astronomy and religion were integrally linked, and the Maya believed that the sun, the moon, and the stars were deities who

102.   D. Webster, *The Fall of the Ancient Maya: Solving the Mystery of the Maya Collapse* (London: Thames & Hudson, 2002), 78.

103.   Cf. Prudence M. Rice, *Maya Political Science: Time, Astronomy, and the Cosmos* (Austin: University of Texas Press, 2004), 284.

104.   With an increased understanding of Maya hieroglyphs, the previously held assumptions that priests governed their societies had to be rejected. Credit goes in part to T. Proskouriakoff ("Historical Data in the Inscriptions of Yaxchilan, Part 1," *Estudios de Cultura Maya* 3 [1963]: 144–67; idem, "Historical Data in the Inscriptions of Yaxchilan, Part 2," *Estudios de Cultura Maya* 4 [1964]: 177–201) See also Ashmore, "Classic Maya Landscapes," 180. For further example, see William L. Fash, "Changing Perspectives on Maya Civilization," *Annual Review of Anthropology* 23 (1994): 97; Norman Hammond, "Inside the Black Box: Defining Maya Polity," in *Classic Maya Political History: Hieroglyphic and Archaeological Evidence* (ed. T. Patrick Culbert; Cambridge: Cambridge University Press, 1991), 253; Linda Schele and Peter Mathews, "Royal Visits and Other Intersite Relationships among the Classic Maya," in Culbert, ed., *Classic Maya Political History*, 251; Webster, *The Fall of the Ancient Maya*, 217–30.

105.   The complexity of Maya civilization has been adequately demonstrated by, for example, Stephan F. de Borhegyi, "The Development of Folk and Complex Cultures in the Southern Maya Area," *American Antiquity* 21 (1956): 343–56; Hammond, "Inside the Black Box," 253–84; Webster, *The Fall of the Ancient Maya*; Linnea H. Wren and Peter Schmidt, "Elite Interaction During the Terminal Classic Period: New Evidence from Chichen Itza," in Culbert, ed., *Classic Maya Political History*, 199–225. One should also include the informed comparative analysis of Robert McCormick Adams, *The Evolution of Urban Society: Early Mesopotamia and Prehispanic Mexico* (New Brunswick: AldineTransaction, 2005).

106.   Ashmore, "Classic Maya Landscapes," 171.

affected human destiny.[107] Beliefs such as these, however, are common among ancient societies, including those of the ancient Near East. The Aten, for example, symbolized the sun in ancient Egypt. Archaeologists and anthropologists of ancient Maya, however, initially read this obvious symbolism as convincing evidence that the society was essentially theocratic.

Maya use of ritual was not necessarily uncommon. They used rituals to preserve the order of the natural world and to obtain advice from the gods. Maya kings and queens used rituals to reaffirm the divine right of the monarchy.[108] From the monuments, city layout, and even ball courts used to re-enact past military victories or others of a conquering nature, it is obvious that rituals, which were given religious significance, were important to the society.[109] Human sacrifice, which often involved captives, was considered a dramatic and potent means of communicating with the divine world and for the nobles to demonstrate their power and generosity to their supporters.[110]

The economy in Classic Maya was largely subsistence based,[111] with the household unit being the basic unit of production.[112] With high population numbers, food production moved beyond traditional slash and burn techniques into terrace farming.[113] In many suitable locations, hill-slopes were terraced. In flatter areas, fields were raised and were dissected by veins of water, together signifying the waffle-like patterns on a crocodile's back, which symbolized the cosmogonic floating crocodilian earth-city.[114]

107.   Cf. Heather Irene McKillop, *The Ancient Maya: New Perspectives* (Understanding Ancient Civilizations; Santa Barbara, Calif.: ABC-CLIO, 2004), 263. See also the larger work of Patricia A. McAnany, *Living with the Ancestors* (Austin: University of Texas Press, 1995).

108.   McKillop, *Ancient Maya*, 221–23.

109.   Note also Ashmore ("Classic Maya Landscapes," 185), who states that the natural landscape provided order and meaning for the individuals of a Maya society.

110.   Cf. Arthur A. Joyce, "Sacred Space and Social Relations in the Valley of Oaxaca," in Hendon and Joyce, eds., *Mesoamerican Archaeology*, 202.

111.   McKillop, *Ancient Maya*, 127–30; Cynthia Robin, "Social Diversity and Everyday Life within Classic Maya Settlements," in Hendon and Joyce, eds., *Mesoamerican Archaeology*, 162–63.

112.   Cf. McKillop, *Ancient Maya*, 122.

113.   Ibid., 127. For further reference, see Paul F. Healy et al., "Caracol, Belize: Evidence of Ancient Maya Agricultural Terraces," *Journal of Field Archaeology* 10 (1983): 397–410. See also the larger work of Peter D. Harrison and B. L. Turner, eds., *Ancient Maya Agriculture* (Austin: University of Texas Press, 1978).

114.   Cf. Ashmore, "Classic Maya Landscapes," 172–73, note Figure 7.3; D. E. Puleston, "The Art and Archaeology of Hydraulic Agriculture in the Maya

Farmers often doubled as artisans and produced items for exchange—such as, subsistence goods and resources, tools, and other miscellanea of basic daily life—while more specialized artisans lived in or near royal courts.[115] "At these expanded social and economic scales," writes Ashmore, "political economy bound farmer, artisan and king in larger networks of exchange and obligation. Considering political economy illustrates ways in which these networks exceed local forms of differentiation and integration."[116] As trade became more important, Maya economy consisted of the prestige or ritual economy and the subsistence economy. "These two spheres of the economy may have had different systems of production, distribution (including trade), and use."[117] The prestige economy included production and distribution of goods and resources for the royal Maya and other elites. Most of these item types have been recovered from tombs.[118] The subsistence economy included goods and resources used in the basic daily life of all classes of Maya society.[119] The increased appreciation for trade by the elite helped develop the role of the occupational specialist, who produced items beyond those needed in daily household activities.[120]

Deities often represented agricultural and subsistence-based concerns.[121] For instance, Kinich Ahau, the sun god (also known as god G) transforms himself into a jaguar each night as he travels through Xibalba (the underworld). The Maize god, or god E, may be known as Hun Hunahpu from the *Popol Vuh* (a sixteenth-century Quiché Maya text), or Hun Nah Yeh. This god "sometimes has his head flattened like a mature maize ear. Alternatively, he is shown as a foliated Maize God with a maize ear emerging from a human head. The resurrection of Hun Hunahpu symbolizes the planting and growth of a new maize crop. His death by decapitation is a metaphor for the harvesting of corn and for death."[122]

Lowlands," in *Social Process in Maya Prehistory* (ed. Norman Hammond; London: Academic Press, 1977), 449–76.

115.   Ashmore, "Classic Maya Landscapes," 144, 74–80; McKillop, *Ancient Maya*, 119–22.

116.   Ashmore, "Classic Maya Landscapes," 177; McKillop, *Ancient Maya*, 130.

117.   McKillop, *Ancient Maya*, 114. For further discussion on the economy, see Ashmore, "Classic Maya Landscapes," 174–80.

118.   In addition, note that access to trade luxury goods appears to have been limited to the elite (cf. McKillop, *Ancient Maya*, 118).

119.   Ibid., 114.

120.   Ibid., 119–22.

121.   Webster discusses Maya deities in *The Fall of the Ancient Maya*, 147–46.

122.   McKillop, *Ancient Maya*, 218.

Initial proposals of a theocratic structure in Maya civilization were based on the magnificent architecture of and the seeming centrality of Maya buildings, such as temples, and a misunderstanding of their social purposes. At first, the layout was believed to serve a primarily religious function. The focus of early archaeological efforts on the temples led to an unbalanced understanding of Classic Maya society.[123] When archaeologists turned to households, the previously held ideas of a temple-centered "state" became increasingly discarded.[124] Moreover, as Maya hieroglyphs became better understood, investigators gained a better understanding of the social and political structures of the society and also of the importance and function of the royalty.[125] It is now understood that temple-pyramids were part of a central complex, or plaza, containing royal palaces and other public ceremonial and administrative buildings.[126] In Calakmul, for example,

> The domestic and productive socio-spatial world constructed by Calakmul's architects replicated the political-ideological order represented in monumental images… [A]t the base of the temple-pyramid St. II labored the most common of artisans in the royal court, the producers of utilitarian stone tools from local chert. As one proceeded up the pyramid, higher-status artisans produced items such as cloth and imported shell objects. At the pinnacle of the pyramid was a palace and temple complex, where some of the most important families of the royal court oversaw other people's production, consumed the products of their labor, and expended these goods in the name of politics and rituals for the gods… By largely excluding productive activities from their palaces, Calakmul's royalty set their homes (their palaces) apart from other people's homes in a quite vivid way—a royal home consumed a distinctive lifestyle enabled by the labor undertaken in other people's homes.[127]

Once thought to be evidence of priestly rule, monuments are now recognized as deliberate manifestations of the social-political realm.[128]

---

123.   Robin, "Social Diversity," 149.

124.   Ibid., 149–50.

125.   Schele and Mathews, "Royal Visits," 226–52.

126.   Cf. McKillop, *Ancient Maya*, 234–41; Robin, "Social Diversity," 154, 60; Webster, *The Fall of the Ancient Maya*, 154–55.

127.   Robin, "Social Diversity," 156. This observation highlights the social stratification that existed not only in Calakmul, but also in Maya societies more generally (cf. Webster, *The Fall of the Ancient Maya*, 143–46).

128.   Cf. W. Ashmore, "Site-Planning and Concepts of Directionality among the Ancient Maya," *Latin American Antiquity* 2 (1991): 199–226; idem, "Monumentos políticos: Sitio asentamiento, y paisaje alrededor de Xunantunich, Belice," in *Anatomía de una civilización: Aproximaciones interdisciplinarias a la cultura Maya*

Nobles manipulated religious beliefs to legitimate their prestige and power.[129] For instance, A. Joyce writes, "As the Classic period progressed, nobles at Monte Alban and other sites in the Oaxaca Valley increasingly erected portraits of themselves and their ancestors in public art."[130] At the same time, there was a need for the nobles to "encourage" the loyalty of the individuals in their realms. "Commoners...contributed to the social negotiation of power since they had some choice over which nobles they supported. Commoners could also express resistance by contacting the sacred via household rituals without the assistance of elites."[131] Religion was not the property of the elite, nor did it obligate individuals to a specific ruler. It did not control the political realm but was a tool used by both ruler and ruled for personal or collective gain. It is also important to note that religion was not the property of the priests.[132] It is interesting, as Webster observes, that Classic Maya texts have yet to yield an unambiguous term designating "priest."[133]

Yathrib/Medina

The *Constitution of Medina* reads:

> In the name of God! The Merciful, the Compassionate! This is a writing of Muhammad the prophet between the believers and Muslims of Quraysh and Yathrib (sc. Medina) and those who follow them and who crusade along with them. They are a single community distinct from other people.[134]

Several key transitions must be acknowledged when discussing Yathrib/ Medina as a possible theocracy. Islam, as Muhammad taught it and as the precursor to modern Islam, was not yet the dominant form of

---

(ed. A. Ciudad Ruiz et al.; Madrid: Sociedad Española de Estudios Mayas, 1998), 161–83; idem, "Classic Maya Landscapes," 169–86; Joyce, "Sacred Space," 205–7; Robin, "Social Diversity," 151; Saburo Sugiyama, "Governance and Polity at Classic Teotihuacan," in Hendon and Joyce, eds., *Mesoamerican Archaeology*, 97–123; Webster, *The Fall of the Ancient Maya*, 115–16.

129.   Cf. Joyce, "Sacred Space," 198, 203, 205–8.

130.   Ibid., 208. See also McKillop, *Ancient Maya*, 226; Webster, *The Fall of the Ancient Maya*, 102.

131.   Joyce, "Sacred Space," 195.

132.   Cf. ibid., 193–95.

133.   Webster, *The Fall of the Ancient Maya*, 149.

134.   Translation by W. Montgomery Watt, *Muhammad: Prophet and Statesman* (London: Oxford University Press, 1961), 94. Cited in Hamid Dabashi, *Authority in Islam: From the Rise of Muhammad to the Establishment of the Ummayads* (New Brunswick: Transaction, 1989), 54.

religion, though it was related to the then dominant form of Arabic religion.[135] The social organization of cities remained tribal-based to a large extent; cities were not strictly political entities defined in terms of geography. This does not mean that a theocracy requires the latter. What should be understood is that the systems of government were still in transition from tribal leadership and politics to those of a state.[136] This in part created a vacuum (for lack of a better word) that was fertile for Muhammad's pioneering social-political reorganization.

Initially, Muhammad was motivated by a concern over the changing moral and social climate in Mecca, for example, the exploitation of the poor by the leaders of the Quraysh.[137] Control of Mecca, the Kaaba, and thus the *hajj*, or holy pilgrimage, had made the leading tribe in Mecca prosperous.[138] This concern, Lapidus writes,

> [w]as...an implicit challenge to all the existing institutions of the society—worship of gods and the economic life attached to their shrines, the values of tribal tradition, the authority of the chiefs and the solidarity of the clans from which Muhammad wished to draw his followers. Religion, moral belief, social structure, and economic life formed a system of ideas and institutions inextricably bounded [*sic*] up with one another.[139]

To see Muhammad's motivation as strictly religious is to miss entirely the revolutionary events that would lead to the later Islamic empire. Armstrong argues,

> [Muhammad] taught the Arabs no new doctrines about God: most of the Quraysh were already convinced that Allah had created the world and would judge humanity in the Last Days, as Jews and Christians believed.

135.   Cf. Karen Armstrong, *Islam: A Short History* (Modern Library Chronicles; New York: Modern Library, 2000), 4–5; Ira M. Lapidus, *A History of Islamic Societies* (2d ed.; Cambridge: Cambridge University Press, 2002), 28–39.

136.   This led to a number of revolts against the different incumbent leaderships—most notably the ʿAbbasid revolt again the Umayyads. Cf. Lapidus, *A History of Islamic Societies*, 51–60. Note also Khaldun (*The Muqaddimah*, 1:428), who writes, "It is thus clear that the caliphate at first existed without royal authority. Then, the characteristic traits of the caliphate became mixed up and confused. Finally, when its group feeling had separated from the group feeling of the caliphate, royal authority came to exist alone."

137.   Cf. Lapidus, *A History of Islamic Societies*, 21.

138.   For further reference, see Armstrong, *Islam: A Short History*, 3–14; Fred M. Donner, "Muhammad and the Caliphate: Political History of the Islamic Empire up to the Mongol Conquest," in *The Oxford History of Islam* (ed. John L. Esposito; New York: Oxford University Press, 1999), 5–10; Lapidus, *A History of Islamic Societies*, 20–27.

139.   Lapidus, *A History of Islamic Societies*, 21.

Muhammad did not think that he was founding a new religion, but that he was merely brining the old faith in the One God to the Arabs, who had never had a prophet before. It was wrong, he insisted, to build a private fortune, but good to share wealth and create a society where the weak and vulnerable were treated with respect. If the Quraysh did not mend their ways, their society would collapse (as had other unjust societies in the past) because they were violating the fundamental laws of existence.[140]

The Quraysh drove Muhammad out of Mecca because of the criticisms he leveled against their social and economic injustices. Representatives of Yathrib, however, took him in, agreeing to follow his teachings and inviting him to become the de facto ruler and arbiter of disputes in the town.[141] This act eventually gave Muhammad political and judicial control over the town. It also eventually gave him economic control over the territory, which resulted in several skirmishes with the leading Jewish clans who had previously held some sway over the economic sphere. Yathrib became known as Medina (from Arabic *madinat al-nabi*, "city of the prophet" or "the prophet's city") after Muhammad took up residence there in 622 CE.[142] From there, Muhammad used religion to give new meaning to traditional virtues and social institutions.[143] His integration of social and religious concerns made possible "a new religious sensibility and the integration of disparate peoples into a new community."[144] Because he was given political and judicial control in Yathrib, he was able to establish legal precedents for appropriate social and religious postures. He consolidated his control over the town's disparate population and extended the town's power and influence in Arabia.[145]

Tribes and tribal bloodlines were still the main form of social organization during this time. Yet in Yathrib, the kinship form of society was becoming increasingly obsolete, which made it a perfect match for Muhammad's view of social organization. As Muhammad was concerned with economic injustices, this view of social organization offered itself capable of addressing the changing economy. "Agricultural rather than pastoral needs governed its economy. Its social life came increasingly to

140. Armstrong, *Islam*, 4.
141. See also Donner, "Muhammad," 9. For further reference, Muhammad's move has become known as the *hijra*, or emigration from Mecca (ibid., 8–9). Muhammad lived there from 622–632 CE.
142. As noted by ibid., 9.
143. Cf. Armstrong, *Islam*, 4–6.
144. Lapidus, *A History of Islamic Societies*, 29.
145. Donner, "Muhammad," 9–10.

be dictated by spatial proximity rather than by kinship. Also, [Yathrib] had a large Jewish population, which may have made the populace as a whole more sympathetic to monotheism."[146] While there, Muhammad gave life to his view of social organization and formed a social-political unit with the various peoples attached to the town. This unit was referred to as an *ummah*, a term that before Muhammad's death took on increasingly political, religious, and social overtones.[147]

So important to Muhammad was the concept of *ummah* that he gave legal definition to the unit in the *Constitution of Medina*.[148] "[It] first appears in the document in article 1, which deals with the Muslims of Quraysh and Yathrib, and with those who joined and strove together with them, i.e., the Jews. Concerning all these groups it is stated: *innahum ummatun wâḥidatun min dûni l-nâs*—they are one *umma*, to the exclusion of—or apart from—[all other] people."[149] The locution *umma wâḥida* in article 1 implies that the Muslims of Quraysh and Yathrib, as well as the Jews, constituted a single unity sharing the same religious orientation.[150] "It is thereby clear that the new unity is designed to be based not only on common sacred territory but also on common faith."[151]

Thus, Muhammad redefined social solidarity and organization from tribal affiliation determined by bloodlines to an affiliation, a group feeling, defined by "faith," which was also membership within the *ummah*.[152] As Dabashi observes,

> In Medina, Muhammad first managed to exemplify the most fundamental substance of his message, the brotherhood of man, by unifying the *Muhajirun* and *Ansar* in a sacred bond of brotherhood. This was a remarkable event in the early development of Islam because for the first time a new unit of social solidarity, the Islamic community, was created against the traditional tribal loyalty and bondage.[153]

146.   Lapidus, *A History of Islamic Societies*, 22–23.

147.   Cf. ibid., 23–24.

148.   Uri Rubin, "The 'Constitution of Medina': Some Notes," *StIsl* 62 (1985): 12. For a translated copy of the full text, see Frederick M. Denny, "Ummah in the Constitution of Medina," *JNES* 36 (1977): 40–42.

149.   Rubin, "Constitution of Medina," 13.

150.   For further reference to the terminology, see article 25 and the discussion of it at length by ibid., 13–18.

151.   Ibid., 13.

152.   Cf. Dabashi, *Authority in Islam*, 48–49, 54. Compare also Khaldun's discussion (*Muqqadimah*, 1:264–65, 374; 2:120, 267, 302–5) of group feeling. He defines this as the fundamental aspect of social organization and so social identity.

153.   Dabashi, *Authority in Islam*, 54.

Through the Quran, in its oral state, and through the *Constitution of Medina*, Muhammad established social, economic, and political norms.[154] According to Lapidus,

> The translation of monotheistic values into the principles of a reformed Arabian society, and the formation of a new community with its own congregational life and ritual and legal norms, made Islam a new religious community alongside the old. This was the umma, the brotherhood that integrated individuals, clans, cities, and even ethnic groups into a larger community in which religious loyalties encompassed all other loyalties without abolishing them, and in which a new common law and political authority regulated the affairs of the populace as a whole. In a fragmented society he integrated otherwise anarchic small clans into a larger confederacy and built a 'church'-like religious community and an incipient imperial organization.[155]

One need not be Muslim to be a part of this *ummah*. Jews, Muslims, and pagans could be members of this "tribe."[156] Based on article 25 of the *Constitution*, Serjeant proposes that the Jews composed an *ummah* alongside that of the Muslims, as opposed perhaps to being part of the same group.[157] Denny, however, who describes Serjeant's theory as "extreme but fascinating," writes,

> In the Constitution it says 'the *dhimmah* of God is one' (no. 15). This probably means that all the members of the *ummah* have equal protection which the *ummah* as a whole guarantees under God. This looks very much like a tribal sort of arrangement, with the difference that the *ummah* itself is the tribe, a supertribe, with God and Muhammad as final arbiters and authorities.[158]

Tribes who pledged their allegiances to Muhammad became members of a larger brotherhood.[159] Muhammad's control of the economy was shown in part by the taxes given to him, which he regarded as signs of membership within the Muslim community.[160]

154. Cf. Lapidus, *A History of Islamic Societies*, 26.
155. Ibid., 28–29.
156. Armstrong, *Islam*, 14; Denny, "Ummah in the Constitution of Medina," 43; Rubin, "The 'Constitution of Medina' Some Notes," 12–13.
157. R. B. Serjeant, "The Constitution of Medina," *Islamic Quarterly* 8 (1964): 13. As discussed in Denny, "Ummah in the Constitution of Medina," 44.
158. Ibid., 46–47. For reference, *dhimmah* means "covenant, security, guarantee"; the term commonly refers to a covenant given by God and Muhammad recognizing the right of non-Muslims to practice their religions, as well as protection of ethnic and religious minorities.
159. Armstrong, *Islam*, 14. See also Khaldun's discussion of group feeling in Khaldun, *Muqqadimah*, 1:414–28.
160. See Lapidus, *A History of Islamic Societies*, 28.

Functionally, the *Constitution* was a political-military document of agreement intended to safeguard Medina and its connected peoples.[161] And according to article 39 of the *Constitution*, Medina was defined as sacred and the *ummah* was called upon to protect the sacred territory.[162] The context of the *ummah* in articles 39, 44, and 47 of the *Constitution* has been linked by Serjeant (through an analysis of *ḥaram* to *ḥawṭah* in contemporary South Arabia) to the traditional Arabian pattern of establishing sanctuaries, called "sacred enclaves" centered on the cult of a local god.[163] For Denny, this is the most significant point for understanding the meaning of the term *ummah* in the Arabian context. "Kinship, while important in designating the parties to the agreement, was not the main binding tie of the *ummah* of Medina. Religion, as represented by the authority of God and his Prophet, was of greater importance, as can be seen especially when the Qurʾānic data and the *Sīrah* are considered."[164] Regarding the *ummah*, Rubin states, "That the main basis of the new unity was to be a territorial one is indicated in article 39: 'the inner part (*jawf*) of Yathrib is sacred (*ḥarâm*) for the people of this document.['] In making the territory of Medina a protected *ḥarâm*, Muhammad put it on a level with the *ḥarâm* of Mecca."[165]

With the conquest of Mecca in January 11, 630 CE, Muhammad firmly established his authority over the entire Arabian Peninsula. In addition to the agricultural- and trade-based economy in Medina, he also controlled the Meccan economy, which was also agricultural- and trade-based. There may have been a greater emphasis on the latter in Mecca because it benefited from holy pilgrimages to the Kaaba, which created a meeting

161. See also Denny, "Ummah in the Constitution of Medina," 44; Rubin, "Constitution of Medina," 9.

162. Rubin, "Constitution of Medina," 12. He writes, "The two articles preceding the declaration of the *ḥarâm* (no. 37, 38) also deal with the subject of protection. Both the Jews and the Muslims must finance the war expenses by paying the *nafaqa*, and they must help each other against whoever fights the people of this document" (ibid.).

163. R. B. Serjeant, "Haram and Hawtah, the Sacred Enclave in Arabia," in *Mèlanges Taha Hussein* (ed. Abdurrahman Badawi; Cairo: Dar al-Maaref, 1962), 41–58. As noted by Denny, "Ummah in the Constitution of Medina," 45.

164. Ibid., 44. See also W. Montgomery Watt, *Muhammad at Medina* (Oxford: Clarendon, 1956), 241–42.

165. Rubin, "Constitution of Medina," 10. Regarding the statement in article 39, Rubin (10 n. 27) writes, "This statement was included in the *ṣaḥîfa* allegedly preserved in the scabbard of ʿAlî's sword." See also ʿAbd al-Razzâq, IX, 263; Bukhârî, III, 26, IV, 122, 124–25, VIII, 192, IX, 119–20; Muslim, IV, 115, 217; Abû Dâwûd, I, 469.

point for several caravan routes through the area. Thus, it can be said that before his death in 632, Muhammad had established a new form of social solidarity in pre-Islamic Arabia, and consolidated and unified the peninsula religiously and politically. Muhammad was a military commander and the political leader of Muslim society. He was the religious leader who intervened between the *ummah* and Allah.[166] Dabashi writes further,

> Initially starting, for example, from a 'spiritual' authority over a limited group of individuals, Muhammad extended his authority, in due course, to encompass 'political' and 'religious' domains. By 'spiritual,' the reference here is to authority over nonmaterial, mental, intellectual, sentimental, or emotional aspects of an individual or community. This should be distinguished from religious authority, which refers to Muhammad as the central figure of the institutionalized form of Islamic beliefs and rituals.[167]

It is clear that Muhammad controlled the social, economic, and political spheres of Medina and its environs and later of Mecca and its environs. He set up social organization in Medina to be that of a community defined in terms of a social-religious community. Thus, it appears that Muhammad's system of government was theocratic in nature. Whether or not this designation holds will be clear after the working definition of theocracy is addressed below.

Calvin and Geneva

At the apex of a clash between France and Berne, Geneva was economically and geographically the linchpin of Northern Savoy.[168] The French and the Swiss both sought to expand their territories to include Savoy when it abandoned a historic alliance with them and fled to the emperor, Charles V. Furthermore, "The city straddled one of three routes between Imperial possessions in Italy and the Low Countries."[169] Therefore, whoever controlled the route controlled communications and the transport of economic goods through the area. It should come as no surprise then that such international forces were in part responsible for Geneva's political struggles.

When Geneva pursued independence from the Duke of Savoy, it found a ready ally in Berne, which not only sought territory from Savoy but also had already embraced the Protestant Reformation.[170] This alliance

---

166. Dabashi, *Authority in Islam*, 56.
167. Ibid., 58.
168. William B. Naphy, *Calvin and the Consolidation of the Genevan Reformation* (Louisville: Westminster John Knox, 1994), 21.
169. Ibid.
170. Ibid., 20.

gave Geneva the strength it needed to break away. And in October of 1534, the *Petit Conseil* deposed of the bishop by vote because the bishop was also the Duke's vassal in the city (in this sense, the bishop played a dual role, religious officer and vassal[171]). W. Naphy writes, "The magistrates clearly viewed themselves as competent to act in this manner and considered their authority paramount in delineating the correct relationship between Geneva's Church and State."[172] He states that when the Genevans overthrew the bishop they broke with their Catholic faith; not only had they been excommunicated, they had, from the perspective of the bishop, committed treason. The city could no longer return to Savoy, the bishop, or the Catholic Church; this reality made certain the popular acceptance of the Reformation.[173] The religious identity of the city was in transition and this, in addition to other social, economic, and political struggles, was one of the reasons for social disagreements within the city. The embracing of the Reformation required the governing leaders of the city to cut off the Catholic Church's economic influence.[174] The magistrates reapportioned the Church's revenues to state institutions, such as the hospitals and schools that they created to replace those previously run by the Church.[175]

Geneva's religion differed from its French-speaking neighbors with whom it shared a common language and culture. It instead shared the religion of its German-speaking neighbors. Despite the differences, the similarities with its neighbors helped it become a Protestant outpost in Catholic Europe during the Reformation;[176] it was in this situation that the city of Geneva became home to Calvin.[177] In addition, others, like Calvin—many of whom were French immigrants—also sought in Geneva a location outside the jurisdiction of the Catholic Church because of its shared language and culture with other French-speaking states.

---

171.   Bishops taking part in judicial and administrative functions was not new here. From the time of at least Constantine, bishops had been given some judicial and administrative functions. Hans A. Pohlsander, *The Emperor Constantine* (New York: Routledge, 1996), 28.

172.   Naphy, *Calvin and the Consolidation*, 20.

173.   Ibid.

174.   Ibid., 19–20.

175.   Ibid., 18.

176.   Bernard Cottret, *Calvin: A Biography* (trans. M. Wallace McDonald; Grand Rapids: Eerdmans, 2000), 160, 162.

177.   Regarding Calvin's influence, Naphy (*Calvin and the Consolidation*, 144) writes that Calvin was no theocratic totalitarian, nor the "last bastion against rampant immorality in Geneva."

The city's government was comprised of several councils: the *Petit Conseil* (Small Council, consisting of four syndics and twenty-one councilors), the *Conseil des Soixante* (Council of Sixty, an extension of thirty-five men to the Small Council, drawn from the Two Hundred, whose functions were primarily diplomatic functions), the *Conseil des Deux Cents* (Council of the Two Hundred, responsible for the final selection of the syndics and for voting members into the Small Council and the Council of Sixty), and a *Conseil Général* (General Council/ Assembly, consisting of all citizens and bourgeoisie who elected the treasurer and Lieutenant and who were called upon to approve all new laws).[178] The four syndics, with the aid of the *Petit Conseil*, wielded executive power in the city.[179]

These councils were often a source of antagonism for Calvin. Calvin wanted to establish a state religion under the Reformation,[180] yet the councils had just broken the economic power of the previous Church to consolidate their own authority. He wanted autonomy from the civic authorities for the Church, but in the collective mind of the councils, independence was ultimately won when the civic authorities put the Church under civic control, making it, in a sense, an institution of the state. Calvin and his ministers fought the civic authorities to maintain the Church's independence from the encroachment of the councils.[181] Cottret writes, "Although they interpenetrated each other more than today, the religious and political powers, the ministry and the magistracy, were never one and the same. Calvin indeed had to fight step-by-step to maintain the autonomy of the church against the ascendancy of the councils."[182] The councils generally perceived Calvin's defensive attempts as threats to rebuild what the city overthrew to gain independence.[183]

178. Cottret, *Calvin*, 162–63; Naphy, *Calvin and the Consolidation*, 38–41.
179. Cottret, *Calvin*, 162–63. Naphy (*Calvin and the Consolidation*, 146) states that the *Petit Conseil* was Geneva's supreme governing body.
180. Naphy, *Calvin and the Consolidation*, 222.
181. Cottret, *Calvin*, 164. Naphy (*Calvin and the Consolidation*, 222) adds Calvin's ultimate aim was the creation of a Protestant State Church developed by the Reformation.
182. Cottret, *Calvin*, 159.
183. Cottret (ibid.) writes, "Calvin was a Reformer. This does not imply that he was always followed. Some of his ideas, even in the ecclesiastical field, remained dead letters, for example his preference for monthly and not quarterly celebration of the Lord's Supper. In civil matters he was neither an omniscient dictator nor a demiurge, nor even a great legislator who endowed his adopted city with its laws and institutions. His role remained more modest; he accompanied more often than initiated the evolution of the city."

The antagonism between Calvin and the civic authorities resulted in his exile from the city during 1538–41 CE. On a superficial level, they punished Calvin for refusing to conduct Easter Eucharist as ordered by the magistracy.[184] At a deeper level, the event was the result of a continuation of divisions arising from disputes over who held the ecclesiastic authority in Geneva. The ministers (i.e. clergy) wanted independence from the magistracy to rule over religious matters. The magistrates believed they should hold the same rights over the freedoms of the pulpit, as did other Swiss republics. Naphy notes:

> The central disputed issue at the beginning of the crisis in 1538 was whether or not the magistracy had the power to order changes to the religious practices of Geneva without consulting the ministers or getting their approval, as they did when they ordered the ministers to conform to the Bernese practices in April 1538. The ministers protested but were warned not to meddle in political matters. This act, though provocative from the ministers' viewpoint, was not inconsistent with the earlier actions of the magistrates in establishing the Reformation. It is useful to recall that even the previous governing group, dominated by future Guillermins, had refused to allow excommunication to be used as a tool for coercing citizens into signing the Confession... The actions of the magistrates after the expulsion of Calvin and Farel, in fact, provide further evidence of their desire to limit the independence of the ministry. Thus, for the first time the ministers were to be salaried employees of the State.[185]

In 1541 Calvin returned from his exile with a set of ordinances he composed, hoping for a commitment to them on the part of the city's political authorities. These were intended to safeguard the Church's independence by stipulating the Church existed within a distinct religious sphere and contained its own method of discipline.[186] Such safeguards distinguished the Church from the civil government and spiritual transgressions would be the sole responsibility of the Church to punish. Although the ordinances appear to have prompted some changes, they were not to the extent Calvin had wanted. As a result, the councils divided the Church into four offices (pastors, doctors, elders, and deacons) and set up a consistory, or ecclesiastical court that was half-lay and half-pastoral, to watch the "morals and beliefs" of the faithful. In spite of the ministers' desire for independence, this court was not autonomous from the civic authorities. From its members, "Two members of the consistory

184. Naphy, *Calvin and the Consolidation*, 34.
185. Ibid., 33–34.
186. Who controlled the power of excommunication stood at the center of the debate/struggle. Was it a religious punishment, or did it fall under civil jurisdiction? See Cottret, *Calvin*, 159.

came from the Small Council, four from the Sixty, and six from the Two Hundred. They were named by the Small Council and approved by the Two Hundred."[187]

Calvin's lack of total social, economic, and political control is revealed in the continuing struggle he and his ministers had with the civic authorities. Naphy observes that the pastors showed an amazing ability to underestimate the effect of their own actions. They were unwilling to concede anything to the sensibilities of the native Genevans. "This lack of compromise meant that many of Geneva's ruling elite had little choice but to fight what they perceived as ministerial arrogance by open resistance."[188] Thus, the Church became an arena for public debate and violent disturbances. "[T]he single most important means available to Calvin for shaping Genevan minds and mores was not the Consistory, but the pulpit."[189] By controlling the pulpit, Calvin controlled a primary means of communication and public indoctrination.[190] "The only fora of dissent which then remained to his opponents were the councils, the General Assembly, and the streets."[191] Because it was believed that the Church controlled access to salvation, the Church was an easy route to the popular collective mind. Yet as previously noted, even Calvin did not have free reign there.[192] The administrative councils of Geneva sought to control what could be expressed from the pulpit, and the Church's ability to withhold sacraments (such as baptism).

While he did preach generally about immorality and unethical conduct, Calvin used his sermons to voice specific and personal attacks against Geneva's political leaders.[193] The attacks apparently went both ways. In 1554 Calvin responded to criticisms leveled against his authority in the Church by attacking those who made them—namely, leading citizens of Geneva—criticizing them in turn of disobeying the Church.[194] His actions reflect the continuing conflict between the French ministers and members of Genevan society, as well the increasing support and membership the "Calvinist" political party was enjoying.[195] Continuing

187. Ibid., 166 n. 20.
188. Naphy, *Calvin and the Consolidation*, 153.
189. Ibid.
190. Naphy (ibid., 154) says, "the only means of…"
191. Ibid., 223.
192. Naphy also notes very little is known about the effect of Calvin's preaching on Genevan society (ibid., 154).
193. Ibid.
194. Ibid., 12–13.
195. On the conflict between the ministers and Genevan citizens, see ibid., 144–66, 208. Calvin could make such attacks without an immanent fear of civil

factions and divisions—driven by social, political, and economic forces—marked the political context.[196]

With the arrival of a large number of French bourgeoisie immigrants, the control of the incumbent bourgeoisie—that is, the Perrinists—became increasingly unstable. While some native Genevans rallied around the Perrinists in their opposition to these immigrants, the city ultimately tolerated the immigrants because it was riddled with extravagant debt and the immigrants brought in money and support for the Reformation.[197] The large number of immigrants provided the city with an increased amount of money and talent, making the Perrinists in a sense superfluous and expendable.[198] Then, in 1555, the city discarded a significant section of its elite, comprising Perrinists, providing room in government for the newly supported French bourgeoisie—though this was not the initial intent.

Thus when Calvin "gained power" in 1555 it was not as the authority of a government, nor was it necessarily Calvin himself who gained power.[199] Rather, Calvin's supporters gained control of the administrative councils from the Perrinists—though they did not fully attain this control, according to Naphy, until 1557.[200] This meant that Calvin could influence in some manner certain decisions of the administrative councils, though he did not control the councils. With the political councils filled by individuals who agreed for the most part with Calvin's ideas, Calvin looked more likely to win victories for the Church, to reorganize the Church and defend its autonomy from temporal powers.[201] Nevertheless, the councils still maintained their autonomy from the Church's control to make whatever decisions they deemed necessary and appropriate for Genevan society.

To be clear, "Calvinist" does not mean "a minion of Calvin."[202] As "Perrinist" is a term proposed by modern scholars to indicate an individual loyal to Perrin or who shares his outlook, "Calvinist" refers to one

punishment—especially after his return from exile—because of his growing support not only in the local city but in the international sphere as well (224).

196.   Ibid., 43.
197.   For reference, see ibid., 225.
198.   Ibid., 226, 228.
199.   Naphy notes the ability of the Calvinists to control the citizens of Geneva was not pervasive (ibid., 213–14).
200.   Ibid., 208, 213. Even still, the Calvinists were not able to impose their will on all Genevans (213–14).
201.   Cottret, *Calvin*, 158.
202.   The Calvinist party in many ways followed in the tradition of the Articulants of a few years before.

who is either loyal to Calvin or who shares his outlook for the city (a "sort of" loyalty, due to the tenuous political climate).[203] Some elders, for instance, who gained control of the administrative councils from the Perrinists had extensive personal contact with the French ministers and began to share similar political and social outlooks (e.g. the relationship of the city to Berne and the state of the Church with relation to the civic authorities).[204] "Calvinist" and "Perrinist," then, are modern designations for what amount to political parties within an already-established political structure; neither Calvin nor his supporters altered the political and social structures of Geneva to bring them under the authority of the Church.[205] The political structure remained intact, while the shared outlook of the new leaders, an outlook defining them as Calvinists, only offered some influence on decisions made in the councils.[206] Consequently, what changed within the political structure were certain (ideological) loyalties of the bourgeoisie.[207]

With the Calvinists in the majority, Calvin could influence the decisions of the councils—notably to establish the independence of the Church from the civic authorities.[208] For the most part, both the civic authorities in Geneva and Calvin appear to have shared the same goal in the Reformation. While one can classify the Reformation as a religious resistance, it was also, and maybe even more so, a social and political movement.[209] It is likely for this reason that following Calvin's exile and return, the city essentially tolerated Calvin and his ministers. Calvin himself did not determine major changes within the city; rather, forces

203. Naphy (*Calvin and the Consolidation*, 221–22) makes a distinction between Calvinist and French minister. The Calvinists appear to be a political party who share similar ideas to Calvin and the ministers under him and who also longed for a change from dominant political control held by the Perrinists. He writes further (219), "The unity, size, and grip on political power held by the Perrinists may explain the Calvinist faction to some degree. The influence of the Perrinists was so pervasive that it effectively suffocated the political ambitions of almost everyone outside their own bloc. Thus, many people, denied power by the Perrinists, had a vested interest in curbing or eradicating their power."

204. Ibid., 220–21.

205. Ibid., 208.

206. As a possible modern example, President George W. Bush appears to share political and social outlooks with the conservative, evangelical religious groups that comprise a large portion of his support base. His decisions as President are no doubt influenced by this relationship. However, one would be remiss to say that the U.S. is a theocracy under President Bush.

207. Naphy, *Calvin and the Consolidation*, 224–28.

208. See also Cottret, *Calvin*, 193–96.

209. Ibid., 104.

surrounding the broader Reformation and the city's struggle for independence and stability brought on such changes.

Geneva therefore does not appear to have been a theocracy under Calvin.[210] While Protestantism was the dominant form of religion, Calvin did not directly control the religious, social, economic, or political spheres of Geneva. The Reformation was a movement that was much more complex and multifaceted than Calvin and his sermons, and it was a process through which the city asserted its new identity as a Protestant republic.[211]

Islam and Post-Revolutionary Iran

Preliminary Remarks on Jurisprudence and the Faqih. M. Kamrava defines *faqih*, or the Islamic supreme religious-jurist, as an individual or a group of individuals who hold ultimate authority.[212] M. Amjad defines the term as a reference to one who is an expert in jurisprudence.[213] Ibn Khaldun, a Medieval Arab scholar of history and sociology in the field of Muslim history, and one whose work remains influential today, defines "jurisprudence" as follows:

> Jurisprudence is the knowledge of the classification of the laws of God, which concern the actions of all responsible Muslims, as obligatory, forbidden, recommendable, disliked, or permissible. These (laws) are derived from the Qurʾân and the Sunnah (traditions), and from the evidence the Lawgiver (Muḥammad) has established for knowledge of (the laws). The laws evolved from the (whole) of this evidence are called 'jurisprudence' (*fiqh*).[214]

Because the traditional structure of the caliphate ended by 1924, the *faqih* took on the role and function similar to the caliph, especially following the Iranian revolution in 1979. The *faqih* insured the stability of the governing structure and system through the help of God (Allah), who granted *fiqh* to the *faqih* (*fiqh* means "true understanding" and "religious jurisprudence"[215]). This defined "understanding," *fiqh*, extends beyond religious law; that is, though the function of the *faqih* belongs primarily to religious law, the *faqih* is also concerned with the laws and

210. See also ibid., 159; Naphy, *Calvin and the Consolidation*, 144.

211. Naphy, *Calvin and the Consolidation*, 43.

212. Kamrava, *Political History*, 92–93.

213. Mohammed Amjad, *Iran: From Royal Dictatorship to Theocracy* (New York: Greenwood, 1989), 157.

214. Khaldun, *Muqqadimah*, 3:3.

215. Ervand Abrahamian, *Khomeinism: Essays on the Islamic Republic* (Berkeley: University of California Press, 1993), 11.

conditions of worldly politics and societies.[216] This concern is based on a belief that all law belongs fundamentally to God, and that the *faqih*, in his understanding, recognizes that worldly laws and politics have often been removed and redirected from their original divine intent. Therefore the *faqih* must safeguard the society by preserving religious law and the religious faithful from those laws and politics that do not allow humanity to manifest the divine's intent. The *faqih* does this partly by guiding individuals in the proper application of the *shariʿa*, or religious laws, to everyday life and society.[217]

To be sure, modern use of the term "jurisprudence" is not confined strictly to the definition applied to it by Ibn Khaldun. His definition, however, is important in that it highlights jurisprudence as a system, theory, and philosophy of law—the nature of which is important as a model for understanding the relationship of law and society within an Islamic framework. Ibn Khaldun traced the idea and structure of law to the Lawgiver (Muhammad), to whom the divine mediated law for religion and society.[218] Divine mandate and divine will became law for the material world through Muhammad's mediation. When Muhammad departed from the material world, his mediation continued when a successor took on his role, and so on.

According to Ibn Khaldun, religious law is intended to censure the evils—for example, tyranny and injustice—that result from the actions of secular political authorities.[219] The *faqih*, who preserves the laws, purifies the political authority of all possible actions, results, and consequences that can be defined as evil or as leading a society or an individual toward evil. While what one might term the secular-oriented, civic authorities govern the mundane and everyday activities of the society, ultimately the *faqih* rules.[220] Religious laws govern the actions and decisions of the

216.   Khaldun, *Muqqadimah*, 2:5 n. 442.
217.   Cf. Amjad, *Iran*, 35–36.
218.   Amjad (*Iran*, 33) states that in Islam, politics and religion were intertwined. Muhammad was both the head of state and administrator of religious affairs. Because the tradition allowed for a variety of interpretations of the law, the religious structure recognized only those whom Muhammad had taught, which qualified them to interpret the law. See also Khaldun, *Muqqadimah*, 3:3–4.
219.   Khaldun, *Muqqadimah*, 1:391.
220.   The term "secular" may be inappropriate. Part of the effect of a theocracy on society is a process of de-secularizing—with a modern sense defining the root word, secular. My intention is to distinguish between the structural elements of government that depend upon a theocracy and those that do not but have been subsumed by a theocracy. "Secular-based" refers to those elements that do not depend upon the existence of a theocracy but can be found in any number of governmental structure types.

political structure, even the structure itself, and it is the *faqih* who interprets and maintains those laws.[221] Fidelity to the state insures fidelity to
religious law because religious law animates the political authority.[222]
Religious law, in other words, is not a separate *religious* law but is simply the law, and the civic authorities are tools of the *faqih*.[223]

The mere perception that a religious law comes from the divine is
not enough alone to maintain a people's adherence to it.[224] Ibn Khaldun
believed that group feeling inspires adherence and obedience to a religious law, insuring that members of the group obey the law because the
law in part defines the collective self-identity of the group (compare the
ummah). Group feeling results initially from blood relationship or something corresponding to it:[225] "(Respect for) blood ties is something natural
among men, with the rarest exceptions. It leads to affection for one's
relations and blood relatives, (the feeling that) no harm ought to befall
them nor any destruction come upon them."[226] If the direct relationship
between individuals is close and each shares a respect for the other(s),
feelings of solidarity are both inherent and readily attainable; they are
inherent in the very structure of the relationship itself.[227]

221.   It is noteworthy that the Islamic notion of government is a positive and not
a negative one. Government and the power contained within it, as well the law, are
the products of God. For this reason, the ruler is obligated by and to the law to
defend, uphold, maintain, and enforce the law. Cf. Bernard Lewis, *The Political
Language of Islam* (Chicago: University of Chicago Press, 1988), 25, 31.

222.   Ibn Khaldun, for instance, writes, "You agree that observance of the religious laws is a necessary thing. Now, that is achieved only through group feeling
and power, and group feeling, by its very nature, requires (the existence of) royal
authority" (*Muqqadimah*, 1:392).

223.   Cf. R. Khomeini's discussion (*Islam and Revolution: Writings and Declarations of Imam Khomeini* [trans. Hamid Algar; Berkeley, Calif.: Mizan, 1981], 60–
87) of the *faqih*. For further reference, see also Lewis, *Political Language*, 28.

224.   Khaldun, *Muqqadimah*, 1:390.

225.   Ibid., 1:264–65, 374; 2:120, 267, 302–5.

226.   Ibid., 1:264.

227.   Khaldun writes, for instance, "[The Bedouins] defense and protection are
successful only if they are a closely-knit group of common descent. This strengthens
their stamina and makes them feared, since everybody's affection for his family and
his group is more important (than anything else). Compassion and affection for one's
blood relations and relatives exist in human nature as something God put into the
hearts of men. It makes for mutual support and aid, and increases the fear felt by the
enemy" (ibid., 1:263). Thus, the nomadic group is closer to purity and divine intent
than is a city (1:282–83).

Revolution in Iran

> A body of laws alone is not sufficient for a society to be reformed. In order for law to ensure the reform and happiness of man, there must be an executive power and an executor. For this reason, God Almighty, in addition to revealing a body of law (i.e., the ordinances of the *sharīʿa*), had laid down a particular form of government together with executive and administrative institutions.[228]

In December of 1979 the revolutionaries in Iran, after overthrowing the U.S.-backed shah,[229] gave birth to a new constitution that committed political power to the Shiʾi clergy—though this turn of events was not necessarily due to original intentions.[230] Approved by popular referendum, this constitution ultimately invested authority in a *faqih*.[231]

To begin with, Khomeini had focused revolutionary ideologies not on religion and doctrinal matters but on issues of class struggle and private

228. Khomeini, *Islam and Revolution*, 40.

229. According to A. Farazmand (*The State, Bureaucracy, and Revolution in Modern Iran: Agrarian Reform and Regime Politics* [New York: Praeger, 1989], 18, 169), many Iranians believed the shah's regime was a U.S. creation and that Iran was virtually a U.S. colony.

230. Jahangir Amuzegar, *The Dynamics of the Iranian Revolution* (Albany: State University of New York Press, 1991), 24; Gene Burns, "Ideology, Culture, and Ambiguity: The Revolutionary Process in Iran," *Theory and Society* 25 (1996): 358. According to S. Nasr (*The Heart of Islam: Enduring Values for Humanity* [New York: HarperSanFrancisco, 2004], 176), the Shiʾi clergy were in a position to assume power in part because of their economic independence.

231. E. Abrahamian, "The Making of the Modern Iranian State," in *Comparative Politics at the Crossroads* (ed. Mark Kesselman et al.; Lexington, Mass.: D. C. Heath & Co., 1995), 693–95, 716–19; Eric Hooglund, "The Gulf War and the Islamic Republic," *MERIP Reports* (1984): 32. Abrahamian (*Khomeinism*, 34) also notes that the infrastructure of the new constitution was borrowed from the French Fifth Republic with Montesquieu's separation of powers. "Superimposed on this conventional constitution was Khomeini's concept of *velayat-e faqih*. Khomeini, described as the Supreme Religious Jurist, was given the authority to dismiss the president, appoint the main military commanders, declare war and peace, and name senior clerics to the Guardian Council (Shawra-ye Negahban), whose chief responsibility was to ensure that all laws passed by Parliament conformed to the sacred law." Also note that within the initial years of its power the Islamic Republican Party (IRP) was able to use the *faqih* to exclude many of its former revolutionary allies from power (see Abrahamian, *Khomeinism*, 83; Kamrava, *Political History*, 94). Lewis (*Political Language*, 28) states the most innovative aspect of the political system devised by Khomeini was his doctrine of the "Authority of the *Faqīh*." This doctrine established the authority of the *faqih* over all social, religious, and political decisions.

property that were of immediate concern to the majority.[232] These important economic issues were the initial rallying points for calls to revolution, and to these he offered a divine resolution. While the Shah was taking lands from his subjects, Khomeini argued that Islam safeguarded private property and everyone's right to own it, an important issue to social classes such as the bazaaris who were increasingly deprived economically by the monarchy's encouragement of and investment in foreign businesses.[233] He won the support of the poor masses by proclaiming that within an Islamic republic there was no poor and no destitution or depravity. Everyone in this republic would own private property, and everyone would share in economic freedoms and have access to economic successes. To usher in this new society, Khomeini proclaimed that it was the responsibility of all sacred Muslims to oppose all monarchies. Most kings, he argued, had been criminals, mass murderers, and oppressors.[234] This republic respected the privacy of an individual's home—privacy toward which the shah's regime had increasingly been showing disrespect.[235] "This society," Abrahamian writes, "the exact opposite of Pahlavi Iran, would be free of want, hunger, unemployment, slums, inequality, illiteracy, crime, alcoholism, prostitution, drugs, nepotism, corruption, exploitation, foreign domination, and, yes, even bureaucratic red tape. It would be a society based on equality, fraternity, and social justice."[236] Khomeini promised a society in which the economy was just and social and economic equality were divinely ordained. In his declaration issued at Neauphle-le-Chateau on January 12, 1979, he asserted,

> The demands of the oppressed people of Iran are not restricted to the departure of the Shah and the abolition of the monarchy. Their struggle will continue until the establishment of an Islamic Republic that guarantees the freedom of the people, the independence of the country, and the attainment of social justice. It is only through the departure of the Shah and the transfer of power to the people that tranquility will return to our beloved country, and it is only though the establishment of a government of Islamic justice, confirmed and supported by the people and functioning with their full and active participation, that the vast cultural, economic,

232. Abrahamian, *Khomeinism*, 16–17.
233. Ibid., 37; Burns, "Ideology, Culture, and Ambiguity," 359.
234. As noted by Abrahamian, *Khomeinism*, 24. See also Khomeini's declaration from Najaf, dated October 31, 1971, on the incompatibility of the monarchy with Islam (*Islam and Revolution*, 200–211).
235. Abrahamian, *Khomeinism*, 37, 41.
236. Ibid., 32.

and agricultural damage inflicted by the corrupt regime of the Shah can be repaired and the reconstruction of the country for the benefit of the working and oppressed classes can begin.[237]

Revolutionary conditions in Iran were created by a massive influx of landless peasants to the cities.[238] This urbanization out-paced industrialization and created high levels of poverty and destitution, as shown in the number of sprawling slums, shanty-towns, and squatter settlements. According to Abrahamian, urban population growth in Iran between the years 1956 and 1977 was astronomical. Tehran, for instance, grew from 1,512,000 to 4,500,000. Isfahan grew from 254,000 to 670,000. Mashad grew from 241,000 to 670,000. Shiraz grew from 170,000 to 416,000. And Qom grew from 96,000 to 246,000. He notes that by the year 1976 nearly half of Iran's population resided in urban centers.[239] Despite the rise of industrialization between 1953 and 1978, the shah's regime tended to overlook the plight of the workers, who were often exploited by their employers.[240] When the regime did address their plights, it was often slow to address important issues demanding immediate attention. Khomeini rebuked the shah's monarchy because it expended time and money on superficialities while letting human conditions worsen. Humans were dying of hunger.[241] Thus Khomeini, without being overtly religious in revolutionary doctrine, addressed the problems he saw developing due to this out-of-balance society. He rallied the urban poor by promising that the revolution would usher in a new era of social justice. These promises, along with Khomeini's pledge that God was on the side of the poor, spoke directly to the issues held in prominent concern.[242] This was in opposition to the practices of the shah, who favored "pomp and circumstance" over the welfare of his people:

237. Khomeini, *Islam and Revolution*, 247.

238. Amjad (*Iran*, 131) believes the petty bourgeoisie created the conditions for revolution in 1979, but Abrahamian's argument and the evidence it contains is much more convincing.

239. Abrahamian, *Khomeinism*, 69–70.

240. Ibid., 23.

241. Khomeini, *Islam and Revolution*, 201.

242. Dariush Zahedi, *The Iranian Revolution Then and Now: Indicators of Regime Instability* (Boulder: Westview, 2000), 115. He writes further (118–19) that after using the support of the poor for the positive outcome of the revolution, Khomeini redefined the term *mostazafin*, which was an ethnic category for deprived masses (or, dispossessed and/or disinherited), to be a label for the regime's supporters, including wealthy bazaar merchants. Khomeini had acquired the support of the poor with declarations such as, "Islam belongs to the *mostazafin*," and "Islam will eliminate class differences." Yet with the term redefined, the poor were once

> One should commemorate a ruler who, when he hears that an anklet has
> been stolen from a non-Muslim woman living under the protection of
> Islam, wishes to die of shame; who, when he thinks that someone may be
> going hungry in his realm, suffers hunger voluntarily himself. One should
> commemorate a rule that uses the sword to protect its people and protects
> them from fear. But as for a regime founded on oppression and thievery
> whose only aim is to satisfy its own lustful desires—only when it is
> overthrown can the people celebrate and rejoice.[243]

With the revolution in full swing, groups who had joined the revolution as a result of Khomeini's charisma and promises of social and
economic justice could only watch as he secured the authority of the
clerics.[244] Khomeini's public declarations, while not oblivious to doctrinal matters, were primarily concerned with social-political issues.[245] He

again marginalized. See also E. Abrahamian, *The Iranian Mojahedin* (New Haven:
Yale University Press, 1989), 22; idem, *Khomeinism*, 52.

243.   Khomeini, *Islam and Revolution*, 200.

244.   Burns ("Ideology, Culture, and Ambiguity," 358) states that rebellions
against the shah in Iran did not involve widespread calls for a theocracy. In fact,
most were surprised at the ultimate outcome of the revolution. N. Nabavi (*Intellectuals and the State in Iran: Politics, Discourse and the Dilemma of Authenticity*
[Gainesville: University Press of Florida, 2003], 149) adds that the secular intellectuals had been effectively silenced during the year following the revolution. Initially,
support for the revolution headed by Khomeini existed because the revolution
represented many of the values the secular intellectuals had been preaching for the
previous two decades. They were left without an effective voice, however, when the
new elite, as Nabavi phrases, turned against them. Adding a further perspective,
Amuzegar (*Iranian Revolution*, 24) writes, "The mass movements (against the
monarch) were not essentially religious. In fact, a large number of people who
followed Khomeini were not necessarily practicing Moslems. Nor did they agree
with Khomeini's idea of an Islamic republic."

245.   Abrahamian, *Khomeinism*, 16–17. There was also a shared rejection of
Western influences in Iran. See R. Horsley ("Religion and Other Products of
Empire," *JAAR* 71 [2003]: 19) who describes the revolution being in part due to a
general Islamic rejection of Western impositions into Iranian society. See also
Khomeini's address to Monsignor Bugnini, Papal Nuncio (November 12, 1979, in
Islam and Revolution, 278–85). Nabavi (*Intellectuals and the State in Iran*, 144–45)
claims the backing of the revolution by the secularist intellectuals was also a
response to the Western ideologies and their perceived incursion into Iranian society
through the Shah. The revolution was considered to embody all those qualities that
could withstand imperialism. In addition, A. Ashraf ("Charisma, Theocracy, and
Men of Power in Postrevolutionary Iran," in *The Politics of Social Transformation in
Afghanistan, Iran, and Pakistan* [ed. Myron Weiner and Ali Banuazizi; Syracuse:
Syracuse University Press, 1994], 118) states that once Khomeini and his leaders
were in power they purged, imprisoned, and executed members of the modern
middle class. Zahedi (*The Iranian Revolution*, 100) claims that Khomeini and his

later began to act more obviously on his plans for developing an Islamic Republic. "In fact, Khomeini succeeded in gaining power mainly because his public pronouncements carefully avoided esoteric doctrinal issues. Instead, they hammered away at the regime on its most visible political, social, and economic shortcomings."[246] It was for these shortcomings that Khomeini vowed resolution.[247]

Once Khomeini and his supporters established the Assembly of Experts, the group's first action was to name Khomeini the first *faqih*.[248] In declaring him the supreme jurist-consult in the new constitution, they gave Khomeini powers more extensive than even the previous shah had enjoyed.[249] Conscious of his new position's initial fragility, he placed rivals[250] in competing positions within the newly established governing structure to preserve his own authority. This setup became an elaborate system of checks and balances within each ministry, bureau, and department.[251]

Khomeini and his followers further established his control when the clergy, who had been his students, created the Islamic Republican Party (IRP) in 1979. They initially created the party to attain political power and establish clerical rule, as Kamrava states.[252] Hooglund observes that the IRP developed into an effective political organization comprised of cleric and lay political activists, though each shared the vision of a government guided by Islamic principles and headed by men trained in Shi'i religious law.[253] Amjad adds that the IRP did not have much trouble

clerics held utter contempt for the middle class and what they stood for even though they had participated in the revolution.

246. Abrahamian, *Khomeinism*, 16–17.

247. It is of interest to note that after using the support of the poor masses to drive the revolution, Khomeini's attention seemingly turned to focus on the middle class. Abrahamian (ibid., 58) writes, "Although Khomeini has often been hailed as the champion of the deprived masses, his own words show him to be much more the spokesman of the propertied middle class. For this reason alone the Islamic Revolution can be considered a bourgeoisie revolution."

248. Kamrava, *Political History*, 92–93.

249. Ibid., 94. According to W. Spellman (*Monarchies 1000–2000* [Globalities; London: Reaktion, 2001], 113), to step further back in the history of this development, the Grand National Assembly in Turkey abolished the caliphate in 1924. In Khomeini's time, therefore, the *faqih*, under the new constitution, took on the additional role and functions of the caliphate.

250. Not necessarily rivals with Khomeini, but person A whose rival was person B was given a position in government of the same level and authority as person B.

251. Kamrava, *Political History*, 96–97.

252. Ibid., 87.

253. Hooglund, "The Gulf War and the Islamic Republic," 32.

gaining control over the mosques and other religious institutions, especially since such institutions supported a political rule by "one of their
own."[254]

Once established, the IRP was quick to establish material power and
secure clerical authority. It imprisoned all those who spoke out against
the new Islamic Republic, as shown by the imprisonment of Tudeh party
leaders.[255] And in 1981–82 more extreme measures were taken when
mass political executions of the Mojahedin and others were carried out
after the Mojahedin failed in its attempt to overthrow the government of
the Islamic Republic.[256] Khomeini's government effectively demonstrated its control of the military, and more generally, the social-political
realm.

Khomeini used Friday prayer leaders to help establish his regime's
authority. Amjad writes,

> Ayatollah Khomeini chose the Friday prayer leaders (Imam Jomeh)
> mainly from among IRP members and supporters, hence giving his tacit
> approval to the IRP. Friday prayers are a combination of regular prayers
> and speeches (Khotbeh) about the recent development of the Islamic
> community given by Friday prayer leaders in each city.[257]

These prayer leaders used the prayers as a time to pledge allegiance to
the revolution and to Khomeini—propaganda given religious legitimation.[258] Once Khomeini's power and authority were fully entrenched and
unchallenged (or incapable of being effectively threatened), Friday
prayers became a means of indoctrination through which clergy voiced
support for the government and the government announced policy
decisions to the public.[259]

As Kamrava notes, the religious fervor that swept through the nation
after the fall of the monarchy fueled the IRP's political power. As religious fervor grew, so did the popularity of the IRP.[260] By the time those

254. Amjad, *Iran*, 132.
255. Abrahamian, *Khomeinism*, 89–90.
256. Ibid., 130–31. Abrahamian notes in addition that over 1,000 people were
shot. "The victims included not only members of the Mojahedin but also royalists,
Bahais, Jews, Kurds, Baluchis, Arabs, Qashqayis, Turkomans, National Frontists,
Maoists, anti-Stalinist Marxists, and even apolitical teenage girls who happened to
be in the wrong street at the wrong time" (ibid.).
257. Amjad, *Iran*, 132–33.
258. Amjad notes (ibid.) that Friday prayer imams were chosen mainly from
IRP members and supporters.
259. Kamrava, *Political History*, 86–87.
260. Ibid., 90.

who sought to disavow the authority of the IRP acted, it was already too late; the party had successfully taken control. Once established, the party entrenched the government's power in a material base and strictly enforced obedience to the government.[261]

The IRP's control over the nation's security forces facilitated this transition into a material power base. The group purged those in the army who showed any signs of disloyalty to the new constitutional structure. In addition, because most of the current officers were young, the new government indoctrinated them before their commission—an added element in their training. In addition, the IRP created an office of government whose sole purpose was to watch over the army and make sure they properly performed Islamic rituals.[262]

Under Khomeini's authority, clerics thoroughly "de-secularized" the society, and the Shiʾi jurists gave the legal system new criminal, civil, commercial, and moral codes.[263] The government purged the education system of any teachers and students not deemed sufficiently Islamic and also revised textbooks to conform to religiously accepted interpretations. Clerics occupied executive positions in all government ministries and military organizations. Furthermore, "Participation in regular communal prayers and abstinences from alcoholic beverages, drugs and illicit sex [were] considered essential for proving one's Islamic worthiness."[264]

The revolution of 1979 paved the way for a theocracy in Iran when the religious institution subsumed the political institution.[265] Religious law became political law,[266] and the clerics governed Iran under the ultimate

261.   See also Hamid Dabashi, *Theology of Discontent: The Ideological Foundations of the Islamic Revolution in Iran* (New York: New York University Press, 1993), 417.

262.   Hooglund, "The Gulf War and the Islamic Republic," 35–36.

263.   For extended reference on the religious-political nature of the legal system, see Khomeini's discussion (*Islam and Revolution*, 94–104) of the integral relationship between the *shariʿa* and the *faqih*.

264.   Hooglund, "The Gulf War and the Islamic Republic," 35.

265.   According to Lewis (*Political Language*, 5), while political domination could be maintained for a while through mere force, it cannot be maintained indefinitely. Religion, Islam specifically, was a source of legitimation for government for Muslims. Legitimation, Lewis notes, is most effective when "the ruling authority derives its legitimacy from Islam rather than from merely nationalist, patriotic, or even dynastic claims—still less from such Western notions as national or popular sovereignty."

266.   Lewis states (ibid., 72) that in Muslim vocabulary there is no distinction between law and holy law. "The *shariʿa* is simply the law, and there is no other."

authority of a *faqih*.[267] Khomeini's government controlled the society, economy, and politics, as well as the military and security forces.[268] It controlled the educational institutions, which it used to indoctrinate students to the proper social, political, and religious posture. Iran's theocracy developed from within, it was successful because much of Islam was already part of the dominant culture.[269]

A Working Definition of "Theocracy"

In any discussion of ancient or modern theocracies, it is important to maintain a measured approach. Despite modern Western tendencies to see a theocracy as imposing severe limitations upon individuals and their freedoms,[270] a theocracy is not uniquely a structure that limits or confines either. Nor should one consider it antiquated or anti-scientific in nature. These are *not* qualifying characteristics of a theocracy. Though a society might take on these characteristics, they do not in and of themselves make a society theocratic.[271]

267.　The *faqih* could decide ultimately who was able to serve in public administrative and executive offices. More recently, the Council of Guardians, composed of six religious jurists appointed directly by the *faqih*, was created. This council assesses the qualifications of those aspiring for public offices. In March 1996, for example, this council rejected 44 percent of those seeking offices in Iran's parliamentary elections, and in 1997 it allowed only four of the more than 230 individuals who expressed an interest in running for the presidency actually to run. Cf. Zahedi, *The Iranian Revolution*, 105.

268.　Amjad, *Iran*, 147–56.

269.　A possible additional Islamic theocracy is described by M. Johnson ("The Economic Foundations of an Islamic Theocracy—the Case of Masina," *The Journal of African History* 17 [1976]: 481–95). According to Johnson (483–85), an Islamic teacher going by the name of Sheku Ahmadu overthrew the overlords in Masina and established a theocratic governing structure controlling the economy, politics, and military. More research, however, is necessary to answer definitively whether or not Masina was a theocracy.

270.　For a sampling of references contending that theocracies place limits on individuals and their freedoms, see Frederick Clarkson, *Eternal Hostility: The Struggle between Theocracy and Democracy* (Monroe: Common Courage, 1997), 2–4; Eric Gorski, "Hart Warns of Theocracy Trap," *Denver Post* (November 5, 2005); Sandy Rapp, *God's Country: A Case against Theocracy* (Haworth Women's Studies; Binghamton: Haworth, 1991), 89–91; Ginger Thompson and Nazila Fathi, "For Honduras and Iran, World's Aid Evaporated," *The New York Times* (January 11, 2005).

271.　In fact, as Webster states, theocratic "states" are fundamentally similar to ethnohistorically known "secular" ones ("On Theocracies," 817).

Moreover, defining a theocracy as an ideology or a perception (as in a ruled people perceiving their ruler to be divine) alone is inconclusive and imprecise.[272] And, sadly enough, standard dictionary definitions give us no more information than stating that a theocracy involves government by priests or ministers or representatives of the gods—insufficient definitions at best.[273] For comparative examples, and as noted above, virtually *every* ancient Near Eastern society believed its monarchy to be of divine origin in one form or another: societies saw the monarch as a divine incarnation (e.g. Egypt), a divine mediator (e.g. Babylonia and Assyria), or the divinely adopted son (e.g. Israel). Yet one would be wholly misguided to claim that all societies of the ancient Near Eastern world were theocratic. Consequently, claimed divine origins alone, which can be entirely distinct from the concept of divine rule, do not uniquely define theocracies.[274] As Webster states,

> I am in complete disagreement with the contentions that supernatural manipulation by itself can support or justify a hierarchical social structure. Such a view cannot be reconciled with widespread anthropological opinion that sociopolitical institutions in general are fundamentally adaptive solutions to systematic stresses, and thus cuts the ground from under any attempt to evaluate culture change in processual terms, especially cultural-ecological ones.[275]

What are the common elements that we can draw from the case studies, whether from a positive or negative perspective? In Classic Maya, apart from ceremonialism, there is no evidence that any religious institution maintained an authority that extended over the social, economic, and political realms. As Webster has noted above, the existence of ceremonialism alone in Maya is not enough to justify a hierarchical social or political structure. Instead, it appears that a monarchy was the system of government and the basis for any social-political system. Moreover, there is no evidence of a dominant system or code of religious law that could have become either part of or the dominant form of law in the society.

In Medina, Muhammad, as the religious authority, maintained authority over the social, economic, and political realms. The authority over these latter was socially legitimated by the citizens of Medina. These realms did not exist separately from the religious realm but became

---

272. See also ibid., 815–17.
273. See also ibid., 813.
274. As a related note, Webster (ibid., 812) states that a fundamental premise for theocracies is that the people under a theocratic structure believe the structure provides the necessary functions for the whole of society.
275. Ibid., 816.

extensions of it—the latter which was also the socially dominant form of religion. Furthermore, there was no clear distinction between religious law and political law. That was so because in the *Constitution of Medina* and in Muhammad's decisions as arbiter, religious laws became laws. In addition, Muhammad's control over trade and his control over Medina's military illustrate his authority over the economy and his control over material power.

Calvin's authority seems ultimately to have been restricted to the realm of the Church. His authority did not extend over the social, economic, or political realms. While he could influence some decisions of the councils, his level of impact does not show him to be an authority over the councils but something more akin to a social-religious activitist or lobbyist. The laws of the Church were not the laws of Geneva.

In Iran, a new constitution was created in which Khomeini was named *faqih*. Thus, not only was he *the* religious authority, he was given authority over the social, economic, and political realms of Iran. With this authority, he (with the aid the IRP) "de-secularized" the society by imprisoning all who spoke out against the new government, purging the education system of materials deemed not sufficiently Islamic, incorporating political policies and announcements in Friday prayers, and purging the military of those who showed any signs of disloyalty to the new constitutional structure. The constitution rooted the authority of the religious institution in the social, economic, and political realms. Religious law was incorporated into the country's law code, which in turn made obedience to the religious institution and its leaders the obligation of every obedient citizen.

On the basis of these common elements and on the common structural components taken from the definitions above, we can define a theocracy principally as a social-political context governed by a dominant religious institution or authority that holds authority over and administers the social, economic, and political spheres or realms of a society. There is, in addition, no clear distinction between religious law and civic or political law because the fundamental, ideological basis for virtually all law is situated in the divine authentication of the religious institution and authority. The legitimation of a theocratic authority is rooted in not only the fundamental bases of the religion but also in the society more generally—authority in a theocracy is a socially legitimated authority.[276] In addition, this authority extends to a society's material and physical power base.[277] A precise definition of theocracy, therefore—and one that

276. Ibid., 815.
277. Ibid., 812–13.

is appropriate for a social-scientific study—must account and accommodate for these things because, as Bourdieu so studiously asserts, using "state" as a reference to a unified social space,

> the genesis of the state is inseparable from the process of unification of the different social, economic, cultural (or educational), and political fields which goes hand in hand with the progressive constitution of the state monopoly of legitimate physical and *symbolic* violence. Because it concentrates an ensemble of material and symbolic resources, the state is in a position to regulate the functioning of the different fields...[278]

To explain the concept in question further, for a theocracy to exist, divine rule is necessary. This initial statement presents a paradox, of course, and requires additional explanation: the dominant religious structure manifests the perception of a divine rule. As the case studies of Medina and Iran have shown, the political institution in a theocracy has an obvious connection with the divine (in whatever way the religion defines the concept of the divine). The religious institution legitimates the ruling authority as an extension of divine control over the social, economic, and political realms and physical (economic, military, etc.) and symbolic (values, beliefs, ideologies, etc.) power.[279] Moreover, it "legitimates social institutions by bestowing upon them an ultimately valid ontological status, that is, by *locating* them within a sacred and cosmic frame of reference."[280] This legitimation[281] (or act of legitimating) uses the inherent structure, organization, and value systems of a religion, creating and validating an infrastructure for the social and political body.[282] This

278. Bourdieu, *Practical Reason*, 33, emphasis in original.

279. Berquist, *Judaism in Persia's Shadow*, 241; Bourdieu, *Cultural Production*, 7, 39, 101, 258; Webster, "On Theocracies," 813.

280. Peter L. Berger, *The Sacred Canopy: Elements of a Sociological Theory of Religion* (1967; New York: Anchor Books, 1990), 33.

281. Berger notes, "There is both an objective and a subjective aspect to legitimation. The legitimations exist as objectively valid and available definitions of reality. They are part of the objectivated 'knowledge' of society. If they are to be effective in supporting the social order, however, they will have to be internalized and serve to define subjective reality as well. In other words, effective legitimation implies the establishment of symmetry between objective and subjective definitions of reality. The reality of the world as socially defined must be maintained externally, in the conversation of men with each other, as well as internally, in the way by which the individual apprehends the world within his own consciousness. The essential purpose of all forms of legitimation may thus be described as reality-maintenance, both on the objective and the subjective levels" (ibid., 32).

282. Cf. Karl Marx, "The German Ideology," in *The Marx–Engels Reader* (ed. Robert C. Tucker; New York: W. W. Norton, 1978), 187.

process confirms the political authority through the religious institution. In comparison, this legitimation and subsequent processual confirmation was lacking in Classic Maya and Geneva.

Thus, a theocracy is an institutional governing order that exercises social, economic, political, and religious authority over a society.[283] It is a product of a dominant (or dominating) religion, an institution it uses in part to legitimate its exercise of authority. It produces or redefines the social-political order as one that draws legitimation and a basis for meaning from the religious order. This is where the definitions discussed in the first half of this chapter fall short. These define a theocracy primarily as an ideology while failing to define it as a complex managerial or governing system for administering material and symbolic power. While Josephus admits to the limitations of the term's definition, and Assmann's definition is on the right track, neither is capable of bearing the weighty responsibility of an objective social-scientific definition. A theocracy administers and defines the superstructure and the infrastructure of a society. Its stability rests upon the strengths of the systems and institutions underlying it that necessitate the theocratic organization.[284] It is a system of government, and for this reason, the authority of a theocracy possesses the socially legitimated knowledge that contains individual or group resistances within tolerable limits and enforces political obedience.[285] Consequently, the institutional order, which is by necessity religious, embodies this authority and not, in comparison, the single individual or the individual's charisma.

The charisma and authority that a ruler takes on—even though these are thought to be products of the individual—are qualities of the office.

---

283.   See also Cancik's informed discussion ("Theokratie und Priesterherrschaft," 65–77) on the political element(s) of a theocracy, which he develops in part through the initial phrasing of "theocracy" by Josephus. For further reference on the religious and political aspects of a theocracy, see Abrahamian, *Khomeinism*, 32–44; Amjad, *Iran*, 131; Burns, "Ideology, Culture, and Ambiguity," 369–70; Cottret, *Calvin*, 159; Hooglund, "The Gulf War and the Islamic Republic," 31–37; Joseph J. Spengler, "Economic Thought of Islam: Ibn Khaldun," *Comparative Studies in Society and History* 6 (1964): 268–306; Paul Valliere, *Modern Russian Theology: Bukharev, Soloviev, Bulgakov—Orthodox Theology in a New Key* (Grand Rapids: Eerdmans, 2000), 134; Weber, *Economy and Society*, 1158–63; Webster, "On Theocracies," 815–22.

284.   Webster, "On Theocracies," 824.

285.   Cf. Berger (*Sacred Canopy*, 29–32), who discusses the activities of socialization, social control, and legitimation at length. See also Marx's discussion of the purpose of political governments in "On the Jewish Question," in Tucker, ed., *The Marx–Engels Reader*, 43–44.

"Socially recognized charisma (alleged or presumed)...goes with the job."[286] Quite simply, a governed body may replace a particular ruler without disturbing the system of government because the ruler is merely the symbolic head or face given to a "bureaucratic" office. I am not presenting anything new here. One can say the same of virtually any system of government: a monarchy, for example, does not cease to be a monarchy if the monarch dies or is replaced. The ruler does not legitimate a monarchy; it is an institutional order legitimated by the society to exercise authority by controlling physical and symbolic power and including other areas of authority.[287] It makes and enforces laws for a society. In a theocracy, these laws are divine laws.[288]

286. Webster, "On Theocracies," 821.
287. On physical and symbolic power, see Bourdieu, *In Other Words*, 133, 38; idem, *Cultural Production*, 101, 40.
288. Cf. Abrahamian, *Khomeinism*, 43–45.

Chapter 5

WAS YEHUD A THEOCRACY?

With the working definition of theocracy before us, it is now possible to turn our final thoughts to issues of governance in Yehud. The previous chapter drew out several common elements necessary for a theocracy from both the positive and negative case studies; I will begin with the "core" of these elements and build upon them.[1] To begin with, the religious institution exercises control over the social, economic, and political spheres or realms of a society—a control that is legitimated by the underlying social systems and institutions requiring a theocratic organization. It exercises control over the physical and symbolic power in a society. The governed social body over whom this power is exercised validates the institution's control by accepting the institutional authority's claim to the power. The political ruler—who usually represents the office itself—must be legitimated as the social and political authority in some way by the dominant religious institution. In addition, the religious laws of the dominant religious institution determine, define, and distinguish the social and political laws of a theocracy.

Visions of Physical and Symbolic Power

While the Persian government may have practiced a certain level of tolerance, there is no clear evidence that Yehud was given autonomy or that it was the empire's "golden child": a territory and people the imperial king so desperately longed to see free.[2] The biblical texts claim

---

1. A theorist of structuralism might refer to these elements as objective structures (cf. Bourdieu, *In Other Words*, 123).

2. The presence of fortresses within the province and surrounding territories seems to suggest imperial control. See Neh 2:8; 7:2 (regarding הבירה). So also Carter, *Emergence of Yehud*, 282, 320; Edelman, *The Origins of the 'Second' Temple*, 75, 146 (regarding fortresses being fire-signal stations); Fried, "The Political Struggle," 61–73; Hoglund, *Achaemenid Imperial Administration*, 165–69, 207–12,

that Yahweh chose Cyrus as his servant to re-establish the glory of an ideological Israel (cf. 2 Chr 36:22–23 || 1 Esd 2:1–2; see also Ezra 1:1–11; 4:3–5; 5:13–14; Neh 1:3–2:11; Isa 44:28; 45:1, 13). Yet, apart from a strictly *golah*-religious explanation, given to us by the Persian-period biblical texts, there is no evidence that Cyrus had a particular fondness for the Babylonian Jewish diaspora or Israel. Furthermore, one should not quickly overlook and dismiss Yehud's proximity to Egypt, an area that rebelled repeatedly against its imperial overlords (cf. *Hist.* 7.5). While Yehud itself may not have been the linchpin to Persia's military involvement with the rebellious area, it makes little sense to grant autonomy to a nearby province and allow for its possible, unmediated involvement in future revolts. It is correct to propose that Yehud held some strategic military value for the empire and that actions in the province were done in part to increase that value.[3] The exact extent of this value, however, remains difficult to determine.[4]

220–25; Lipschits, "Achaemenid Imperial Policy," 35–40 (contra fortresses and imperial fortification); Meyers, "The Persian Period," 516. For reference, compare Horsley's claim ("Religion and Other Products," 26) that the Persian empire set up a temple-state in Yehud that continued as part of imperial order under the Hellenistic and Roman empires.

    3. For reference, Lipschits ("Achaemenid Imperial Policy," 35–40) suggests that Yehud held little or no military-strategic value. He is highly critical of Hoglund who, in 1992, had proposed that Yehud held a significant value level (*Achaemenid Imperial Administration*).

    4. Lipschits ("Achaemenid Imperial Policy," 35–40) contra Fried ("The Political Struggle," 61–73), Hoglund (*Achaemenid Imperial Administration*, 165–69, 207–12, 220–25), and Meyers ("The Persian Period," 516), among others, argues that Yehud could not have held any significant military-strategic value. Lipschits ("Achaemenid Imperial Policy," 36) states that most scholars reach their conclusions based on Greek texts, Ezra–Nehemiah, and "a basic assumption regarding the strategic importance of Judah." In turn, he attempts to show how the archaeological records tell a different story. While I would agree that Yehud was not the linchpin of any imperial military strategy or presence, Lipschits' alternative, which focuses on the city of Jerusalem, remains problematic. "The agreement of the Persians to build fortifications in Jerusalem and to alter the status of the city to the capital of the province was the most dramatic change in the history of the city after the Babylonian destruction in 586. However, we know nothing about the reasons for this change. *The most logical explanation is that the Persian authorities agreed to the request (of the Judeans/Jerusalemites/some representatives of the Judeans/Nehemiah?) when they realized that, besides its status as the ideological and literary center, Jerusalem had already become the fiscal center of the province...*" (40 [emphasis mine]). His proposal seems to rest implicitly on the idea that the primary direction of empire–province interaction was that the socio-economic actions of the province prompted imperial policies. It also is also problematic in its statement that Jerusalem was the

In other words, no evidence exists that demonstrates that the province of Yehud was free of the imperial control found in the other areas of the Persian empire. Neither does any evidence, apart from the biblical texts, demonstrate that the *golah* community obtained such freedom through, for theoretical example, revolutionary struggle or other conscious action. Both Medina and Iran offer informative examples: because a theocracy was a new development in both contexts, it required obvious changes in the social, economic, and political realms of the societies. Since the territory of Yehud was not under a theocracy before the Persian period, it would be necessary for us to see evidence of changes on the social, economic, and political levels that reflect the structuring and development of a theocracy. That one can establish a line of governors within Yehud (cf. Table 2, p. 90) requires one to look first to the more established system of government within the empire—that is, administration under satraps and governors—rather than to the priesthood for political leadership.

Ezra–Nehemiah implies that the *golah* community held an important place in the Persian empire, a place which elevated the community's freedoms and imperial status. However, Yahwists such as those from Samaria (or Samerina generally) seeking to help rebuild the Jerusalem temple did not address the *golah* community as political authorities but as equals (cf. Ezra 4:2–3).[5] It also seems highly unlikely that this petition

---

ideological center of the province, if one defines ideology as a unifying system of beliefs, attitudes, and values expressed in the superstructure of a culture.

5. There is a growing corpus of epigraphic evidence demonstrating that from 587 B.C.E. onward, Yahwists existed in the provinces and regions surrounding Yehud. As cited by Kessler, "Persia's Loyal Yahwists," 95. For Ashdod, see A. Lemaire, "Épigraphie et Religion En Palestine à l'époque achéménide," *Transeu* 22 (2001): 110; J. Naveh, "An Aramaic Ostracon from Ashdod," *ʾAtiqot* 9/10 (1971): 200–201. For Galilee, see J. Briend, "L'édit de Cyrus et sa valeur historique," *Transeu* 11 (1996): 33–44; I. Eph'al, "Changes in Palestine During the Persian Period in Light of Epigraphic Sources," *IEJ* 48 (1998): 110; Sean Freyne, *Galilee from Alexander the Great to Hadrian, 323 BCE to 135 CE: A Study of Second Temple Judaism* (Wilmington, Del.: University of Notre Dame Press, 1980), 24–25; A. Lemaire, *Histoire et Administration de la Palestine à l'époque perse* (ed. Ernest-Marie Laperrousaz and André Lemaire; La Palestine à l'époque perse; Paris: Cerf, 1994), 40–41; idem, "Épigraphie et Religion," 99. For Gaza, see Eph'al, "Changes in Palestine," 114; idem, "Épigraphie et Religion," 111; Joseph Naveh, "Aramaic Ostraca and Jar Inscription from Tell Jemmeh," *ʾAtiqot* 21 (1992): 49–53. And for south and southwest Idumea, see I. Beit-Arieh, "Edomites Advance into Judah," *BAR* 22, no. 6 (1996): 28–36; Eph'al, "Changes in Palestine," 11; Lemaire, *Histoire et Administration*, 30; idem, "Épigraphie et Religion," 11; J. Naveh, "Published and Unpublished Aramaic Ostraca," *ʾAtiqot* 17 (1985): 114–21.

to aid in rebuilding the temple was a petition to set the Jerusalem priesthood in power over Yehud.[6]

While the biblical texts suggest that the Jerusalem high priests and other religious figures controlled the province, it seems clear at this point (see also the discussion in Chapter 3) that the authors had ulterior motives. The intent of the biblical authors was to define their society as they thought it should be; the alleged social policies and visions of the texts reflect an ideal longing. Apart from ideological claims, however, no clear social-political development for a theocratic structure in Yehud is apparent. Of the four case studies, the closest parallel for our purposes here would be Classic Maya, notably that the religious texts were used as propaganda. The difference is that in Maya, political rulers used religious inscriptions as propaganda while in Yehud, members of the *golah* community used religious ideologies as propagandistic petitions for control over symbolic power. While this act might initially suggest a possible later development into a theocracy, what we have discussed to this point of the structure and the infrastructure of Yehud does not confirm one.[7] Instead, the biblical texts seem to be petitions for control over symbolic power in the province, but it was a power that the imperial bureaucratic institution ultimately controlled.[8]

6. D. Petersen (*Zechariah 9–14 and Malachi* [OTL; Louisville: Westminster John Knox, 1995], 6–15) states that Jerusalem was the ritual center. While Jerusalem might be a ritual center for a Yahwistic cult in Yehud, there is no certainty that it was *the* ritual center for all Yahwistic cults in the Persian empire or even in Palestine.

7. See, for instance, the discussion in Chapter 3.

8. Berquist's suggestion that Ezra brought a Pentateuchal law canonized within a symbolic framework ultimately controlled by the Persian empire may be relevant here. He ultimately suggests that control over symbolic power lay with the imperial government. "Just as Persian constructed Yehud through its symbolic universe, Persia would have maintained its control over the province through an emphasis on order, including symbols of cosmic harmony. One would expect Yehud to produce literature that emphasized such order, including wisdom literature and other explanations of creation" (*Judaism in Persia's Shadow*, 134). And further, "Legal codes are sets of symbols creating a universe of proper relations among humans, but they also construct a symbolic relationship between the lawgiver and the legal adherent. Israel's heritage of law marked one of its greatest and longest-lasting legacies, but in the Persian period it was much newer and more dynamic" (137). And finally, "The internal/external paradox of the Pentateuch reflects well the nature of canonicity. A canon tells one's own story but in a normative way. The canon, through the external process of a community's insistence upon it, forces itself to be the reader's story, displacing other stories and identities. The Persian Empire provided this identity for Yehud, along with the laws that gave specific guidance in daily life. This story provided the official symbolic universe for Yehud's corporate life" (139).

The *golah* authors laid claim to the religious traditions of Yahwism, using their "ownership" of such traditions, along with their own religious ideologies, to exercise religious-ethnic exclusion in Yehud.[9] The land, they argued, belonged to those to whom Yahweh had given it, that is, the ones who remained faithful.[10] And yet, according to the authors, being "faithful" was not possible for everyone. The true remnant consisted of those who had been exiled, and, as a result, Ezra–Nehemiah rejects the *am haʾaretz* (cf. Ezra 9:1–15; Neh 10:28–31). This divisive policy would imply for the province of Yehud a superstructure based entirely on *golah* ideologies alone. However, the extent to which the authors were effective in redefining citizenship or were accurate in their social portrayals remains in question. Their portrayal of the religious situation may not be entirely accurate either. Many 'people of the land' likely considered themselves to be Yahwists in one fashion or another—despite the claims of the *golah* authors. It is unlikely that everyone accepted the determinative claims of the newly arrived immigrants or their new version of Yahwism. After all, theirs was a version based in significant part on the rejection of the people already in the land of Yehud (note the implications of Ezra 10:1–44; Neh 13:1–30). Thus, it is not entirely clear that the biblical texts reflect even the dominant religion of the people in Yehud. If they did, we might have seen a situation similar to Muhammad's "restructuring" of Yathrib in its beginnings. Even there, however, Muhammad moved well beyond religious ideology by establishing control over the social, economic, and political realms. We are without evidence that the *golah* community was able to do likewise.

Weinberg proposed that the *golah* community successfully altered the social, economic, and political landscapes through their control of private property.[11] But, as noted previously, his argument cannot overcome a defeating number of weaknesses.[12] Short of Morgenstern's unacceptable theories of rebellion in Yehud,[13] nothing exists that could adequately explain the necessary and radical altering of the social, economic, and political landscapes of Yehud, from an imperial province into a theocracy, by the *golah* community. If a successful revolution had occurred,

9. So also Davies, "Exile! What Exile? Whose Exile?," 138.

10. For instance, note that the so-called Golah Lists seem to be comprised primarily of those "exiled" (Ezra 2:1–67; Neh 7:4–69).

11. This argument is a common theme throughout a number of his published articles. For the translated collection, see Weinberg, *Citizen-Temple Community*.

12. See the discussion of Weinberg's theory in "J. Weinberg's Bürger-Tempel-Gemeinde" in Chapter 3 (p. 109).

13. Morgenstern, "Jerusalem—485 BC," 101–79; idem, "Jerusalem—485 BC (Continued)," 15–47; idem, "Jerusalem—485 BC (Concluded)," 1–29.

one would expect to see textual or annalistic evidence of the community winning the support of the so-called masses, the *am ha'aretz*. The immediate concern over intermarriage in Ezra–Nehemiah would have retreated from the forefront because in a *golah*-controlled and theocratic context, it would have simply been law.[14] But no such evidence exists. Neither is there any evidence that the biblical texts, the religious ideologies they were products of, or the *golah* religious "institution" generally were forces that shaped the infrastructure of the province. As was seen in the case studies of Yathrib/Medina and Iran, this was one ingredient necessary for a theocracy.

Political Rulers and the Religious Institution

In Yehud, while it is possible (*though not proven*) that the high priests of the *golah* community in Jerusalem controlled formal religion in the province, ultimately it was an imperially appointed official and an imperially administered system that controlled the judicial and political realms.[15] The case study of Calvin and Geneva may prove useful here.

14. By that, I mean that the issue would have seemed less important to the authors. For example, one rarely sees any extensive discussion within the biblical texts regarding the enforcement of laws that were already a part of everyday society. The seemingly dramatic concern regarding the foreign women and children suggests that the texts reflect an attempt to establish the prohibition against intermarriage as a law for Yehud. Neh 13 looks like a plea (enforced with violence): "And I contended with them and cursed them and beat some of them and pulled out their hair; and I made them take an oath in the name of God, saying, 'You shall not give your daughters to their sons, or take their daughters for your sons or for yourselves. Did not King Solomon of Israel sin on account of such women? Among the many nations there was no king like him, and he was beloved by his God, and God made him king over all Israel; nevertheless, foreign women made even him to sin. Shall we then listen to you and do all this great evil and act treacherously against our God by marrying foreign women?'" (Neh 13:25–27). In his informed analysis of high priests of Jerusalem, VanderKam (*From Joshua to Caiaphas*, 53–54) notes that even some of the aristocratic priests practiced intermarriage. This would seem to indicate that a theocracy as dictated by the religious laws described in the biblical texts did not exist.

15. For a listing of governors, see again Table 2 (p. 90). There is also no certainty that the new Yahwism that the *golah* community brought with it into Yehud was the dominant form of the religion in the province. Granted, a discussion regarding the valuation of Yahwistic forms cannot be confirmed on a defined scale; there is simply not enough evidence. Yet the theoretical possibility that there were competing forms must be acknowledged. Doing so recognizes that Yahwism continued to be practiced in the area of Yehud before the entrance of the *golah* community and, by extension, that the community was itself not the sum of Yehud's society.

As a religious authority, Calvin could not escape functioning under the authority of a political body he did not control. Likewise, the high priests from the *golah* community also had to function under the authority of the imperial administrative system, which included the local governor. While the religious texts of the *golah* community lay claim, in varying levels, to three of Yehud's governors (Sheshbazzar, Zerubbabel, and Nehemiah), these individuals and the others in addition to them were validated in their positions by and through the imperial political system and not any religious one. As it is, apart from the propositions of the biblical texts (cf. Hag 1:1; Zech 3:1–10; 6:11–13),[16] there is no compelling evidence that supports high-priestly control over the political institution and systems in Yehud.[17]

Instead, the extra-biblical evidence, as discussed in Chapters 2 and 3, weighs strongly in favor of Persian-appointed governors in Yehud and a lack of autonomy on the part of the province. Any confirmation therefore of the existence of a theocracy in the province depends partly on whether the Persian-period biblical texts are accurate in their social-historical observations—especially in their portrayal of the social roles and functions of the Jerusalem cult and its priesthood. The culture portrayed was not the whole culture of Yehud. As previously noted, one might see a possible parallel between the function of the Maya hieroglyphic inscriptions and the *golah*-oriented biblical texts. On a certain level, both served a propagandistic purpose intended to legitimize claims to land, raw materials, and authority over others.

The following passage from Nehemiah (13:23–31) demonstrates this as Nehemiah, in the text, imposes dramatic boundary lines within the society (seemingly of Jerusalem and its environs [cf. Neh 11:1–36]):

> In those days also I saw Jews who had married women of Ashdod, Ammon, and Moab; and half of their children spoke the language of Ashdod, and they could not speak the language of Judah, but spoke the

16. As Philip R. Davies ("The Intellectual, the Archaeologist and the Bible," in *The Land That I Will Show You: Essays on the History and Archaeology of the Ancient Near East in Honour of J. Maxwell Miller* [ed. J. Andrew Dearman and M. Patrick Graham; Sheffield: Sheffield Academic Press, 2001], 245) notes, the biblical writers presented two cultures within the texts: their monotheistic culture, and the indigenous "fertility religion" culture practiced by those considered outside their group. In other words, the biblical authors projected a very specific face onto the history of Yehud.

17. And even the suggestions of this nature by the Persian-period biblical texts can be easily explained as descriptions of an ideal reality, not one that currently existed. See also the section "Proposed Governing Structure(s) after Nehemiah" in Chapter 3 (p. 109).

language of various peoples. And I contended with them and cursed them and beat some of them and pulled out their hair; and I made them take an oath in the name of God, saying, "You shall not give your daughters to their sons, or take their daughters for your sons or for yourselves. Did not King Solomon of Israel sin on account of such women? Among the many nations there was no king like him, and he was beloved by his God, and God made him king over all Israel; nevertheless, foreign women made even him to sin. Shall we then listen to you and do all this great evil and act treacherously against our God by marrying foreign women?" And one of the sons of Jehoiada, son of the high priest Eliashib, was the son-in-law of Sanballat the Horonite; I chased him away from me. Remember them, O my God, because they have defiled the priesthood, the covenant of the priests and the Levites. Thus I cleansed them from everything foreign, and I established the duties of the priests and Levites, each in his work; and I provided for the wood offering, at appointed times, and for the first fruits.

There is reason to be skeptical of the presentation of not only Yahwism but also of Yehud that the biblical texts give.[18] For instance, they tend to ignore the governors and other officials in Yehud though the extra-biblical evidence tells us they existed (cf. AP 30/31 [regarding Bagohi]; see also Table 2, p. 90). Moreover, their discussion of Yehud's political systems is almost entirely absent. Neither are they entirely concerned with the economic systems of the province. They say next to nothing about how Yehud met the imperial requirements that the empire imposed upon its territories, such as taxes and corvée labor.[19] Nehemiah (5:4–12)

18. Against the portrayal of the reality of Yahwism, as monolithic, given by the biblical texts, for example, the archaeological evidence from Wadi ed-Daliyeh, Elephantine, āl-Yāhūdu, Ashdod, Galilee, Gaza, and Idumea demonstrate that Yahwism existed throughout the general area, and not Jerusalem alone. The biblical texts, however, argue that Jerusalem was the central authority of Yahwism. For the archaeological evidence referred to, see Beit-Arieh, "Edomites Advance into Judah," 28–36; Cross, "Papyri of the Fourth Century," 22–26; Eph'al, "Changes in Palestine," 110, 111, 114; Leith, "Israel among the Nations," 367–419; Lemaire, *Histoire et Administration*, 30, 40–41; ibid., "Épigraphie et Religion," 11, 99, 110–11; Naveh, "Aramaic Ostraca," 49–53. See also the discussions of related evidence in Briend, "L'édit de Cyrus," 33–44; Cross, "Discovery of the Samaria Papyri," 110–21; Freyne, *Galilee from Alexander the Great to Hadrian*, 24–25; Gropp, *Samaria Papyri*; Kaptan, *The Daskyleion Bullae*; Kraeling, *Brooklyn Museum Papyri*; Leith, *Wadi Daliyeh Seal Impressions*; Naveh, "An Aramaic Ostracon," 200–201; ibid., "Published and Unpublished Aramaic Ostraca," 114–21; Pearce, "New Evidence," 399–411; Porten, "Religion of the Jews," 116–21; Porten and Yardeni, "Ostracon Clermont-Ganneau 125 (?)," 451–56.

19. Darius's inscription at Susa (DSf lines 28–30) mentions that the imperial government used a temple workforce from Babylonia as corvée labor. See also the discussion of imperial requirements of provinces (e.g. taxes) in Chapter 2.

mentions a concern for the debtor practices of the community, but the concern, if it is valid beyond being strictly textual, is religiously motivated and comprises only a minute part of a larger economic system. Nehemiah's abstention from the governor's tax (Neh 5:13–16) is more self-aggrandizing than useful for our understanding of the economic setting of Yehud. We are left without any evidence that any religious "institution" in Yehud (particularly of the *golah* Yahwistic cult) controlled the social, economic, and political realms.

Based on the evidence discussed in Chapter 2, it is also unlikely that the imperial government granted autonomy to the province of Yehud or the city of Jerusalem.[20] That is a gesture that is so far without precedent in the history of the Persian empire.[21] Just as some of the Babylonian priests and scribes claimed that Cyrus was the chosen of Marduk (cf. the Cyrus Cylinder), so some of the Jewish scribes claimed the same of Cyrus under Yahweh (cf. Ezra 1:1–8; Isa 44:28; 45:1, 13):

> Marduk [   ] turned (?) towards all the habitations that were abandoned and all the people of Sumer and Akkad who had become corpses; [he was recon]ciled and had mercy (upon them). He surveyed and looked throughout all the lands, searching for a righteous king whom he would support. He called out his name: Cyrus, king of Anshan; he pronounced his name to be king over all (the world). He (Marduk) made the land of Gutium and all the Umman-manda bow in submission at his feet. And he (Cyrus) shepherded with justice and rightouesness all the black-headed people, over whom he (Marduk) had given him victory. Marduk, the great lord, guardian (?) of his people, looked with gladness upon his good deeds and upright heart. He ordered him to march to his city Babylon. He set him on the road to Babylon and like a companion and friend, he went at his side. His vast army, whose number, like the water of the river, cannot be known, marched at his side fully armed. He made him enter his city Babylon without fighting or battle; he saved Babylon from hardship. He delivered Nabonidus, the king who did not revere him, into his hands. All the people of Babylon, all the land of Sumer and Akkad, princes and governors, bowed to him and kissed his feet.[22]

> Thus says the LORD to his anointed, to Cyrus, whose right hand I have grasped to subdue nations before him and strip kings of their robes, to open doors before him—and the gates shall not be closed: I will go before you and level the mountains, I will break in pieces the doors of bronze and cut through the bars of iron, I will give you the treasures of darkness

20. Compare also Torrey (*Chronicler's History*, xxvii) who argues that the central importance of the *golah* community and of the city of Jerusalem were fantasies of the Chronicler.

21. As noted in the discussion of Chapter 2.

22. *COS* 2:315, translation by M. Cogan.

and riches hidden in secret places, so that you may know that it is I, the LORD, the God of Israel, who call you by your name. For the sake of my servant Jacob, and Israel my chosen, I call you by your name, I surname you, though you do not know me. I am the LORD, and there is no other; besides me there is no god. I arm you, though you do not know me, so that they may know, from the rising of the sun and from the west, that there is no one besides me; I am the LORD, and there is no other. I form light and create darkness, I make weal and create woe; I the LORD do all these things. … I have aroused Cyrus in righteousness, and I will make all his paths straight; he shall build my city and set my exiles free, not for price or reward, says the LORD of hosts. (Isa 45:1–7, 13)

These texts are propaganda, used by imperial government and the texts' respective provinces, communities, and cults.[23] The claims made—if they even apply to the situation in Yehud under discussion—do not lend credence to the belief that the imperial government granted political autonomy to its provinces.[24] Rather, the empire's continual struggle against the Greeks and the Egyptians, for related example, illustrates that the empire focused on expanding its borders and increasing its material base, in order to control its territories, not to grant autonomy to conquered areas.[25] Those actions are not consistent with the portrayal of the imperial king as a passive, divine servant.

Temple, Texts, and Politics

An underlying theme throughout the Persian-period biblical texts, as noted in Chapter 3, is the importance and central location of the Jerusalem temple.[26] According to the biblical texts, Yahweh directed world

23. Fried, *Priest and the Great King*, 177–83.

24. For example, there is strong evidence that the Persian imperial government maintained a significant presence in Babylonia (cf. BE 1 33:12; BRM 1 101:5 [as noted by CAD]; *Dar*. 27:3; 338:4, 14; MA 9, 40; PBS 8/2 162:8, 18; 13 64:11). See also Cook, *Persian Empire*, 83; Dandamaev and Lukonin, *Culture and Social Institutions*, 90; Stolper, *Entrepreneurs and Empire*, 58. Also note the New Year's Festival program in *ANET*, 331–34. Herodotus (*Hist.* 3.92, 97) describes the tax system that Darius instituted in Babylonia, which demonstrated that imperial territories were required to provide the empire with material resources.

25. Young ("Consolidation," 71, 78) remarks that the reign of Xerxes marked the end of expansion development for the Persian empire: "[T]he whole of Achaemenid history from 479 B.C. onwards could be described as…a holding operation in the face of challenges from rebellious subjects, ambitious satraps and external enemies."

26. E. Stern ("The Religious Revolution in Persian-Period Judah," in Lipschits and Oeming, eds., *Judah and the Judeans in the Persian Period*, 203–4) proposes—in an initial argument—that the inscriptions found on fragments of wine jars, imported by the Babylonian and Egyptian diasporas, demonstrates the authority and

events specifically to bring about the restoration of the temple and the *golah* community;[27] in addition, only the members of the *golah* community, in all its sociological–theological–philosophical nuance and human composition,[28] were the accepted citizens of this society (cf. Ezra 2; Neh 7).[29] The biblical texts often ignore or exclude the existence of those peoples not included in their unique definition of society.[30]

True power was not in the hands of the imperial king, the biblical authors argue following in the tradition of the Deuteronomistic and prophetic viewpoints, but it was in the hands of Yahweh, who directed

centrality of the Jerusalem temple. Even if it were true that the wine was imported from the region surrounding Jerusalem, this is not evidence of the temple's centrality. In making this argument, would not one also be required to make a similar conclusion of more modern times after recognizing that modern religious groups import for religious purposes olive oil from the "Holy Land"? There may be good reason for the Yahwists in Babylonia and Egypt to want to maintain a traditional connection to Jerusalem—preserved as such through ceremonies and imports—but tradition does not equal authority. The small number of the fragments, furthermore, is itself not enough to demonstrate a widespread practice of importing.

27. On a related issue, Ezra 7:12–26 states that a significant amount of money was given to the Judeans from the imperial storehouses. Lester L. Grabbe ("The 'Persian Documents' in the Book of Ezra: Are They Authentic?," in Lipschits and Oeming, eds., *Judah and the Judeans in the Persian Period*, 554) adds the figures and arrives at about 15 per cent of the annual imperial revenue—a figure, he concludes, that is wholly unrealistic. It would seem, then, that Ezra exaggerates the importance of the *golah* in order to legitimate (within the narrative) the *golah*'s claim to authority.

28. Torrey's remarks about the Chronicler are pertinent here. "His special interests and motives keep cropping out in all contexts. *Foremost among them is his insistence on the true Israel, limited and exclusive.* It is not too much to say that the whole great history, with its endless lists and tables, was planned with Ezra 2:59–63, 4:1–5, and Neh 7:5 definitely in mind. The motives and tendencies which have their clearest expression in the Chronicler's story of the Restoration are in evidence in the earlier part of the history…" (*Chronicler's History*, xi [emphasis mine]). See also Garbini, *History and Ideology*, 126.

29. This tendency is also seen in scholarship. Weinberg ("Das Bēit ʾAbōt"), for example, argues that the *bet abot* structure was the operative infrastructure for all of Yehud (*bet ab* = a social structure, to be sure, but also one that takes on religious intonations in the Persian-period biblical texts). As a biblical example, Ezek 11 claims that Yahweh went into exile with the people, by that classifying the people of Yahweh as those who endured exile from the land.

30. History can tell us that when strong exclusivist ideologies become real social forces, they often result in bloodshed when the select group attempts to pattern a social order after themselves. There is no evidence that this became a real threat in Yehud. While the *golah* community controlled its membership, there is no evidence it controlled the social order.

the imperial king.[31] This claim, however, ignores the broader social world from which the community benefited. Perhaps more importantly, it also misrepresents the agendas and policies of the Persian empire.[32] Texts such as the Behistun Inscription (cf. DB 1:9–17) do not portray an imperial government eager to allow the local inhabitants of its territories to (re)gain their political autonomy. For instance,

> Says Darius the King: Within these countries, the man who was loyal, him I rewarded well; him who was evil, him I punished well; *by the favor of Ahuramazda these countries showed respect toward my law; as was said to them by me, thus it was done.*[33]

When the biblical texts speak of governors and other imperial officials, it is typically within a religious framework—of which Jerusalem and its temple are the center—and with religious vocabulary. For example, Sheshbazzar plays a theologically infused role in the narrative, leading "the return," bringing with himself the Jerusalem temple's utensils (cf. Ezra 1:8, 11; 5:14; see also 1 Esd 2:11–12, 15; 6:18, 20).[34] He was also credited with laying the foundation of the Jerusalem temple (Ezra 5:16). He is the transitional figure, the one through whom the texts link the Judean–Yahwistic past to the present moment of Yehud under the Persian empire.[35] Apart from this theological role, the biblical authors see no need for him.

Other significant figures are Zerubbabel and Joshua. Zerubbabel is claimed to have been from the Davidic line (cf. 1 Chr 3:9–19),[36] and Joshua, from the Zadokite line, is described as the direct descendant of

31. It seems to me that the temple is the central symbol for this claim because it (in idea) embodies the reassurance that Yahweh will maintain the appropriate covenants, giving the *golah* community unarguable claim to the land.

32. See also the section on "Imperial Administration and Governing Officials" in Chapter 2 (p. 37).

33. DB 1:17–19, emphasis mine; translated by Roland G. Kent, *Old Persian Grammar, Texts, Lexicon* (2d ed.; New Haven: American Oriental Society, 1953), 116–34.

34. Grabbe ("The 'Persian Documents'," 546) states that it is unlikely that the Babylonian empire would have preserved and catalogued the temple utensils. While this may have been the case, there is not enough evidence to conclude either way. As an additional note, this return of utensils and exiles seems to me to be presented as a religious procession possibly paralleling the procession to Zion (cf. Ps 24:1–10).

35. In addition, P. Ackroyd (*The Temple Vessels—A Continuity Theme: Studies in the Religion of Ancient Israel* [VTSup 23; Leiden: Brill, 1972], 172–80) argues that the giving of utensils to Sheshbazzar connects the second temple to the first.

36. While both link Zerubbabel to David, the Chronicler and Haggai appear to differ on whose son he is. Compare 1 Chr 3:17–19 and Hag 1:12.

the last high priests of the first Jerusalem temple.[37] In this sense, Zerubbabel is the continuation of the Davidic covenant, and Joshua may symbolically connect the coming second temple to the idealized Solomonic temple. With these two figures, the authors of Haggai and Zechariah bridged (in theory) the temporal gap following the 586 B.C.E. exile (which brought about the destruction of the Jerusalem temple) to show that Yahweh had preserved his chosen people (cf. Hag 1:1, 12, 14; 2:2, 4; Zech 6:9–15). Zerubbabel and Joshua, as noted in Chapter 3, represent not only the ideal positions of authority as hoped for by the authors, they also represent what the authors believed to be the manifestation of a prophetic fulfillment in progress: Yahweh did not abandon his people—a people whose membership was strictly regulated in Ezra–Nehemiah.[38]

In the world described by the Persian-period biblical texts, the problems with the governing structure(s) highlighted in this investigation seem to fade away. One might even be caught up in the crescendo of what seem to be theocratic aspirations. These texts proclaim that one need not look for any social or political evolution because Yahweh stirred up people and systems to produce the appropriate society (cf. Hag 1:14–15). This was no earthly evolution but divine creation! The seed of David and the high priest built the altar, began the foundation of the temple, and led the people in the Festival of Booths (Ezra 3:2–11).[39] A learned Yahwistic scribe—also a priest according to Neh 8:9; 12:26— was appointed by the Persian government to establish the law of the land (Ezra 7:1–28). The "cupbearer" (Nehemiah) of the Persian emperor rebuilt the walls of the holy city, restructured the cult and its priesthood, and, along with Ezra, purified the community of foreign elements (Neh 2:17–3:32; 13:1–31). Everything prefaced what the authors believed was to come: Yahweh's ultimate intent was the glorification of a religiously defined body and its installation as a national kingdom with an international presence.[40] All of that, however, describes an ideal reality, not one

37. On the matter of Joshua and his lineage, see VanderKam, *From Joshua to Caiaphas*, 18–42. For further reference, note that Zadok was appointed high priest by Solomon, according to 1 Kgs 2:35.

38. See also the discussion in the section "Zerubbabel and Joshua: A Diarchy?" in Chapter 3 (p. 95).

39. Thus, Sheshbazzar is not the only individual credited with laying foundations of the temple (compare Ezra 5:16).

40. For instance, see Deut 27:1–11; Neh 1:7–11. With Deut 27:4–8 one might compare Ezra 3:2–3 concerning the building of an altar. Furthermore, what is not being proposed here is that the Judean nation ever was a world leader; instead, the authors believed that the nation was a world authority and that Yahweh intended for it to be so again.

that existed during the Persian period.[41] The biblical obsession with the temple forgoes any attention to the immediate realities of the social, economic, and political realms. What we seem to have, then, are cultic texts concerned with cultic aspirations. It is interesting that in the case studies revealing theocracies, the focus of those involved was not so much on centralizing a religion as it was on establishing control over the very realms that the biblical texts seem to neglect.

Furthermore, the Jerusalem temple was not the only temple to receive imperial attention.[42] Where this attention was given—and where we have documentation of this—the temple complexes (lands, buildings, people, etc.) were considered commodities by the imperial government. The *Demotic Chronicle* offers further confirmation of the authority of the imperial government over local temples. According to this chronicle, Cambyses displayed the Persian king's power over the temples in Egypt by substantially cutting their allotted portions of income and supplies.[43] Darius later restored the portions of the temples and took a more conciliatory attitude toward the cults.[44] One finds further evidence in the archival text of Darius at Susa, which tells of the imperial government calling up a temple workforce from Babylon to serve as corvée labor (cf. DSf lines 28–30).[45] In addition, Darius commanded Udjahorresnet to (re)furnish the Temple of Neith (cf. Udjahorresnet's inscription, line 45) after it failed to receive resources from Cambyses.[46] At no point do we see actions that suggest an imperial policy or tendency granting political autonomy to local temples. From this evidence, it appears that the economic well-beings of various temples were partly dependent upon policies of the imperial government.

41. I discussed in more detail the Persian-period biblical texts as describing an ideal reality throughout Chapter 3.

42. I have also addressed this in Chapter 2.

43. Cook, *Persian Empire*, 49. Cook notes that one need ask no further why Cambyses's memory was damned in Egypt.

44. Ibid. See also Udjahorresnet's inscription, line 45.

45. Kent, *Old Persian Grammar*, 142–44. Note also Briant, *From Cyrus to Alexander*, 401–402. The practice of corvée labor is further evidenced in the *urāšu* officials from the Murašû archive (cf. MA, nos. 9, 40; MS, no. 59).

46. See also Fried, *Priest and the Great King*, 68–74; Lichtheim, *Ancient Egyptian Literature*, 3:38–40. A letter by Yedanyah, from Elephantine, states that Cyrus did more than just stop sending resources, "Our ancestors built that temple in Yeb back during the time of the kings of Egypt, and when Cambyses came into Egypt, he found it already built. *They pulled down the temples of the Egyptian gods*, but no one damaged anything in that temple" (AP 30/31 [emphasis mine]).

With that in mind, rebuilding the Jerusalem temple may not only have won favor with the local population, it also served an imperial purpose and agenda.[47] Temples were sometimes included within imperial policies because of their possible benefit to the imperial government. There is evidence that they were used as "banks" and/or locations for melting down and repackaging precious materials such as silver and gold[48]—uses that were somewhat common to the general area.[49] Restored temples throughout Babylonia and Egypt, for comparison, did not secure political authority for their priests.[50] Instead, the temples were important to the Persian imperial government for their use as mechanisms of social control and possibly as custodians of imperial financial interests in their local areas (district or provincial).[51] It is with the imperial government that such concerns begin.

It seems that we can safely say the Jerusalem temple institution did not exist outside imperial control and jurisdiction. Yehud was important to the Persian empire not for its religious value but for the strategic and

47. This conclusion is based on the portrayals of the relationship between the imperial government and temples in, to name a few sources as referenced in CAD [see esp. *zazakku*], ABL 465 r. 4; BE 8 42:1; 10 101.26, 36; TCL 9 136:7; YOS 6 198:10, 238:17. In each of these, the imperial government is portrayed as having direct control over the administration of the temple (i.e. apart from the strictly religious matters).

48. See, for instance, O. Eissfeldt, "Eine einschmelzstelle Am Tempel zu Jerusalem," *Forschungen und Fortschritte* (1937): 163–64 (republished in idem, *Eine einschmelzstelle Am Tempel zu Jerusalem* [Kleine Schriften II; Tübingen: Mohr, 1963], 107–9); Schaper, "Jerusalem Temple," 528–39; idem, "Temple Treasury Committee," 200–206; C. Torrey, "The Foundry of the Second Temple of Jerusalem," *JBL* 55 (1936): 247–60; idem, "The Evolution of a Financier in the Ancient Near East," *JNES* 2 (1943): 295–301.

49. Cf. BE 10 101.26, 36; TCL 9 147:6–7; 12 117:8; YOS 6 224:2; 7 19:19, 59:17, 140:25, 190:17, 198:2; as well as YOS 7 7 i 11 (as noted in CAD [*gitepatu*; PN *ša muḫḫi quppa* ‖ *rēš šarri bēl piqitti*]; Oppenheim, "A Fiscal Practice," 117 [TCL 9 147:607 references]). Note also Fried, *Priest and the Great King*, 41–42; Oppenheim, "A Fiscal Practice," 116–20; Schaper, "Jerusalem Temple," 528–39; ibid., "Temple Treasury Committee," 200–206.

50. So also Fried, *Priest and the Great King*, 8–107 (106–7).

51. M. Dandamaev, *A Political History of the Achaemenid Empire* (Leiden: E. J. Brill, 1989), 362–66; Hornblower, *Mausolus*, 161–63; Leith, "Israel among the Nations," 379, 96–97; Schaper, "Jerusalem Temple," 528–39; ibid., "Temple Treasury Committee," 200–206; Christopher Tuplin, "The Administration of the Achaemenid Empire," in *Coinage and Administration in the Athenian and Persian Empires: The Ninth Oxford Symposium on Coinage and Monetary History* (ed. Ian Carradice; Oxford: Oxford University Press, 1987), 149–53.

financial purposes it could offer, among other social, political, and economic reasons.[52] It also seems most probable that the imperial government did not intend Nehemiah, for instance, to carry out a *golah*-focused religious agenda but to establish an inland fortress (cf. Neh 2:8)[53] and to set up a financial administration—activities that were part of his function as governor. Nehemiah's focus on other strategic, economic, and social reforms—if it is portrayed accurately—does not reflect his religious alignment but conforms to a pattern of transforming the empire–province relationship.[54] To be sure, more social-political activity took place within the province than what the *golah*-oriented biblical texts portray. Concern for the political and economic stability as well the defense of the empire itself was behind the imperial actions within the empire's provinces.[55] Nevertheless, the authors of the biblical texts do not favor this use or depiction of their temple. Deutero-Isaiah may have set the stage when he claimed that Cyrus was the מְשִׁיחַ (Isa 45:1) and Yahweh's designee to subdue kings and restore the people of Yahweh.[56] While Cyrus, if he was aware of it, may have used Isaiah's description of himself to his advantage—political propaganda similar to that found in Babylonia on the Cyrus Cylinder[57]—he did not intentionally establish his empire,

52. Hoglund, *Achaemenid Imperial Administration*, 243.

53. See also Fried, *Priest and the Great King*, 193–200.

54. So also Hoglund, *Achaemenid Imperial Administration*, 243.

55. Smith (*Palestinian Parties*, 62) writes that the royal patronage of the cult of Yahweh ended with the Assyrian and Babylonian conquests. The belief of the texts, that Yahweh called Cyrus to do his will, may be an attempt by the authors and redactors to maintain royal patronage of the court in some manner.

56. Josephus even has Cyrus believing himself to be the fulfillment of Deutero-Isaiah's prophecy (*Ant.* 11.5–6).

57. Fried (*Priest and the Great King*, 179–83), referring to Isaiah's designation of Cyrus as the messiah (cf. Isa 45:1), states that the servant songs in Isaiah reveal a *quid pro quo* between Cyrus and Deutero-Isaiah (who seems to represent the Babylonian Jews). On the other hand, the Cyrus Cylinder makes no reference to Yehud, Jerusalem, or the Jerusalem temple. There is a small section in which these might have been very generally included (but note the focus remains primarily on Babylonia and its gods and temples). It states, "By his exalted [word], all the kings who sit upon thrones throughout the world, from the Upper Sea to the Lower Sea, who live in the dis[tricts far-off], the kings of the West, who dwell in tents, all of them brought their heavy tribute before me and in Babylon they kissed my feet. From [Ninev]eh (?), Ashur and Susa, Agade, Eshnunna, Zamban, Meturnu, Der, as far as the region of Gutium, I returned the (images of) the gods to the sacred centers [on the other side of] the Tigris whose sanctuaries had been abandoned for a long time, and I let them dwell in eternal abodes. I gathered all their inhabitants and returned (to them) their dwellings" (*COS* 2:315, translation by M. Cogan).

contrary to Isaiah's claim, to benefit the "people of Yahweh."[58] Should such descriptions have been written by the political-religious authority, like Khomeini and his followers in Iran, which in this case would have been Cyrus and the imperial government, the descriptions would have read differently.

Deutero-Isaiah stated that the Persian ruler expanded his territories, prompted by a religious motivation and a concern brought on by Yahweh (cf. Isa 44:28; 45:1, 13). Yet the religious ideologies of the texts do not account for the broader concerns of the province. They define Yehud according to what might be described as a *golah* theology (cf. Zech 2:1–13) and not as an imperial province of the Persian empire. Yet Yehud functioned politically as a province, perhaps even socially, defined on many levels by the Persian empire's administrative framework and policies.[59] The Persian-period biblical texts, in their failure to present accurately the social and political realities of the province, cannot be accepted as evidence for a theocracy in Yehud. They describe not the realities of government but an idealized restoration of a nation governed by Yahweh. For this reason, if we label Yehud a theocracy, we do so based on biblical ideologies alone. Yet such a definition is inadequate. One finds a contrast for this portrayal of Yehud in the case study of Medina. There a theocracy developed on a fundamental concern for the social, economic, and political infrastructure of the community. On the other hand, the biblical texts make dramatic religious claims about a much-narrowed view of the state of things (confined primarily to Jerusalem) and generally ignore the social, economic, and political realms entirely.

Provincial Law and the Political Order

There is some suggestion that the imperially appointed satraps had some authority over local temples.[60] Cook, for instance, writes,

> The satrap in Egypt was also made responsible on the King's behalf for ensuring that candidates for appointment as temple superintendants were

58. As a point of interest, Fried (*Priest and the Great King*, 182) states that Xenophon (*Oec.* 4.8) suggests that Cyrus may have permitted the Jews to return because the emperor abhorred uncultivated land.

59. Even if one does not agree with his conclusion that Ezra brought a version of Pentateuchal law to Yehud, Berquist's suggestion mentioned above (*Judaism in Persia's Shadow*, 134–39) that the Persian imperial government controlled symbolic power in the empire is pertinent here.

60. Cook, *Persian Empire*, 71; Fried, *Priest and the Great King*, 106–7.

suitable; a missive in demotic from the satrap Farnadata to the priests of Khnum refers to Darius' orders and shows that confirmation of the priests' choice was not a mere formality. One temple superintendant was actually dismissed at El Hibeh in 513 B.C.[61]

One learns from Ezra–Nehemiah that Sheshbazzar (Ezra 5:14; see also 1 Esd 2:12; 6:20), Zerubbabel (Neh 12:47), some unnamed predecessors (Neh 5:15), and Nehemiah (Neh 8:9; 10:1; 12:26) were governors. Including extra-biblical evidence of bullae and seals, Elnathan, Yeho-ʿezer, Ahzai, Bagohi, and Yehezqiyau are included in the list of Yehud's governors.[62] Based on this evidence, and on the discussions from the previous chapters (esp. Chapters 2 and 3), it is difficult to see how the leaders of the Jerusalem cult (members of the *golah* community) could have redefined the entire judicial system of the province according to their version of Yahwistic religious law. There is no evidence that these were able to gain control over the political realm of the province.

Ezra 7:25–26 might be interpreted as a commission to establish Yahwistic law as the law of the land. Should that be true, then the introduction of this law might suggest a possible theocracy for Yehud. Yet the phrase "law of the king" within the passage implies that the imperial law was the parameter within which any local must fit.[63] For this reason, Berquist's suggestion that Persian imperial desires for a harmonious and integrated society were given mythic-religious dimensions within Pentateuchal law is possible though not certain:[64]

> Perhaps the best example of the ritual construction of reality was Ezra's public reading of the law. This brought the Persian-canonized Pentateuchal law into the public mind, thus shifting the ideological basis for activity. The public reading also formed the conception of power groups within Yehud, because it was the public event that sacralized the presence of the elders who came to run Yehud. By equating the law of God and the law of the emperor, Ezra encouraged allegiance to Persia.[65]

Bearing in mind that scholars generally accept that the Persian imperial government incorporated local laws into an imperial law, Berquist's suggestion seems to require one to accept that a relatively new law was

---

61. Cook, *Persian Empire*, 71. Again, see also P. Berlin 13540, 13572, 13582, for additional reference. In P. Berlin 13540, Pherendates, satrap of Egypt, dismisses two candidates for Lesonis (priest), who, as Fried (*Priest and the Great King*, 81) notes, provided an accounting of temple finances (from 3 years) to the satrap.
62. See again also Table 2, p. 90.
63. See also Briant, *From Cyrus to Alexander*, 510–11, 956–57.
64. Berquist, *Judaism in Persia's Shadow*, 139.
65. Ibid., 143.

introduced in Yehud, if indeed this Pentateuchal law was the handiwork of the *golah* community and its leaders. One can also say that if Ezra, whose existence remains debated,[66] was given permission or freedom by the imperial government to establish a theocracy,[67] this permission would have been unique in the Persian empire.[68] As shown in Chapter 2, the imperial administrative system was composed of satraps, governors, and judges, and son on, who, while making allowances for local customs, governed and arbitrated under the authority of and within the parameters of imperial law. The imperial government ultimately set the basis for law and politics within the empire.

A passage from Herodotus (*Hist.* 3.31) demonstrates that the imperial government maintained control over the judicial system:

> The royal judges are a picked body of men among the Persians, who hold office till death or till some injustice is detected in them. This is the only limitation on their term of office. They judge suits among the Persians and are the interpreters of the ancestral statutes, and everything is referred to them.

Porten's description of the general (imperial) judicial system in Elephantine offers further aspects:

> "Judges" appeared regularly in the contracts as one of the three parties before whom a complainant might bring a suit or register a complaint, the other two being lord and prefect (*TAD* B2.3:13, 24; B3.1:13, 19; B3.2:6; B3.12:28; B4.6:14; B7.1:13). In a case involving an inheritance they are called "judges of the king" [i.e. royal judges] (*TAD* B5.1:13) and in a petition seeking redress of grievances they are "judges of the province" (*TAD* A5.2:4, 7). When named, they were always Persian—Pisina (*TAD* A3.8:2), Bagadana (*TAD* A6.1:5–6), Damidata (*TAD* B2.2:6), Bagafarna and Nafaina (*TAD* A5.2:6)—and once Babylonian—Mannuki.[69]

---

66. For example, Clines, *Ezra, Nehemiah and Esther*, 10–16; Grabbe, "The 'Persian Documents'," 554; Myers, *Ezra, Nehemiah*, 57–63; Rudolph, *Esra und Nehemia*, 73–77; Williamson, *Ezra, Nehemiah*, 97–105.

67. To be clear, Berquist does not argue that Yehud was a theocracy. I am merely using his suggestion to move back into the larger discussion of this investigation.

68. Garbini (*Myth and History*, 110) states that instead of being interpreted literally, the actions of Ezra should be read as later allegorical creations by scribes who sought to account for the fundamental division between the teachers of the Law and the priests during the Hellenistic period. He finds no evidence within the written materials for the person of Ezra. Compare Grabbe ("The 'Persian Documents'," 532–33) with Ahlström (*The History of Ancient Palestine*, 888).

69. B. Porten, *The Elephantine Papyri in English: Three Millennia of Cross-Cultural Continuity and Change* (Documenta et Monumenta Orientis Antiqui 22; Leiden: Brill, 1996), 136 n. 19. As quoted by Fried, *Priest and the Great King*, 92.

Here we have a glimpse of what might be considered a general frame-work of the Persian empire's judicial system. Furthermore, the various discussions of the *dātabaru* official (cf. BE 9 83:18, 84:11; PBS 2/1 1:14, 34:13, 185:15 [also Persian **dātabara-* in PF 1272]) also confirm the imperial function of judges within the Persian empire. Judges within the empire, to be clear, were appointed by the imperial government and it was to that government, not local temples or religious law codes, that they were ultimately responsible.

Regarding the judicial system in Yehud (possibly even *eber-nahara[h]*), Ezra 7:25 states,

> And you, Ezra, according to the God-given wisdom you possess, appoint magistrates and judges who may judge all the people in the province Beyond the River who know the laws of your God; and you shall teach those who do not know them.

Would these magistrates and judges have been any different from those appointed throughout the empire?[70] Perhaps Fried says it best:

> If Ezra 7:25–26 was part of a genuine commission from the Persian king Artaxerxes to a person named Ezra...then Ezra's assignment...was to appoint judges and magistrates. Like the ones in Egypt, they would have been Iranian and would have judged first according to the *dāta* of the king and his representatives (the satrap or governor) and second accord-ing to the *dāta* of the god. The former term refers to positive law, created by edict. The latter term refers to "natural" law. Judges would not have judged according to a law code; the law collections were not *codes* in the modern sense. Rather, they would have made their decisions according to their socially constructed concepts of right, fairness, and justice. These would necessarily be Persian concepts—not Jewish![71]

Concluding Remarks

By restoring peoples exiled from their lands by the Babylonians (and probably even the Assyrians),[72] Cyrus created a social-economic base that was, in theory, less likely to make trouble in paying taxes or fulfilling

---

70. Fried suggests that these appointees also served as the "eyes and ears" of the king. "That judges would be chosen directly by the king (or his agent) rather than by the satrap is reminiscent of Xenophon's remark on the installation of local garrison commanders. These were chosen directly by the king as well, not by the satrap. The garrison commanders were appointed directly by the king (or his agent) so that they would serve as 'eyes and ears' of the king within the satrapy. It appears the same function is attested here for the royal judges" (*Priest and the Great King*, 217 n. 26).

71. Ibid., 220.

72. *ANET*, 316; *COS* 2:315.

other obligations. It was for its own benefit that the imperial government permitted the *golah* community, among innumerable others, to return and eventually allowed the community to rebuild the Jerusalem temple.[73]

While the Jerusalem temple served an obvious religious function for a particular (local) cult, the Persian empire had a pattern of using temples for imperial reasons apart from religion.[74] And although the text of Ezra–Nehemiah rejects any claim or access to the temple by peoples outside the *golah* community (cf. Ezra 4:1–3; Neh 10:28–39), Persian-appointed officials administrated temples throughout the Persian empire,[75] and it is likely that the same was true for Yehud. Consequently, though one may conclude that provinces and satrapies ran finances through the temples, one should not conclude that the temples ran their respective provinces; the king's appointees represented imperial authority over the temples.[76] There is no reason to assume that what was true for temples in Babylonia and Egypt was not also true for the temple(s) in Yehud.

Was Yehud a Theocracy?

As defined, a theocracy is principally a social-political context governed by a dominant religious institution or administrative authority that, by virtue of its control over government, holds authority over and administers the social, economic, and political spheres or realms of a society. This authority is not a superficial connection—as one can make through various religious-ideological statements or ceremonies—but is deep-rooted within the social, economic, and political realms of a society and is, as a result, legitimated by that society. Moreover, there is no clear distinction between religious law and law (see below).

---

73. It is possible (though speculative to a large part) that, as Xenophon suggests, the imperial government restored peoples to "cultivate" the land (*Oec.* 4.8).

74. The temple, according to Ahlström (*The History of Ancient Palestine*, 841–42, 847), displayed imperial authority in the province. Moreover, he states that the temple was a moneymaking venture bound to the economics of the empire because it remained under the authority of imperial law.

75. Ibid., 849–50; Fried, *Priest and the Great King*, 32–33, 106. See also P. Berlin 13540, 13572, 13582.

76. Such as the *zazakku* official (cf. YOS 6 198:10, 238:17; BE 8 42:1; TCL 9 136:7 [as cited in CAD]), the *rēš šarri bēl piqitti* (cf, YOS 6 224:2; 7 19:19, 59:17, 140:25, 190:17, 198:2; TCL 9 147:6–7; 12 117:8; *Dar.* 216:3; *I.Cyr.* 271:14; CT 22.131.10–11 [as cited in CAD; Oppenheim, "A Fiscal Practice," 117 [CT 22.131.10–11 and TCL 9 147:607 references]), the *gitepatu* (Persian = * *gaθupati-*) official (cf. BE 10.101.26, 36 [see also Torrey, "The Evolution," 299]), and possibly, by extension, the יוֹצֵר official (cf. Zech 11:13; Lam 4:2; Isa 30:14; compare *Hist.* 3.96]). Regarding the יוֹצֵר official, see also Torrey, "The Evolution," 299.

What was true for much of the Persian empire, that the imperial government maintained a careful eye over its territories, that it appointed and monitored officials in the administrative system, at even the provincial and district levels, appears to have been true for Yehud. Furthermore, as previously discussed, there is no evidence that the high priests in Jerusalem, as the authorities of the Yahwistic religious institution in the city, became authorities over the social or political realms; there is also no clear evidence that these were the authorities over the whole of the religious realm in the province.

In addition, while we may know some of the basic elements of the economy—grain, wine, oil, trade, and so on.[77]—there is not enough evidence to conclude definitively regarding any authority. What appears from the text of Nehemiah is that the imperial tax system was operational in Yehud (cf. Neh 5:4–15). This would suggest some level of imperial influence in the economic system. Concerning the political realm, it is clear that imperially appointed administrative officials governed and administered the province.[78] No power or political vacuum existed in Yehud, allowing the priesthood to claim power.[79] And of the social realm more generally, there is no evidence that the Yahwistic religious authorities in Jerusalem exercised authority over social interactions and systems in the province. On the other hand, it seems apparent from Ezra–Nehemiah that the imperially appointed governor was able to dictate various social norms and policies.[80] It is still highly questionable that the local law of the province was in fact a Yahwistic religious law or that the provincial law was defined and legitimated by a dominant religious institution or authority. This last is important because in a theocracy no clear distinction between religious law and civic or political law exists; the fundamental, ideological basis for virtually all law is situated in the divine authentication of the religious institution and authority. Additionally, from the comparative evidence of judges and other officials (e.g. satraps and governors) appointed by and answerable to the imperial government, and as even suggested by the text of Ezra (7:25–26), law within province appears to have functioned within the framework of an imperial system. When all of these factors are taken together, when theocracy is recognized as a system of government, one is left with the obvious conclusion that Yehud was not a theocracy during the Persian period.

77. Cf. Carter, *Emergence of Yehud*, 250–56.
78. As noted above and in Chapters 2 and 3.
79. Fried, *Priest and the Great King*, 183; VanderKam, *From Joshua to Caiaphas*, 110–11.
80. As noted above and in Chapter 3.

Of the case studies earlier in this investigation, Yehud finds its closest parallels in Classic Maya and Geneva, which were not theocracies in part because the religious institution was not a social-political authority and did not govern over the social, economic, and political realms. In those locations, religious texts and ceremonies were used as propaganda or vehicles for social protest. The Persian-period biblical texts, as we have discussed them, seem to fit most comfortably in either or both of those roles. Certainly, the *golah*-Yahwistic religion and its institutional body had a place in the society of Yehud, but it was not a place of governing authority.

A Representative Theocracy in Yehud?

To this point, I have addressed whether or not Yehud was a theocracy in the full sense of the term. The conclusion, clearly, is that it was not. Yet what about a representative theocracy, as defined by Assmann? As noted in Chapter 4, Assmann states that in a representative theocracy the priests function as rulers and priests. Furthermore, a representative theocracy does not compete with an earthly kingdom but forms the kingdom's "condition" when the governing structure absorbs metaphors and models of the divine–human relationship. Since Assmann has already differentiated his representative theocracy from what he terms a "direct" theocracy, one does not need to pursue how a representative theocracy fails to meet the necessary criteria for a proper theocracy. As discussed in Chapter 3 and in this chapter above, there is no evidence that the priests functioned as political leaders in Yehud. In fact, there is no certainty that they even "ruled" over all Yahwists in the province.

When Assmann states that a representative theocracy forms a polity's "condition," he seems to be describing the superstructure. Because the theocracy does not "compete with the kingdom" it defines the ideological legitimation for functions and systems at work in the social order—even if those functions and systems are more characteristic of a monarchy (or other polity). The social-political context in Yehud hardly meets even this particular criterion for a representative theocracy. This criterion requires one to assume that the viewpoints expressed in the biblical texts were in fact those socially legitimated by the entire province and even the imperial government by extension. Yet, as this investigation has shown, the texts were the products of a specific minority and were focused on justifying that minority's claims to rights of authority. Beyond that, however, there is no direct evidence that these texts had any influence over the laws, politics, education, and so on, of the province in order to promote the ideology of the texts as being culturally dominant.

Avenues of Further Research

From this investigation, there are important avenues of further research:

One such avenue would focus on the nature of the Persian imperial government's control over the various symbolic powers of societies throughout its empire. There is still a need for scholars to gain a better perspective on the relationship between the Persian empire and its provinces. I foresee that this would help scholars better place, for example, the biblical texts into a proper social-political perspective.[81]

A more extensive cross-cultural comparison of Yahwists from Samerina, Babylonian āl-Yāhūdu, Elephantine, Yehud, and other areas (e.g. Lachish and surrounding territories) would be of significant benefit, where the currently available evidence allows for it. The investigator might invoke social-scientific case studies addressing how religion aided in identity formation. In addition, strong cross-cultural comparisons of the governing systems and structures of the provinces and satrapies in the Levantine area would be fruitful.

A final related but more focused investigation would be one that sought out the common elements of jurisprudence or judicial systems in the provinces of the Persian empire. This would be of benefit not only to the scholar of Yehud but to scholars focusing on other areas that fell under the jurisdiction of the Persian imperial government. The scholar of Yehud could extend the previous investigation by including a social-scientific analysis of the *golah* community and the *am ha'aretz*. This analysis might focus on whether or not issues of jurisprudence were affected by the social division (and whether or not this division, as suggested to us by the biblical texts, existed as a factor in the social-political context of Yehud). Certainly, these areas have been touched upon in this investigation but they are worthy in their own right of further sustained discussions.

81. As noted above, Berquist has offered initial comments on this topic. I am suggesting a further, more sustained and focused discussion.

BIBLIOGRAPHY

Abrahamian, Ervand. *The Iranian Mojahedin*. New Haven: Yale University Press, 1989.
———. *Khomeinism: Essays on the Islamic Republic*. Berkeley: University of California Press, 1993.
———. "The Making of the Modern Iranian State." Pages 693–719 in *Comparative Politics at the Crossroads*. Edited by Mark Kesselman, Joel Krieger, and William A. Joseph. Lexington, Mass.: D. C. Heath & Co., 1995.
Ackroyd, Peter R. *Exile and Resoration: A Study of Hebrew Thought of the Sixth Century B.C.* Old Testament Library. Philadelphia: Westminster, 1968.
———. *The Temple Vessels—A Continuity Theme Studies in the Religion of Ancient Israel*. Supplements to Vetus Testamentum 23. Leiden: Brill, 1972.
Adams, Robert McCormick. *The Evolution of Urban Society: Early Mesopotamia and Prehispanic Mexico*. New Brunswick: AldineTransaction, 2005.
Aharoni, Yohanan. *Investigations at Lachish: The Sanctuary and the Residency (Lachish V)*. Publications of the Institute of Archaeology 4. Tel Aviv: Gateway, 1975.
Ahlström, Gösta W. *The History of Ancient Palestine*. Minneapolis: Fortress, 1993.
Alt, Albrecht. *Judas Nachbarn zur Zeit Nehemia*. Kleine Schriften zur Geschichte des Volkes Israel 2. Munich: Beck, 1953.
———. "Die Landnahme der Israeliten in Palästina." Pages 89–125 in *Kleine Schriften zur Geschichte des Volkes Israel*. Edited by Albrecht Alt. Munich: Beck, 1953.
———. "Die Rolle Samarias bei der Entstehung des Judentums." Pages 5–28 in *Festschrift Otto Procksch zum Sechzigsten Geburtstag*. Edited by Albrecht Alt. Leipzig: A. Deichert & J. C. Hinrichs, 1934.
———. *Die Rolle Samarias bei der Entstehung des Judentums*. Edited by Albrecht Alt. Kleine Schriften zur Geschichte des Volkes Israel 2. Munich: Beck, 1953.
Amjad, Mohammed. *Iran: From Royal Dictatorship to Theocracy*. New York: Greenwood, 1989.
Amuzegar, Jahangir. *The Dynamics of the Iranian Revolution*. Albany: State University of New York Press, 1991.
Andersen, Francis I. "Who Built the Second Temple?" *Australian Biblical Review* 6 (1958): 1–35.
Armstrong, Karen. *Islam: A Short History*. Modern Library ed. Modern Library Chronicles. New York: Modern Library, 2000.
Ashmore, Wendy. "Classic Maya Landscapes and Settlement." Pages 169–91 in Hendon and Joyce, eds., *Mesoamerican Archaeology*.
———. "Monumentos políticos: Sitio asentamiento, y paisaje alrededor de Xunantunich, Belice." Pages 161–83 in *Anatomía de una civilización: Aproximaciones inter-disciplinarias a la cultura Maya*. Edited by A. Ciudad Ruiz, Y. Fernández Marquínez, Ma. J. I. Ponce de León, A. L. García-Gallo, and L. T. Sanz Castro. Madrid: Sociedad Española de Estudios Mayas, 1998.

————. "Site-Planning and Concepts of Directionality among the Ancient Maya." *Latin American Antiquity* 2 (1991): 199–226.

Ashraf, A. "Charisma, Theocracy, and Men of Power in Postrevolutionary Iran." Pages 101–55 in *The Politics of Social Transformation in Afghanistan, Iran, and Pakistan*. Edited by Myron Weiner and Ali Banuazizi. Syracuse: Syracuse University Press, 1994.

Assmann, Jan. *Herrschaft und Heil: politische Theologie in Altägypten, Israel und Europa*. Munich: Carl Hanser Verlag, 2000.

————. *The Mind of Egypt: History and Meaning in the Time of the Pharaohs*. Translated by Andrew Jenkins. New York: Metropolitan, 2002.

Austin, M. M. "Greek Tyrants and the Persians, 546–479 B.C." *Classical Quarterly* 40 (1990): 289–306.

Avigad, Nahman. *Bullae and Seals from a Post-Exilic Judean Archive*. Qedem 4. Jerusalem: Hebrew University, 1976.

————. "A New Class of Yehud Stamps." *Israel Exploration Journal* 7 (1957): 146–53.

————. "Two Hebrew Inscriptions on Wine-Jars." *Israel Exploration Journal* 22 (1972): 1–9.

Avigad, Nahman, and Benjamin Sass. *Corpus of West Semitic Stamp Seals*. Jerusalem: Israel Academy of Sciences and Humanities, Israel Exploration Society, and Institute of Archaeology, Hebrew University, 1997.

Balcer, Jack Martin. "The Athenian Episkopos and the Achaemenid 'King's Eye'." *The American Journal of Philology* 98 (1977): 252–63.

————. *Sparda by the Bitter Sea: Imperial Interaction in Western Anatolia*. Brown Judaic Studies 52. Chico, Calif.: Scholars Press, 1984.

Barag, Dan P. "The Effects of the Tennes Rebellion on Palestine." *Bulletin of the American Schools of Oriental Research* 183 (1966): 6–12.

————. "A Silver Coin of Yohanan the High Priest and the Coinage of Judea in the Fourth Century B.C." *Israel Numismatic Journal* 9 (1986): 4–21.

————. "Some Notes on a Silver Coin of Johanan the High Priest." *Biblical Archaeologist* 48 (1985): 166–68.

Barclay, John M. G. "The Politics of Contempt: Judeans and Egyptians in Josephus' *Against Apion*." Pages 109–27 in *Negotiating Diaspora Jewish Strategies in the Roman Empire*. Edited by John M. G. Barclay. Library of Second Temple Studies 45. London: T&T Clark, 2004.

Barstad, Hans M. "After the 'Myth of the Empty Land': Major Challenges in the Study of Neo-Babylonian Judah." Pages 3–20 in Lipschits and Blenkinsopp, eds., *Judah and the Judeans in the Neo-Babylonian Period*.

Bealey, Frank. *The Blackwell Dictionary of Political Science*. Oxford: Blackwell, 1999.

Becking, Bob. "'We All Returned as One!': Critical Notes on the Myth of the Mass Return." Pages 3–18 in Lipschits and Oeming, eds., *Judah and the Judeans in the Persian Period*.

Bedford, Peter R. "Diaspora: Homeland Relations in Ezra–Nehemiah." *Vetus Testamentum* 52 (2001): 147–65.

————. "On Models and Texts: A Response to Blenkinsopp and Peterson." Pages 1:154–62 in Davies, ed., *Second Temple Studies*.

Beit-Arieh, I. "Edomites Advance into Judah." *Biblical Archaeology Review* 22, no. 6 (1996): 28–36.

Bennett, W. J. Jr., and Jeffrey A. Blakely. *Tell El-Hesi: The Persian Period (Stratum V)*. American Schools of Oriental Research. Winona Lake: Eisenbrauns, 1989.

Berezin, Mabel. "Politics and Culture: A Less Fissured Terrain." *Annual Reviews in Sociology* 23 (1997): 361–83.

Berger, Peter L. *The Sacred Canopy: Elements of a Sociological Theory of Religion*. 1967. New York: Anchor Books, 1990.

Berquist, Jon L. "Constructions of Identity in Postcolonial Yehud." Pages 53–66 in Lipschits and Oeming, eds., *Judah and the Judeans in the Persian Period*.

———. *Judaism in Persia's Shadow: A Social and Historical Approach*. Minneapolis: Fortress, 1995.

Betlyon, John W. The Coinage and Mints of Phoenicia: The Pre-Alexandrian Period. Harvard Semitic Monographs 26. Chico, Calif.: Scholars Press, 1980.

———. "The Provincial Government of Persian Period Judea and the Yehud Coins." *Journal of Biblical Literature* 105 (1986): 633–42.

Blenkinsopp, Joseph. *Ezra–Nehemiah*. Old Testament Library. Philadelphia: Fortress, 1988.

———. *A History of Prophecy in Israel*. 2d ed. Louisville: Westminster John Knox, 1996.

———. *Isaiah 56–66: A New Translation with Introduction and Commentary*. New York: Doubleday, 2003.

———. "The Mission of Udjahorresnet and Those of Ezra and Nehemiah." *Journal of Biblical Literature* 106 (1987): 409–21.

Boardman, John, N. G. L. Hammond, D. M. Lewis, and M. Ostwald, eds. *The Cambridge Ancient History*. Vol. 4, *Persia, Greece and the Western Mediterranean, c. 525 to 479 B.C.* Cambridge: Cambridge University Press, 1988.

Bourdieu, Pierre. *The Field of Cultural Production*. Edited and translated by Randal Johnson. New York: Columbia University Press, 1993.

———. *In Other Words: Essays toward a Reflexive Sociology*. Translated by Matthew Adamson. Stanford: Stanford University Press, 1990.

———. *Practical Reason: On the Theory of Action*. Stanford: Stanford University Press, 1998.

Briant, Pierre. *From Cyrus to Alexander: A History of the Persian Empire*. Translated by Peter T. Daniels. Winona Lake: Eisenbrauns, 2002.

———. "L'histoire achéménide: Sources méthodes, raisonnement et modèles." *Topoi* 4 (1994): 109–30.

———. *Histoire de l'Empire perse de Cyrus à Alexandre*. Paris: Librairie Arthème Fayard, 1998.

———. "Pouvoir Central et Polycentrisme Culturel dans l'empire Achemenide." Pages 1–31 in *Achaemenid History*. Vol. 1, *Sources, Structures and Synthesis*. Edited by Heleen Sancisi-Weerdenburg. Leiden: Nederlands Instituute voor het Nabije Oosten, 1987.

———. *Rois, tributs et paysans*, vol. 43.Paris: Centre de recherches d'histoire ancienne, 1982.

Briend, J. "L'édit de Cyrus et sa valeur historique." *Transeu* 11 (1996): 33–44.

Bright, John. *A History of Israel*. 2d ed. Philadelphia: Westminster, 1972.

Bruin, Janet, and Stephen Salaff. "Never Again: The Organization of Women Atomic Bomb Victims in Osaka." *Feminist Studies* 7 (1981): 5–18.

Burns, Gene. "Ideology, Culture, and Ambiguity: The Revolutionary Process in Iran." *Theory and Society* 25 (1996): 349–88.

Campbell, Edward F. "Jewish Shrines of the Hellenistic and Persian Periods." Pages 159–67 in *Symposia Celebrating the Seventy-Fifth Anniversary of the Founding of the American Schools of Oriental Research*. Edited by Frank Moore Cross. Cambridge, Mass.: American Schools of Oriental Research, 1979.

Cancik, Hubert. "Theokratie und Priesterherrschaft: Die mosaische Verfassung bei Flavius Josephus, c. Apionem 2, 157–198." Pages 65–77 in *Theokratie*. Edited by Jacob Taubes. Munich: W. Fink/F. Schöningh, 1987.

Carroll, Robert P. "Ancient Israelite Prophecy and Dissonance Theory." *Numen* 24 (1977): 135–51.

———. "Exile! What Exile? Deportation and the Discourse of Diaspora." Pages 62–79 in Grabbe, ed., *Leading Captivity Captive*.

———. "Twilight of Prophecy or Dawn of Apocalyptic?" *Journal for the Study of the Old Testament* 14 (1979): 3–35.

———. *When Prophecy Failed: Cognitive Dissonance in the Prophetic Traditions of the Old Testament*. New York: Seabury, 1979.

Carter, Charles E. "A Discipline in Transition." Pages 3–36 in *Community, Identity, and Ideology: Social Science Approaches to the Hebrew Bible*. Edited by Charles E. Carter and Carol L. Meyers. Sources for Biblical and Theological Study 6. Winona Lake: Eisenbrauns, 1996.

———. *The Emergence of Yehud in the Persian Period: A Social and Demographic Study*. Journal for the Study of the Old Testament: Supplement Series 294. Sheffield: Sheffield Academic Press, 1999.

———. "The Province of Yehud in the Post-Exilic Period: Soundings in Site Distribution and Demography." Pages 2:106–45 in Eskenazi and Richards, eds., *Second Temple Studies*.

Cataldo, Jeremiah. "The Crippled Ummah: Toward Redefining *Golah* in Ezra–Nehemiah." *Bible and Critical Theory* 4, no. 1 (2008): 6.1–6.17

———. "Persian Policy and the Yehud Community During Nehemiah." *Journal for the Study of the Old Testament* 28 (2003): 240–52.

Chhibber, Pradeep, and Mariano Torcal. "Elite Strategy, Social Cleavages, and Party Systems in a New Democracy: Spain." *Comparative Political Studies* 30 (1997): 27–54.

Childs, Brevard S. *Introduction to the Old Testament as Scripture*. Philadelphia: Fortress, 1979.

Clarkson, Frederick. *Eternal Hostility: The Struggle between Theocracy and Democracy*. Monroe: Common Courage, 1997.

Clines, David J. A. *Ezra, Nehemiah and Esther*. New Century Bible. Grand Rapids: Eerdmans, 1984.

Collins, Randall. "On the Microfoundations of Macrosociology." *American Journal of Sociology* 86 (1981): 984–1014.

Cook, John M. *The Persian Empire*. New York: Schocken, 1983.

Cook, Stephen L. *Prophecy and Apocalypticism: The Postexilic Social Setting*. Minneapolis: Fortress, 1995.

Cottret, Bernard. *Calvin: A Biography*. Translated by M. Wallace McDonald. Grand Rapids: Eerdmans, 2000.

Cowley, A. E. *Aramaic Papyri of the Fifth Century B.C.* Oxford: Oxford University Press, 1923.

Cross, Frank Moore Jr. "Aspects of Samaritan and Jewish History in Late Persian and Hellenistic Times." *Harvard Theological Review* 59 (1966): 201–11.

———. "Discovery of the Samaria Papyri." *Biblical Archaeologist* 26 (1963): 110–21.

———. "Judean Stamps." *Eretz-Israel* 9 (1969): 22–26.

———. "Judaean Stamps." Pages 138–45 in *Leaves from an Epigrapher's Notebook: Collected Papers in Hebrew and West Semitic Palaeography and Epigraphy*. Harvard Semitic Studies 51. Winona Lake: Eisenbrauns, 2003.

———. "The Papyri and Their Historical Implications." Pages 17–24 in Lapp and Lapp, eds., *Discoveries in the Wâdi Ed-Dâliyeh*.

———. "Papyri of the Fourth Century B.C. from Dâliyeh: A Preliminary Report on Their Discovery and Significance." Pages 41–62 in *New Directions in Biblical Archaeology*. Edited by David N. Freedman and Jonas C. Greenfield. Garden City: Doubleday, 1969.

———. "A Reconstruction of the Judean Restoration." *Journal of Biblical Literature* 94 (1975): 4–18.

———. "A Report on the Samaria Papyri." Pages 17–26 in *Congress Volume: Jerusalem 1986*. Edited by John A. Emerton. Supplements to Vetus Testamentum 40. Leiden: Brill, 1988.

———. "Samaria Papyrus 1: An Aramaic Slave Conveyance of 335 B.C.E. Found in the Wâdi Ed-Dâliyeh." *Eretz-Israel* 18 (1985): 7*–17*.

———. "A Reconstruction of the Judaean Restoration." Pages 151–72 in *From Epic to Canon: History and Literature in Ancient Israel*. Edited by Frank Moore Cross Jr. Baltimore: The Johns Hopkins University Press, 1998.

Culbert, T. Patrick, ed. *Classic Maya Political History: Hieroglyphic and Archaeological Evidence*. Cambridge: Cambridge University Press, 1991.

Dabashi, Hamid. *Authority in Islam: From the Rise of Muhammad to the Establishment of the Ummayads*. New Brunswick: Transaction, 1989.

———. *Theology of Discontent: The Ideological Foundations of the Islamic Revolution in Iran*. New York: New York University Press, 1993.

Dandamaev, Muhammad. A. *Persien unter den ersten Achämeniden (6. Jahrhundert V. Chr.)*. Translated by Heinz D. Pohl. Wiesbaden: Reichert, 1976.

———. *A Political History of the Achaemenid Empire*. Leiden: Brill, 1989.

Dandamaev, Muhammad A., and Vladimir G. Lukonin. *The Culture and Social Institutions of Ancient Iran*. Translated by Philip L. Kohl. Cambridge: Cambridge University Press, 1989.

Davies, Graham. *Ancient Hebrew Inscriptions: Corpus and Concordance*. Cambridge: Cambridge University Press, 1991.

Davies, Philip R. "Exile! What Exile? Whose Exile?" Pages 128–38 in Grabbe, ed., *Leading Captivity Captive*.

———. "The Intellectual, the Archaeologist and the Bible." Pages 239–54 in *The Land That I Will Show You: Essays on the History and Archaeology of the Ancient Near East in Honour of J. Maxwell Miller*. Edited by J. Andrew Dearman and M. Patrick Graham. Sheffield: Sheffield Academic Press, 2001.

———. *In Search of 'Ancient Israel'*. Journal for the Study of the Old Testament: Supplement Series 148. Sheffield: JSOT, 1992.

————, ed. *Second Temple Studies*. Vol. 1, *Persian Period*. Sheffield: Sheffield Academic Press, 1991.

de Borhegyi, Stephan F. "The Development of Folk and Complex Cultures in the Southern Maya Area." *American Antiquity* 21 (1956): 343–56.

de Vaux, Roland. *Ancient Israel: Its Life and Institutions*. Translated by John McHugh. New York: McGraw–Hill, 1961.

Denny, Frederick M. "Ummah in the Constitution of Medina." *Journal of Near Eastern Studies* 36 (1977): 39–47.

Descat, Raymond. "Mnesimachos, Hérodote et le Système Tributaire Achémèmide." *Revue des etudes anciennes* 87 (1985): 97–112.

Diakonoff, Igor M. *The Main Features of Ancient Society [Russian]: The Problems of Pre-Capitalist Societies in Eastern Countries*. Moscow, n.p., 1971.

Dion, P. "The Civic-and-Temple Community of Persian Period Judaea: Neglected Insights from Eastern Europe." *Journal of Near Eastern Studies* 50 (1991): 281–87.

Donbaz, Veysel, and Matthew Stolper. *Istanbul Murašû Texts*. Leiden: Nederlands Instituut voor het Nabije Oosten, 1997.

Donner, Fred M. "Muhammad and the Caliphate: Political History of the Islamic Empire up to the Mongol Conquest." Pages 1–61 in *The Oxford History of Islam*. Edited by John L. Esposito. New York: Oxford University Press, 1999.

Douglas, Mary. "Responding to Ezra: The Priests and the Foreign Wives." *Biblical Interpretation* 10 (2002): 1–23.

Dusinberre, Elspeth R. M. "Satrapal Sardis: Achaemenid Bowls in an Achaemenid Capital." *American Journal of Archaeology* 103 (1999): 73–102.

Dyck, Jonathan E. *The Theocratic Ideology of the Chronicler*. Biblical Interpretation Series 33. Leiden: Brill, 1998.

Edelman, Diana. "Dangerous Liaisons: How Hypothetical Sinuballits are Skewing the Dating of Sidonian and Samarian Coinage." Paper presented at the University of Sheffield, 2005.

————. *The Origins of the 'Second' Temple: Persian Imperial Policy and the Rebuilding of Jerusalem*. London: Equinox, 2005.

Eissfeldt, Otto. "Eine einschmelzstelle Am Tempel zu Jerusalem." *Forschungen und Fortschritte* (1937): 163–64.

————. *Eine einschmelzstelle Am Tempel zu Jerusalem*. Kleine Schriften 2. Tübingen: Mohr, 1963.

————. *The Old Testament: An Introduction*. Oxford: Oxford University Press, 1965.

Elayi, Josette. *Sidon, cité autonome de l'Empire perse*. 2d ed. Paris: Idéaphane, 1990.

Eph'al, Israel. "Changes in Palestine During the Persian Period in Light of Epigraphic Sources." *Israel Exploration Journal* 48 (1998): 106–19.

————. "Syria-Palestine under Achaemenid Rule." Pages 4:139–64 in Boardman et al., eds., *Cambridge Ancient History*.

Eskenazi, Tamara C. *Ezra–Nehemiah*. Edited by Carol A. Newsom and Sharon H. Ringe. Expanded ed. with Apocrypha. Women's Bible Commentary. Louisville: Westminster John Knox, 1998.

————. *In an Age of Prose: A Literary Approach to Ezra–Nehemiah*. Atlanta: Scholars Press, 1988.

Eskenazi, Tamara C., and Eleanore P. Judd. "Marriage to a Stranger in Ezra 9–10." Pages 2:266–85 in Eskenazi and Richards, eds., *Second Temple Studies*.

Eskenazi, Tamara C., and Kent H. Richards, eds. *Second Temple Studies*. Vol. 2, *Temple and Community in the Persian Period*. Sheffield: Sheffield Academic Press, 1994.

Fantalkin, Alexander, and Oren Tal. "Re-Dating Lachish Level I: Identifying Achaemenid Imperial Policy at the Southern Frontier of the Fifth Satrapy." Pages 167–97 in Lipschits and Oeming, eds., *Judah and the Judeans in the Persian Period*.

Farazmand, Ali. *The State, Bureaucracy, and Revolution in Modern Iran: Agrarian Reform and Regime Politics*. New York: Praeger, 1989.

Fash, William L. "Changing Perspectives on Maya Civilization." *Annual Review of Anthropology* 23 (1994): 181–208.

Festinger, Leon, Henry W. Riecken, and Stanley Schachter. *When Prophecy Fails*. Minneapolis: University of Minnesota Press, 1956.

Finkelstein, Israel, and Neil Asher Silberman. *The Bible Unearthed: Archaeology's New Vision of Ancient Israel and the Origin of Its Sacred Texts*. New York: Free, 2001.

Francis, E. D. "Oedipus Achaemenides." *The American Journal of Philology* 113 (1992): 333–57.

Freyne, Sean. *Galilee from Alexander the Great to Hadrian, 323 BCE to 135 CE: A Study of Second Temple Judaism*. Wilmington, Del.: University of Notre Dame Press, 1980.

Fried, Lisbeth S. "The ʿAm Hāʾreṣ in Ezra 4:4." Pages 123–45 in Lipschits and Oeming, eds., *Judah and the Judeans in the Persian Period*.

———. "The Land Lay Desolate: Conquest and Restoration in the Ancient near East." Pages 21–54 in Lipschits and Blenkinsopp, eds., *Judah and the Judeans in the Neo-Babylonian Period*.

———. "The Political Struggle of the Fifth-Century Judah." *Transeu* 24 (2002): 61–73.

———. *The Priest and the Great King: Temple–Palace Relations in the Persian Empire*. Biblical and Judaic Studies 10. Winona Lake: Eisenbrauns, 2004.

Gabriel, Johannes. *Zorobabel: ein Beitrag zur Geschichte der Juden in der ersten Zeit nach dem Exil*. Vienna: Mayer & Co., 1927.

Garbini, Giovanni. *History and Ideology in Ancient Israel*. Translated by John Bowden. New York: Crossroad, 1988.

———. *Myth and History in the Bible*. Translated by Chiara Peri. Journal for the Study of the Old Testament: Supplement Series 362. Sheffield: Sheffield Academic Press, 2003.

———. "Nuovi Documenti Epigrafici Dalla Palestina." *Henoch* 1 (1979): 396–400.

Geertz, Clifford. *The Interpretation of Cultures*. New York: Basic, 1973.

Gerson, Stephen N. "Fractional Coins of Judea and Samaria in the Fourth Century BCE." *Near Eastern Archaeology* 64 (2001): 106–21.

Giddens, Anthony. *Central Problems in Social Theory: Action, Structure, and Contra-diction in Social Analysis*. Berkeley: University of California Press, 1979.

Glassner, Jean-Jacques. *Mesopotamian Chronicles*. Edited by Benjamin R. Foster. SBL Writings from the Ancient World 19. Atlanta: Society of Biblical Literature, 2004.

Gorski, Eric. "Hart Warns of Theocracy Trap." *Denver Post*, November 5, 2005.

Gottwald, Norman K. *The Tribes of Yahweh: A Sociology of the Religion of Liberated Israel 1250–1050 B.C.E.* Maryknoll: Orbis, 1979.

Grabbe, Lester L. *Ezra–Nehemiah*. New York: Routledge, 1998.

———. "Josephus and the Reconstruction of the Judean Restoration." *Journal of Biblical Literature* 106 (1987): 231–46.

———. *Judaism from Cyrus to Hadrian*. Minneapolis: Fortress, 1992.

————, ed. *Leading Captivity Captive: 'The Exile' as History and Ideology*. Journal for the Study of the Old Testament: Supplement Series 278. Sheffield: Sheffield Academic Press, 1998.

————. "The 'Persian Documents' in the Book of Ezra: Are They Authentic?" Pages 531–70 in Lipschits and Oeming, eds., *Judah and the Judeans in the Persian Period*.

————. "Pinholes or Pinheads in the *Camera Obscura*? The Task of Writing a History of Persian Period Yehud." Paper presented at the Accademia Nazionale dei Lincei. Rome, March 6–7, 2003.

————. "Sup-Urbs or Only Hyp-Urbs? Prophets and Populations in Ancient Israel and Socio-Historical Method." Pages 95–123 in *'Every City Shall Be Forsaken': Urbanism and Prophecy in Ancient Israel and the Near East*. Edited by Lester L. Grabbe and Robert D. Haak. Sheffield: Sheffield Academic Press, 2001.

Gropp, Douglas M. "The Samaria Papyri from Wadi Ed-Daliyeh: The Slave Sales." Ph.D. diss., Harvard University, 1986.

————. *The Samaria Papyri from Wadi Daliyeh*. Vol. 28, *Introduction*. Edited by Emanuel Tov, Douglas M. Gropp, Moshe J. Bernstein, Monica Brady, James Charlesworth, Peter W. Flint, Haggai Misgav, Stephen Pfann, Eileen Schuller, Eibert J. C. Tigchelaar, and James C. VanderKam. Wadi Daliyeh II and Qumran Cave 4: The Samaria Papyri from Wadi Daliyeh/Miscellanea, Part 2. Oxford: Clarendon, 2001.

Gropp, Douglas M., Moshe J. Bernstein, James C. VanderKam, and Monica Brady. *Wadi Daliyeh II: The Samaria Papyri from Wadi Daliyeh Miscellanea, Part 2 / by Moshe Bernstein ... [et al.] in Consultation with James VanderKam and Monica Brady*. Discoveries in the Judaean Desert 28. Oxford: Clarendon, 2001.

Gros, Jean-Germain. "The Hard Lessons of Cameroon." *Journal of Democracy* 6 (1995): 112–27.

Hamilton, David K. "Organizing Government Structure and Governance Function in Metropolitan Areas in Response to Growth and Change: A Critical Overview." *Journal of Urban Affairs* 22 (2000): 65–84.

Hammond, Mason. "Ancient Imperialism: Contemporary Justifications." *Harvard Studies in Classical Philology* 58 (1948): 105–61.

Hammond, Norman. "Inside the Black Box: Defining Maya Polity." Pages 253–84 in Culbert, ed., *Classic Maya Political History*.

Hanson, Paul D. *The Dawn of Apocalyptic: The Historical and Sociological Roots of Jewish Apocalyptic Eschatology*. 1975. Repr., Philadelphia: Fortress, 1979.

Harrison, Peter D., and B. L. Turner, eds. *Ancient Maya Agriculture*. Austin: University of Texas Press, 1978.

Healy, Paul F., John D. H. Lambert, J. T. Arnason, and Richard J. Hebda. "Caracol, Belize: Evidence of Ancient Maya Agricultural Terraces." *Journal of Field Archaeology* 10 (1983): 397–410.

Hendon, Julia A., and Rosemary A. Joyce, eds. *Mesoamerican Archaeology: Theory and Practice*. Blackwell Studies in Global Archaeology. Malden, Mass.: Blackwell, 2004.

Henshaw, R. A. "The Office of Šaknu in Neo-Assyrian Times I." *Journal of the American Oriental Society* 87 (1967): 517–25.

————. "The Office of Šaknu in Neo-Assyrian Times II." *Journal of the American Oriental Society* 88 (1968): 461–83.

Hoglund, Kenneth G. "The Achaemenid Context." Pages 1:54–72 in Davies, ed., *Second Temple Studies*.

———. *Achaemenid Imperial Administration in Syria-Palestine and the Missions of Ezra and Nehemiah*. Society of Biblical Literature Dissertation Series 125. Atlanta: Scholars Press, 1992.

Hölscher, G. *Geschichte der Israelitischen und Jüdischen Religion*. Giessen: J. Ricker, 1903.

Hooglund, Eric. "The Gulf War and the Islamic Republic." *MERIP Reports* (1984): 31–37.

Hornblower, Simon. *The Greek World 479–323 BC*. New York: Routledge, 1991.

———. *Mausolus*. Oxford: Clarendon, 1982.

Horsley, Richard A. "Religion and Other Products of Empire." *Journal of the American Academy of Religion* 71 (2003): 13–44.

Janzen, David. "The 'Mission' of Ezra and the Persian-Period Temple Community." *Journal of Biblical Literature* 119 (2000): 619–43.

———. "Politics, Settlement, and Temple Community in Persian-Period Yehud." *Catholic Biblical Quarterly* 64 (2002): 490–510.

Jeselsohn, D. "A New Coin Type with Hebrew Inscription." *Israel Exploration Journal* 24 (1977): 77–78.

Joannès, F., and André Lemaire. "Trois tablettes cunéiformes à L'onomastique ouest-sémitique." *Transeu* 17 (1999): 17–33.

Johnson, Marion. "The Economic Foundations of an Islamic Theocracy: The Case of Masina." *The Journal of African History* 17 (1976): 481–95.

Joyce, Arthur A. "Sacred Space and Social Relations in the Valley of Oaxaca." Pages 192–216 in Hendon and Joyce, eds., *Mesoamerican Archaeology*.

Kaiser, Otto. "Freiheit und Bindung in der Attischen Demokratie und der Jüdischen Theokratie: Ein Beitrag zur Bestimmung der Aufgabe der Religion in der Modernen Zivilgesellschaft." Pages 448–64 in *Vergegenwärtigung des Alten Testaments: Beiträge zur Biblischen Hermeneutik—Festschrift für Rudolf Smend zum 70. Geburtstag*. Edited by Christoph Bultmann, Walter Dietrich, and Christoph Levin. Göttingen: Vandenhoeck & Ruprecht, 2002.

Kamrava, Mehran. *The Political History of Modern Iran: From Tribalism to Theocracy*. Westport: Praeger, 1992.

Kaptan, Deniz. *The Daskyleion Bullae: Seal Images from the Western Achaemenid Empire*. Vol. 1, *Text*. Edited by Pierre Briant, Wouter Henkelman, Amélie Kuhrt, Johan de Roos, Margaret C. Root, Heleen Sancisi-Weerdenburg, and Josef Wiesehöfer. Achaemenid History 12. Leiden: Nederlands Instituut voor het Nabije Oosten, 2002.

Kellermann, Ulrich. "Erwägungen zum Problem der Esradatierung." *Zeitschrift für die alttestamentliche Wissenschaft* 80 (1968): 55–87.

Kent, Roland G. *Old Persian Grammar, Texts, Lexicon*. 2d ed. New Haven: American Oriental Society, 1953.

Kenyon, Kathleen M. *Archaeology in the Holy Land*. 3d ed. New York: Praeger, 1971.

Kessler, John. *The Book of Haggai: Prophecy and Society in Early Persian Yehud*. Supplements to Vetus Testamentum 91. Leiden: Brill, 2002.

———. "Building the Second Temple: Questions of Time, Text, and History in Haggai 1.1–15." *Journal for the Study of the Old Testament* 27 (2002): 243–56.

———. "Persia's Loyal Yahwists: Power Identity and Ethnicity in Achaemenid Yehud." Pages 91–121 in Lipschits and Oeming, eds., *Judah and the Judeans in the Persian Period*.

Khaldun, Ibn. *The Muqaddimah: An Introduction to History*. Translated by Franz Rosenthal. 3 vols. New York: Pantheon, 1958.

Khomeini, Ruhollah. *Islam and Revolution: Writings and Declarations of Imam Khomeini*. Translated by Hamid Algar. Berkeley, Calif.: Mizan, 1981.

Kindler, A. "Silver Coins Bearing the Name of Judaea from the Early Hellenistic Period." *Israel Exploration Journal* 24 (1974): 73–76.

Knoppers, Gary N. "Revisiting the Samaritan Question in the Persian Period." Pages 265–89 in Lipschits and Oeming, eds., *Judah and the Judeans in the Persian Period*.

Kraeling, Emil G. *The Brooklyn Museum Aramaic Papyri: New Documents of the Fifth Century B.C. from the Jewish Colony at Elephantine*. New Haven: Yale University Press, 1953.

Krekeler, Achim. "Excavations and Restoration on the Elephantine Island." Pages 69–83 in *The Near East Antiquity*. Amman: Al Kutba, 1992.

Kuhrt, Amélie. *The Ancient Near East c. 3000–330 B.C.* Routledge History of the Ancient World 2. London: Routledge, 1995.

Kundera, Milan. *Testaments Betrayed*. New York: Harper Collins, 1995.

Lane, David. "What Kind of Capitalism for Russia? A Comparative Analysis." *Communist and Post-Communist Studies* 33 (2000): 485–504.

Lapidus, Ira M. *A History of Islamic Societies*. 2d ed. Cambridge: Cambridge University Press, 2002.

Lapp, Paul W., and Nancy L. Lapp. *Discoveries in the Wâdi Ed-Dâliyeh*. Annual of the American Schools of Oriental Research 41. Cambridge, Mass.: Annual of the American Schools of Oriental Research, 1974.

Leith, Mary J. W. "Israel among the Nations: The Persian Period." Pages 367–419 in *The Oxford History of the Biblical World*. Edited by Michael D. Coogan. Oxford: Oxford University Press, 1998.

———. "Seals and Coins in Persian Period Samaria." Pages 691–707 in *The Dead Sea Scrolls Fifty Years after Their Discovery: Proceedings of the Jerusalem Congress, July 20–25, 1997*. Edited by Lawrence H. Schiffman, Emanuel Tov, and James C. VanderKam. Jerusalem: Israel Exploration Society in cooperation with the Shrine of the Book, Israel Museum, 2000.

———. *Wadi Daliyeh: The Wadi Daliyeh Seal Impressions*. Discoveries in the Judaean Desert 24. Oxford: Clarendon, 1997.

Lemaire, André. "Épigraphie et Religion En Palestine à l'époque achéménide." *Transeu* 22 (2001): 97–113.

———. *Histoire et Administration de la Palestine à l'époque perse*. Edited by Ernest-Marie Laperrousaz and André Lemaire. La Palestine à l'époque perse. Paris: Cerf, 1994.

———. "Nabonidus in Arabia and Judah in the Neo-Babylonian Period." Pages 285–98 in Lipschits and Blenkinsopp, eds., *Judah and the Judeans in the Neo-Babylonian Period*.

Lenski, Gerhard, and Jean Lenski, *Human Societies: An Introduction to Macrosociology*. New York: McGraw–Hill, 1987.

Lewis, Bernard. *The Political Language of Islam*. Chicago: University of Chicago Press, 1988.

Lichtheim, Miriam. *Ancient Egyptian Literature*. Vol. 3, *The Late Period*. Berkeley: University of California, 1980.

Lindenberger, James M. *Ancient Aramaic and Hebrew Letters*. Edited by Kent H. Richards. SBL Writings from the Ancient World 4. Atlanta: Scholars Press, 1994.

Lipschits, Oded. "Achaemenid Imperial Policy, Settlement Processes in Palestine, and the Status of Jerusalem in the Middle of the Fifth Century B.C.E." Pages 19–52 in Lipschits and Oeming, eds., *Judah and the Judeans in the Persian Period*.

———. "Demographic Changes in Judah between the Seventh and the Fifth Centuries B.C.E." Pages 323–76 in Lipschits and Blenkinsopp, eds., *Judah and the Judeans in the Neo-Babylonian Period*.

Lipschits, Oded, and Joseph Blenkinsopp, eds. *Judah and the Judeans in the Neo-Babylonian Period*. Winona Lake: Eisenbrauns, 2003.

Lipschits, Oded, and Manfred Oeming, eds. *Judah and the Judeans in the Persian Period*. Winona Lake: Eisenbrauns, 2006.

Machinist, Peter. "The First Coins of Judah and Samaria: Numismatics and History in the Achaemenid and Early Hellenistic Periods." Pages 365–80 in *Achaemenid History*. Vol. 8, *Continuity and Change*. Edited by Heleen Sancisi-Weerdenburg, Amelie Kuhrt, and Margaret C. Root. Leiden: Nederlands Instituut voor Nabije Oosten, 1994.

Margalith, Othniel. "The Political Background of Zerubbabel's Mission and the Samaritan Schism." *Vetus Testamentum* 41 (1991): 312–23.

Marx, Karl. "The German Ideology." Pages 146–200 in Tucker, ed., *The Marx-Engels Reader*.

———. "On the Jewish Question." Pages 26–52 in Tucker, ed., *The Marx-Engels Reader*.

McAnany, Patricia A. *Living with the Ancestors*. Austin: University of Texas Press, 1995.

McEvenue, Sean. "The Political Structure in Judah from Cyrus to Nehemiah." *Catholic Biblical Quarterly* 43 (1981): 353–64.

McEwan, Gilbert J. P. *Priest and Temple in Hellenistic Babylonia*. Freiburger Altorientalische Studien 4. Wiesbaden: F. Steiner, 1981.

McKillop, Heather Irene. *The Ancient Maya: New Perspectives*. Understanding Ancient Civilizations. Santa Barbara, Calif.: ABC-CLIO, 2004.

McLaren, James S. "Theocracy, Temple and Tax: Ingredients for the Jewish–Roman War of 66–70 CE." Paper presented at the Society of Biblical Literature, National Meeting, Atlanta, November 21, 2004.

Meshorer, Y. *Jewish Coins of the Second Temple Period*. Tel Aviv: Am Hassefer & Massada, 1967.

Meshorer, Ya'akov. *Ancient Jewish Coinage*. Vol. 1, *Persian Period through Hasmoneans*. Dix Hills: Amphora, 1982.

Meshorer, Ya'akov, and Shraga Qedar. *Samarian Coinage*. Numismatic Studies and Researches 9. Jerusalem: Israel Numismatic Society, 1999.

Meyers, Carol. "'To Her Mother's House': Considering a Counterpart to the Israelite *Bêt ʿAb*." Pages 39–51 in *The Bible and the Politics of Exegesis*. Edited by David Jobling, Peggy L. Day, and Gerald T. Sheppard. Cleveland: Pilgrim, 1991.

Meyers, Carol L., and Eric M. Meyers. *Haggai, Zechariah 1–8*. Anchor Bible 25B. Garden City: Doubleday, 1987.

Meyers, Eric M. "The Shelomit Seal and the Judean Restoration: Some Additional Considerations." *Eretz-Israel* 18 (1985): 33*–38*.

———. "The Persian Period and the Judean Restoration: From Zerubbabel to Nehemiah." Pages 509–21 in *Ancient Israelite Religion: Essays in Honor of Frank Moore Cross*. Edited by Paul D. Hanson, S. Dean McBride Jr., and Patrick D. Miller Jr. Philadelphia: Fortress, 1987.

Mildenberg, Leo. "On the Money Circulation in Palestine from Artaxerxes II Till Ptolemy I: Preliminary Studies of Local Coinage in the Fifth Persian Satrapy. Part 5." *Transeu* 7 (1994): 63–71.

———. "Yehud: A Preliminary Study of the Provincial Coinage of Judaea." Pages 183–96 in *Greek Numismatics and Archaeology: Essays in Honor of Margaret Thompson*. Edited by Otto Mørkholm and Nancy M. Waggoner. Wetteren: NR, 1979.

Momigliano, Arnaldo. "Persian Empire and Greek Freedom." Pages 140–51 in *The Idea of Freedom: Essays in Honour of Isaiah Berlin*. Edited by A. Ryan. Oxford: Oxford University Press, 1979.

Morgenstern, Julian. "Jerusalem—485 BC." *Hebrew Union College Annual* 27 (1956): 101–79.

———. "Jerusalem—485 BC (Continued)." *Hebrew Union College Annual* 28 (1957): 15–47.

———. "Jerusalem—485 BC (Concluded)." *Hebrew Union College Annual* 31 (1960): 1–29.

Mowinckel, Sigmund. *Studien zu dem Buche Ezra–Nehemiah, I–III*. Skrifter Utgitt Au Det Norske Videnskaps-Adademi I. Oslo II. Hist.-Filos. Klasse, Nu Serie, 3, 5 and 7. Oslo: Universitetsforlaget, 1964.

Myers, Jacob. *Ezra, Nehemiah*. Anchor Bible 14. Garden City: Doubleday, 1965.

Nabavi, Negin. *Intellectuals and the State in Iran: Politics, Discourse and the Dilemma of Authenticity*. Gainesville: University Press of Florida, 2003.

Naphy, William B. *Calvin and the Consolidation of the Genevan Reformation*. Louisville: Westminster John Knox, 1994.

Nasr, Seyyed Hossein. *The Heart of Islam: Enduring Values for Humanity*. New York: HarperSanFrancisco, 2004.

Naveh, Joseph. "Aramaic Ostraca and Jar Inscription from Tell Jemmeh." *ʾAtiqot* 21 (1992): 49–53.

———. "An Aramaic Ostracon from Ashdod." *ʾAtiqot* 9/10 (1971): 200–201.

———. "Dated Coins of Alexander Janneus." *Israel Exploration Journal* 18 (1968): 20–26.

———. "Published and Unpublished Aramaic Ostraca." *ʾAtiqot* 17 (1985): 114–21.

Niditch, Susan. "Legends of Wise Heroes and Heroines." Pages 445–63 in *The Hebrew Bible and Its Modern Interpreters*. Edited by Douglas A. Knight and Gene M. Tucker. Chico, Calif.: Scholars Press, 1985.

Norgaard, Asbjorn Sonne, and Thomas Pallesen. "Governing Structures and Structured Governing: Local Political Control of Public Services in Denmark." *Journal of Public Administration Research and Theory* 13 (2003): 543–61.

Ochs, Elinor, and Lisa Capps. "Narrating the Self." *Annual Reviews in Anthropology* 25 (1996): 19–43.

Oded, B. "Where is the 'Myth of the Empty Land' to Be Found? History Versus Myth." Pages 55–74 in Lipschits and Blenkinsopp, eds., *Judah and the Judeans in the Neo-Babylonian Period.*

Olmstead, Albert T. *History of the Persian Empire.* Chicago: University of Chicago Press, 1948.

Oppenheim, A. Leo. "A Fiscal Practice of the Ancient Near East." *Journal of Near Eastern Studies* 6 (1947): 116–20.

Paglaia, Valentina. "Poetic Dialogues: Performance and Politics in the Tuscan Contrasto." *Ethnology* 41 (2002): 135–54.

Pearce, Laurie. "New Evidence for Jews in Babylonia." Pages 399–411 in Lipschits and Oeming, eds., *Judah and the Judeans in the Persian Period.*

Pelaia, Bruno M. *Esdra e Neemia.* Rome: Marietti, 1960.

Petersen, David L. *Haggai and Zechariah 1–8: A Commentary.* Old Testament Library. Philadelphia: Westminster, 1984.

———. *Zechariah 9–14 and Malachi.* Old Testament Library. Louisville: Westminster John Knox, 1995.

———. "Zerubbabel and Jerusalem Temple Reconstruction." *Catholic Biblical Quarterly* 36 (1974): 366–72.

Petit, Thierry. *Satrapes et Satrapies dans l'empire achéménide de Cyrus le Grand à Xerxés 1er.* Bibliothèque de la Faculté de Philosophie et Lettres de l'Université de Liège. Paris: Les Belles Lettres, 1990.

Plöger, Otto. *Theocracy and Eschatology.* Translated by S. Rudman. Oxford: Blackwell, 1968.

Pohlsander, Hans A. *The Emperor Constantine.* New York: Routledge, 1996.

Porten, Bezalel. "Aramaic Papyri and Parchments: A New Look." *Biblical Archaeologist* 42 (1979): 74–104.

———. *Archives from Elephantine: The Life of an Ancient Jewish Military Colony.* Berkeley: University of California Press, 1968.

———. *The Elephantine Papyri in English: Three Millennia of Cross-Cultural Continuity and Change.* Documenta et Monumenta Orientis Antiqui 22. Leiden: Brill, 1996.

———. "The Religion of the Jews of Elephantine in Light of the Hermopolis Papyri." *Journal of Near Eastern Studies* 28 (1969): 116–21.

———. "Settlement of the Jews at Elephantine and the Arameans at Syene." Pages 451–70 in Lipschits and Blenkinsopp, eds., *Judah and the Judeans in the Neo-Babylonian Period.*

Porten, Bezalel, with Jonas C. Greenfield. *Jews of Elephantine and Arameans of Syene: Aramaic Texts with Translation.* Jerusalem: Hebrew University, 1974.

Porten, Bezalel, and H. Z. Szubin. "'Abandoned Property' in Elephantine: A New Interpretation of Kraeling 3." *Journal of Near Eastern Studies* 41 (1982): 123–31.

Porten, Bezalel, and Ada Yardeni. "Ostracon Clermont-Ganneau 125 (?): A Case of Ritual Purity." *Journal of the American Oriental Society* 113 (1993): 451–56.

———. *Textbook of Aramaic Documents from Ancient Egypt.* Vol. 1, *Letters.* Jerusalem: Hebrew University, 1986. Repr., Winona Lake: Eisenbrauns, 1987.

———. *Textbook of Aramaic Documents from Ancient Egypt.* Vol. 2, *Contracts.* Jerusalem: Hebrew University, 1989.

———. *Textbook of Aramaic Documents from Ancient Egypt.* Vol. 3, *Literature, Accounts, Lists.* Jerusalem: Hebrew University, 1993.

———. *Textbook of Aramaic Documents from Ancient Egypt.* Vol. 4, *Ostraca and Assorted Inscriptions.* Jerusalem: Hebrew University, 1999.

Pritchard, James B., ed. *Ancient Near Eastern Texts Relating to the Old Testament.* Princeton: Princeton University Press, 1950.

Proskouriakoff, Tatiana. "Historical Data in the Inscriptions of Yaxchilan, Part 1." *Estudios de Cultura Maya* 3 (1963): 144–67.

———. "Historical Data in the Inscriptions of Yaxchilan, Part 2." *Estudios de Cultura Maya* 4 (1964): 177–201.

Puleston, D. E. "The Art and Archaeology of Hydraulic Agriculture in the Maya Lowlands." Pages 449–67 in *Social Process in Maya Prehistory.* Edited by Norman Hammond. London: Academic Press, 1977.

Rahmani, L. Y. "Silver Coins of the Fourth Century BC from Tel Gamma." *Israel Exploration Journal* 21 (1971): 158–60.

Rapp, Sandy. *God's Country: A Case against Theocracy.* Haworth Women's Studies. Binghamton: Haworth, 1991.

Rappaport, Uriel. "The First Judean Coinage." *Journal of Jewish Studies* 32 (1981): 1–17.

Redditt, Paul L. "Zerubbabel, Joshua, and the Night Visions of Zechariah." *Catholic Biblical Quarterly* 54 (1992): 249–59.

Renan, Ernst. *Histoire du peuple d'Israël,* vol. 4. Paris, 1893.

Rice, Prudence M. *Maya Political Science: Time, Astronomy, and the Cosmos.* Austin: University of Texas Press, 2004.

Ricke, Herbert, and Serge Sauneron. *Die Tempel Nektanebos' II in Elephantine: Inscriptions Romaines au Temple de Khnoum a Elephantine.* Beiträge zur Ägyptischen Bauforschung und Alterstumkunde 6. Cairo: Schweiz Institut für ägypt Bauforschung und Alterstumkunde, 1960.

Robin, Cynthia. "Social Diversity and Everyday Life within Classic Maya Settlements." Pages 148–68 in Hendon and Joyce, eds., *Mesoamerican Archaeology.*

Root, Margaret C. "From the Heart: Powerful Persianisms in the Art of the Western Empire." *Achaemenid History* 6 (1991): 1–29.

Rubin, Uri. "The 'Constitution of Medina': Some Notes." *Studia Islámica,* no. 62 (1985): 5–23.

Rudolph, Wilhelm. *Chronikbücher.* Handbuch zum Alten Testament 1/21. Tübingen: J. C. B. Mohr, 1955.

———. *Esra und Nehemia samt 3. Esra.* Handbuch zum Alten Testament 20. Tübingen: J. C. B. Mohr, 1949.

Sacchi, Paolo. *The History of the Second Temple Period.* Journal for the Study of the Old Testament: Supplement Series 285. Sheffield: Sheffield Academic Press, 2000.

San Nicolò, Mariano. "Parerga Babylonica XVII. Ein Mühlenbannrecht des Tempels Eanna in neubabylonischer Zeit." *Archiv Orientální* 7 (1935).

Schaeder, Hans H. *Esra der Schreiber.* Beiträge zur Historischen Theologie 5. Tübingen: J. C. B. Mohr, 1930.

Schaper, Joachim. "The Jerusalem Temple as an Instrument of the Achaemenid Fiscal Administration." *Vetus Testamentum* 45 (1995): 528–39.

———. "The Temple Treasury Committee in the Times of Nehemiah and Ezra." *Vetus Testamentum* 47 (1997): 200–206.

Schele, Linda, and Peter Mathews. "Royal Visits and Other Intersite Relationships among the Classic Maya." Pages 226–52 in Culbert, ed., *Classic Maya Political History*.

Serjeant, R. B. "The Constitution of Medina." *Islamic Quarterly* 8 (1964): 3–16.

———. "Haram and Hawtah, the Sacred Enclave in Arabia." Pages 41–58 in *Mèlanges Taha Hussein*. Edited by Abdurrahman Badawi. Cairo: Dar al-Maaref, 1962.

Simon, János. "Electoral Systems and Democracy in Central Europe, 1990–1994." *International Political Science Review* 18 (1997): 361–79.

Smith, Daniel L. "The Politics of Ezra: Sociological Indicators of Postexilic Judaean Society." Pages 1:72–97 in Davies, ed., *Second Temple Studies*.

———. *The Religion of the Landless: A Sociology of the Babylonian Exile*. Bloomington: Meyer-Stone Books, 1989.

Smith, Morton. *Palestinian Parties and Politics that Shaped the Old Testament*. 2d ed. London: SCM, 1987.

Smith-Christopher, Daniel L. *A Biblical Theology of Exile*. Overtures to Biblical Theology. Minneapolis: Fortress, 2002.

———. "The Mixed Marriage Crisis in Ezra 9–10 and Nehemiah 13: A Study of the Sociology of the Post-Exilic Judaean Community." Pages 2:243–65 in Eskenazi and Richards, eds., *Second Temple Studies*.

Soggin, J. Alberto. *A History of Israel: From the Beginnings to the Bar Kochba Revolt, AD 135*. London: SCM, 1984.

Spaer, Arnold. "Some More 'Yehud' Coins." *Israel Exploration Journal* 27 (1977): 200–203.

Spellman, W. M. *Monarchies 1000–2000*. Globalities. London: Reaktion, 2001.

Spengler, Joseph J. "Economic Thought of Islam: Ibn Khaldun." *Comparative Studies in Society and History* 6 (1964): 268–306.

Stager, Lawrence E. "The Archaeology of the Family in Ancient Israel." *Bulletin of the American Schools of Oriental Research* 260 (1985): 1–35.

Stern, Ephraim. *Archaeology of the Land of the Bible*. Vol. 2, *The Assyrian, Babylonian, and Persian Periods (732–332 B.C.E.)*. New York: Doubleday, 2001.

———. *Material Culture of the Land of the Bible in the Persian Period, 538–332 B.C.* Warminster: Aris & Phillips, 1982.

———. "The Persian Empire and the Political and Social History of Palestine in the Persian Period." Pages 78–81 in *The Cambridge History of Judaism*. Vol. 1, *Introduction; the Persian Period*. Edited by W. D. Davies and Louis Finkelstein. Cambridge: Cambridge University Press, 1984.

———. "The Religious Revolution in Persian-Period Judah." Pages 199–205 in Lipschits and Oeming, eds., *Judah and the Judeans in the Persian Period*.

Stockton, David. *The Classical Athenian Democracy*. Oxford: Oxford University Press, 1990.

Stolper, Matthew W. "Babylonian Evidence for the End of the Reign of Darius I: A Correction." *Journal of Near Eastern Studies* 51 (1992): 61–62.

———. *Entrepreneurs and Empire: The Murašû Archive, the Murašû Firm, and Persian Rule in Babylonia*. Publications de L'institut historique et Archéologique Néerlandais de Stamboul. Leiden: Nederlands Historisch-Archaeologisch Instituut te Istanbul, 1985.

———. "The Governor of Babylon and Across-the-River in 486 B.C." *Journal of Near Eastern Studies* 48 (1989): 283–305.

Sugiyama, Saburo. "Governance and Polity at Classic Teotihuacan." Pages 97–123 in Hendon and Joyce, eds., *Mesoamerican Archaeology*.

Swedberg, Richard. *Max Weber and the Idea of Economic Sociology*. Princeton: Princeton University Press, 1998.

Tcherikover, Victor. *Hellenistic Civilization and the Jews*. New York: Atheneum, 1970.

Thompson, Ginger, and Nazila Fathi. "For Honduras and Iran, World's Aid Evaporated." *The New York Times*, January 11, 2005.

Thompson, John Eric Sidney. "The Maya Central Area at the Spanish Conquest and Later: A Problem in Demography." *Proceedings of the Royal Anthropological Institute of Britain and Ireland* 97 (1966): 23–37.

———. *The Rise and Fall of Maya Civilization*. Norman: University of Oklahoma Press, 1954.

Todorov, Tzvetan. *The Morals of History*. Translated by Alyson Waters. Minneapolis: University of Minnesota Press, 1995.

Torrey, Charles C. "The Chronicler as Editor and as Independent Narrator." Pages 208–51 in *Ezra Studies*. New York: Ktav, 1970.

———. *The Chronicler's History of Israel: Chronicles–Ezra–Nehemiah Restored to Its Original Form*. New Haven ed, 1954. Port Washington: Kennikat, 1973.

———. *The Composition and Historical Value of Ezra–Nehemiah*. Beihefte zur Zeitschrift für die alttestamentliche Wissenschaft 2. Giessen: J. Ricker, 1896.

———. "The Evolution of a Financier in the Ancient Near East." *Journal of Near Eastern Studies* 2 (1943): 295–301.

———. "The Exile and Restoration." Pages 285–335 in *Ezra Studies*. New York: Ktav, 1970.

———. "The Foundry of the Second Temple of Jerusalem." *Journal of Biblical Literature* 55 (1936): 247–60.

Tucker, Robert C., ed. *The Marx-Engels Reader*. New York: W. W. Norton, 1978.

Tufnell, Olga. *Lachish II: The Iron Age (Tell Ed-Duwei)*. London: Oxford University Press, 1953.

———. *Lachish III: The Iron Age (Tell Ed-Duwei)*. London: Oxford University Press, 1953.

Tuplin, Christopher. "The Administration of the Achaemenid Empire." Pages 109–66 in *Coinage and Administration in the Athenian and Persian Empires. The Ninth Oxford Symposium on Coinage and Monetary History*. Edited by Ian Carradice. Oxford: Oxford University Press, 1987.

Uffenheimer, Benjamin. *The Visions of Zechariah: From Prophecy to Apocalyptic*. Jerusalem: Kiryat Sepher, 1961.

Ussishkin, David. "Excavations at Tel Lakhish: 1973–1977: Preliminary Report." *Tel Aviv* 5 (1978): 1–97.

Valliere, Paul. *Modern Russian Theology: Bukharev, Soloviev, Bulgakov—Orthodox Theology in a New Key*. Grand Rapids: Eerdmans, 2000.

van Dijk, Jacobus. "The Amarna Period and the Later New Kingdom (C.1352–1069 B.C.)." Pages 272–313 in *The Oxford History of Ancient Egypt*. Edited by Ian Shaw. Oxford: Oxford University Press, 2002.

VanderKam, James C. *From Joshua to Caiaphas: High Priests after the Exile*. Minneapolis: Fortress, 2004.

Vernes, Maurice. *Précis d'histoire Juive depuis les origines jusqu'à l'époque Persane*. Paris: Hachette, 1889.

Vogelsang, W. J. *The Rise and Organisation of the Achaemenid Empire*. Leiden: Brill, 1992.

Watt, W. Montgomery. *Muhammad at Medina*. Oxford: Clarendon, 1956.

———. *Muhammad: Prophet and Statesman*. London: Oxford University Press, 1961.

Weber, Max. *Economy and Society: An Outline of Interpretive Sociology*. Edited by Guenther Roth and Claus Wittich. Translated by Ephraim Fischoff, Hans H. Gerth, A. M. Henderson, Ferdinand Kolegar, C. Wright Mills, Talcott Parsons, Max Rheinstein, Guenther Roth, Edward Shils, and Claus Wittich. New York: Bedminster, 1968.

———. *The Protestant Ethic and the Spirit of Capitalism*. 1930. Translated by Talcott Parsons. Repr., New York: Routledge, 1999.

Webster, David L. *The Fall of the Ancient Maya: Solving the Mystery of the Maya Collapse*. London: Thames & Hudson, 2002.

———. "On Theocracies." *American Anthropologist* 78 (1976): 812–28.

Weinberg, Joel P. "Die Agrarverhältnisse in der Bürger-Tempel-Gemeinde der Achämenidenzeit." *Acta Antiqua* 22 (1974): 473–86.

———. "Das Bēit ʾAḇōt im 6.–4. Jahrhundert v.u.Z." *Vetus Testamentum* 23 (1973): 400–414.

———. "Bemerkungen zum Problem 'Der Vorhellenismus im Vorderen Orient'." *Klio* 58 (1976): 5–20.

———. *The Citizen-Temple Community*. Translated by Daniel L. Smith-Christopher. Journal for the Study of the Old Testament: Supplement Series 151. Sheffield: Sheffield Academic Press, 1992.

———. "Zentral- und Partikulargewalt im achämenidischen Reich." *Klio* 59 (1977): 25–43.

Wellhausen, Julius. *Die kleinen Propheten übersetzt und erklärt*. 3d ed. Berlin: Georg Reimer, 1898.

———. *Prolegomena to the History of Israel*. Scholars Press Reprints and Translations Series. Atlanta: Scholars Press, 1994.

Widengren, Geo. "The Persian Period." Pages 489–538 in *Israelite and Judean History*. Edited by John Hayes and J. Maxwell Miller. Philadelphia: Westminster, 1977.

Williamson, Hugh G. M. *Ezra, Nehemiah*. Word Biblical Commentary 16. Waco: Word, 1985.

———. "Judah and the Jews." Pages 145–63 in *Studies in Persian History: Essays in Memory of David M. Lewis*. Edited by Maria Brosius and Amélie Kuhrt. Leiden: Nederlands Instituut von Het Nabije Oosten, 1998.

Wilson, Robert R. *Prophecy and Society in Ancient Israel*. Philadelphia: Fortress, 1980.

Wittgenstein, Ludwig. *Philosophical Investigations*. Translated by G. Anscombe. 3d ed. New York: Macmillan, 1968.

Wren, Linnea H., and Peter Schmidt. "Elite Interaction During the Terminal Classic Period: New Evidence from Chichen Itza." Pages 199–225 in Culbert, ed., *Classic Maya Political History*.

Yamauchi, Edwin M. *Persia and the Bible*. Grand Rapids: Baker, 1996.

———. "The Reconstruction of Jewish Communities During the Persian Empire." *The Journal of the Historical Society* 4 (2004): 1–25.

Young, T. Cuyler Jr. "The Consolidation of the Empire and Its Limits of Growth under Darius and Xerxes." Pages 4:53–112 in Boardman et al. eds., *The Cambridge Ancient History*.

Žabkar, Louis V. "The Theocracy of Amarna and the Doctrine of the Ba." *Journal of Near Eastern Studies* 13 (1954): 87–101.

Zahedi, Dariush. *The Iranian Revolution Then and Now: Indicators of Regime Instability.* Boulder: Westview, 2000.

Zertal, Adam. "The Province of Samaria (Assyrian *Samerina*) in the Late Iron Age (Iron Age III)." Pages 377–412 in Lipschits and Blenkinsopp, eds., *Judah and the Judeans in the Neo-Babylonian Period.*

INDEXES

INDEX OF BIBLICAL REFERENCES

INDEX OF AUTHORS